AFTA SpringerBriefs in Family Therapy

A Publication of the American Family Therapy Academy

Founded in 1977, the **American Family Therapy Academy** is a non-profit organization of leading family therapy teachers, clinicians, program directors, policymakers, researchers, and social scientists dedicated to advancing systemic thinking and practices for families in their social context.

Vision

AFTA envisions a just world by transforming social contexts that promote health, safety, and well-being of all families and communities.

Mission

AFTA's mission is developing, researching, teaching, and disseminating progressive, just family therapy and family-centered practices and policies.

More information about this series at http://www.springer.com/series/11846

Max Zubatsky • Jackie Williams-Reade
Editors

Self of the Therapist in Medical Settings

A Sociocultural and Systemic Perspective

Springer

AFTA
American Family Therapy Academy

Editors
Max Zubatsky
Department of Family and Community Medicine
Saint Louis University
St. Louis, MO, USA

Jackie Williams-Reade
Department of Counseling and Family Sciences
Loma Linda University
Loma Linda, CA, USA

ISSN 2196-5528 ISSN 2196-5536 (electronic)
AFTA SpringerBriefs in Family Therapy
ISBN 978-3-030-39270-3 ISBN 978-3-030-39271-0 (eBook)
https://doi.org/10.1007/978-3-030-39271-0

This Springer imprint is published by the registered company Springer Nature Switzerland AG
The registered company address is: Gewerbestrasse 11, 6330 Cham, Switzerland

Series Editor's Foreword

The AFTA Springer Briefs in Family Therapy is an official publication of the American Family Therapy Academy. Each volume focuses on the practice and policy implications of innovative systemic research and theory in family therapy and allied fields. Our goal is to make information about families and systemic practices in societal contexts widely accessible in a reader-friendly, conversational, and practical style. AFTA's core commitments to equality, social responsibility, and justice are represented in each volume.

In *Self of the Therapist in Medical Settings: A Sociocultural and Systemic Perspective*, Max Zubatsky and Jackie Williams-Reade provide a much-needed guide for mental health providers entering the world of medicine. Drawing on their own experiences and that of their colleagues, they walk readers through medical culture and practices and the unique challenges behavioral healthcare workers face in these settings. Many readers will be like me, with experience in medical settings only as a patient or family member. Working in this context feels intimidating and confusing, and the practices learned in behavioral health professions often don't fit. Zubatsky and Williams-Reade help readers find their own worth and value in medical settings while demystifying the medical culture. Their practical "dos and don'ts" inspire confidence that one can negotiate this new terrain.

The book calls readers to be self-reflective and examine themselves, anticipating and normalizing personal responses and emotions that will come into play. Several chapters illustrate how our own experiences with healthcare and our social locations (race, gender, etc.) intersect when working as part of a collaborative healthcare team. The book is both optimistic and realistic. It will undoubtedly be required reading for family therapists and other mental health professionals taking their first steps into the challenging and rewarding work in medical settings. It will also be useful to supervisors and colleagues who want to understand and support them. Whether entering the medical world or learning about it, the readers will be inspired and increase their appreciation for this important work.

AFTA Springer Briefs in Family Therapy
Lewis & Clark College,
Portland, OR, USA

Carmen Knudson-Martin

A Publication of the American Family Therapy Academy

Founded in 1977, the **American Family Therapy Academy** is a nonprofit organization of leading family therapy teachers, clinicians, program directors, policymakers, researchers, and social scientists dedicated to advancing systemic thinking and practices for families in their social context.

Vision

AFTA envisions a just world by transforming social contexts that promote health, safety, and well-being of all families and communities.

Mission

AFTA's mission is developing, researching, teaching, and disseminating progressive, just family therapy and family-centered practices and policies.

Preface

As healthcare continues to expand the need for mental health services, therapists are assuming greater presence to provide care to patients and families. Behavioral Health Professionals (BHPs) are being recognized as key providers on integrated care teams and in secondary and tertiary care settings such as endocrinology, pain clinics, geriatrics, and pediatrics. As a result, more graduate programs are teaching basic medical topics, psychopharmacology, and collaborative skills to help integrate new professionals in the field. However, clinicians often find that their personal beliefs, biases, and challenges are often the most difficult barriers to address when working in these settings.

When researching the literature on self-of-the-therapist topics and curriculum, the options out there were much more limited than we had anticipated. The topic comes up so much in training and graduate coursework, yet very few resources address the "real-life" struggles that new (and even seasoned) professionals experience. In our current faculty roles, we hear many personal issues, stories, and reactions of students and new professionals working in the world of medicine. The challenges do not just pertain to the conditions of patients and families but the operational systemic and ecological issues that can impact the care that clinicians provide in these settings. These underlying factors not only play a significant part in how new students, interns, and trainees work with patients but also attend to areas that may activate their own social and cultural experiences.

The development of this volume for us really came out of three impactful experiences. The first was out of an assignment in the Medical Family Therapy Program at Saint Louis University taught by Max. One course on theories and models of Medical Family Therapy requires students to put together a "Self of the Medical Family Therapist" presentation for their colleagues. The student presents a medical issue that either they or another family/close friend has experienced. In the four years of hearing these talks, the depth of vulnerability, new perspectives on culture and spirituality, and personal narratives of the meanings of illness is truly remarkable. It has not only strengthened the trust between each graduate cohort but helps students bring their guard down around illness and disability when working in clinics.

The second influence came out of a similar course and assignment taught by Jackie at Loma Linda University. In her Medical Family Therapy class, students complete a health and illness genogram which traces the transgenerational impact of illness in their lives. These presentations always bring significant revelations to students regarding the often "invisible" role illness plays in their lives. In addition to these insights, Jackie noticed that students' personal stories often intersected with challenges they experienced when providing therapy to patients and families and/or interacting with medical professionals. It became apparent that students' personal experiences were often clouding their abilities to work therapeutically and collaborate effectively. Working with students on these personal responses present in their professional work can be tricky, so writing a volume on these issues can help guide this conversation.

The final impact for this book was through conversations with training students and new professionals at different conferences. We noticed a large gap in the "self-of-the-therapist" training that students and interns encounter in integrated care settings. The field was assuming that new mental health professionals could seamlessly transition into these settings with ease. Hearing the need for more seminars at the Collaborative Family Healthcare Conference on this topic only furthered our curiosity into this area. As a result, the need to develop a guiding text for new professionals was apparent.

This brief can help serve as a valuable resource in mental health and integrated care training for several reasons. First, there is a lack of literature on how the "person" of the therapist is developed in medical training. When many mental health professionals take a biopsychosocial framework into practice, they not only see a more holistic perspective of patient care but also face challenges that cause them to take an introspective look at their own influences and orientation in providing care in a medical system. Second, unlike private practice and many for-profit clinics, medical settings may offer unique challenges and opportunities that therapists often do not anticipate and require new skillsets. For instance, outside of typical clinical duties, there are also operational and financial considerations that mental health professionals may be expected to address when working with underserved populations. Third, there are often unexamined beliefs and biases that therapists may hold about patients, families, medical professionals, and illness at large. Engaging in clinical care requires a reflexive process that looks more closely at one's self, patient and family perspectives, professional values, ethics, and medical culture.

This volume is a starting point for mental health professionals who are looking for self-of-therapist training as they begin their clinical work in a healthcare setting. Several chapters will highlight some of the important yet often unspoken topics that impact the type of care therapists provide to patients and families across a range of diagnoses. Sections will also address how issues such as personal experience with illness, cultural differences, professional burnout, stigma, and differing ethical perspectives of care may impact how professionals work in everyday practice. The last chapter serves as a unique insight into the "self" experiences of seasoned professionals and what advice they offer to the future workforce.

There are some disclaimers that we want to mention from the beginning. First, the concepts, findings, recommendations, and case studies come largely from western cultures of the world. As therapists are assuming more roles in healthcare settings globally, we should also consider the cultural variations seen in behavioral health practice across different countries. Second, we use the terms "medical family therapist" and "behavioral health provider" as overarching roles of mental health professionals in medical settings. There are several mental health disciplines that represent the scope of providers working in medicine. These two terms represent a mental health professional that views a biopsychosocial, systems framework in practice and routinely collaborates with other medical professionals for the care of patients and families. Third, both editors are white academics, where we needed to continually be aware of the power and privilege when explaining certain cultural themes and content. We wanted to be very transparent in how our "self" was impacted through a variety of training and practice situations in healthcare. Our plan to bring diverse authors onto our last chapter of the book was to expand the knowledge and advice that this resource can provide to readers.

Department of Family and Community Medicine
Saint Louis University
St. Louis, MO, USA
Max Zubatsky

Department of Counseling and Family Sciences
Loma Linda University
Loma Linda, CA, USA
Jackie Williams-Reade

Acknowledgments

Max Zubatsky First, I want to thank my coeditor, Jackie Williams-Reade, for agreeing to write on this important topic for behavioral health professionals. Jackie has not only been a great colleague but a wonderful leader in the field around self-of-the-therapist topics though her teaching, research, and clinical work. Her insights and perspectives in this area were invaluable to making this book an important resource to future professionals in medicine.

I also want to thank my family who has supported me through my journey as a student and professional. My parents have given me the advice to always be authentic in both my work and my personal life. Their knowledge has greatly impacted the authenticity I strive to provide to my patients and families in practice. Over the last decade, there have been several life and medical events in my family that have shaped my perspectives of patient care, family resiliency, caregiving, bonding of family members, and spirituality. These situations impacted not only my emotional "self" but my work-life balance at different points of my career. I have been a human and a family member a lot longer than I've been a therapist. Therefore, much of this book was inspired by the personal aspects that impacted my training and emergence as a provider in medicine.

Finally, I want to thank the wonderful students and residents that I have taught over the years. Through many course assignments, clinical rotations, and process groups, I have learned so much from them about the human side of the provider and the similar challenges we all face during very difficult situations. Their authenticity and vulnerability made me realize how valuable we all are to the healthcare system. My hope is that this book is a "pay-it-forward" to future instructors, supervisors, and mentors who can consistently emphasize the use of "self" in their clinical work.

Jackie Williams-Reade I would like to first thank Max Zubatsky for inviting me to be a part of this exciting project. Writing a book has been a goal of mine for several years, and I am grateful to have had the chance to make it a reality on a topic that I am passionate about alongside a valued colleague.

I always think of the phrase "It takes a village" when I think of Medical Family Therapy (MedFT) because it requires so much collaboration and energy to bring about good outcomes. My becoming a MedFT is due to a village of people helping me along the way – family members, patients, colleagues, students, and professors. There are too many to mention, but I'll say a few here. Much of the writing required me to revisit some challenging times in my life due to illness. I must thank my grandma, Doris Williams, for her loving presence in my life in general and throughout the illness and death of my grandpa, Waldo, from pancreatic cancer. His death inspired me to give back to the medical community that supported our family during that time and led me to work in pediatric oncology for several years. For the children, parents, and colleagues I met during that time, thank you for teaching me how to walk alongside those who experience deep suffering. Also, to my MedFT teachers, including professors, patients/clients, colleagues, and students, thank you for the ways you have challenged and supported me along the way to see the impact of illness more clearly and find ways to attend to what I see. And to you the reader, I hope this book helps you feel understood and also challenges you to think differently about yourself and your role as part of the medical team. Thank you for picking up this book and being willing to do the difficult self-of-therapist work that is so important in working with patients and families facing illness.

Both Editors We would like to thank the series editor, Carmen Knudson-Martin, for her continual support and guidance in the process of this book. We are so grateful for her vision and helping to usher us through the process with Springer. She has also given us great freedom to explore the numerous multicultural and systemic issues that impact our work on a regular basis. Additionally, we want to thank Tai Mendenhall for his valuable role as guest editor for the chapters and dedication to help in the editing process for this book. His background as both a clinician in Medical Family Therapy and a writer for learners in medical settings was such a valuable resource in helping us convey this content to our audience.

Contents

About the Editors

Max Zubatsky, PhD is an Associate Professor and Program Director of the Medical Family Therapy Program at Saint Louis University. He is a Licensed Marriage and Family Therapist and State-Approved Supervisor. He completed his doctorate at the University of Minnesota in Family Social Science and his postdoctoral fellowship at the Chicago Center for Family Health. His research interests include geriatrics, caregiving, integrated behavioral health, behavioral health skills of family medicine residents, and provider well-being. He currently directs The Memory Clinic, a specialty clinic in the Center for Counseling and Family Therapy which provides individual and group services to patients and families with memory loss. Max is the Coordinator of Integrated Behavioral Health in the Department of Family and Community Medicine and teaches courses to master's, doctoral, and medical students in several clinical and research areas. He has published over 20 chapters and articles on mental health and medical topics in the field.

Jackie Williams-Reade, PhD is an Associate Professor at Loma Linda University in Loma Linda, CA, where she trains and supervises students in integrated care, conducts and supervises research, and presents nationally on topics related to families and health. She completed her doctorate in Medical Family Therapy from East Carolina University and her postdoctoral fellowship in pediatric palliative care at Johns Hopkins University. Her research interests include the application and advancement of Medical Family Therapy, pediatric illness, utilizing qualitative research to privilege patient and family voices in healthcare, meaning-making and spirituality, and self-of-therapist issues in medical settings. She has over 20 publications, has presented numerous times nationally and internationally on Medical Family Therapy, she is the Administrator of the 600+ member Medical Family Therapy Group on Facebook, and is the founding chair of the Family Therapists in Healthcare Interest Network with the American Association for Marriage and Family Therapy.

Contributors

Jose Bayona, M.D., M.P.H Rundberg Health Center, CommUnityCare Health Centers, Austin, TX, USA

Brittany Huelett, M.S. Department of Counseling and Family Sciences, Loma Linda University, Loma Linda, CA, USA

Tai J. Mendenhall, Ph.D., LMFT Department of Family Social Science, College of Education and Human Development, University of Minnesota, Minneapolis, MN, USA

Stacy Ogbeide, Ph.D., M.S. Department of Family and Community Medicine, UT Health San Antonio, San Antonio, TX, USA

Jackie Williams-Reade, Ph.D. Department of Counseling and Family Sciences, Loma Linda University, Loma Linda, CA, USA

Alison G. Wong, Ph.D., LMFT Department of Marriage and Family Therapy, School of Psychology, Fuller Theological Seminary, Pasadena, CA, USA

Max Zubatsky, Ph.D. Department of Family and Community Medicine, Saint Louis University, St. Louis, MO, USA

Navigating the Culture and Context of Medicine

Max Zubatsky and Jackie Williams-Reade

Entering the world of medicine for the first time is almost the equivalent to being dropped in the middle of an Amazon rainforest. There is no compass, no guide map, and no one to hold your hand to navigate a new territory. The journey requires instincts and the flexibility to be open to the unknown. The experience can be incredibly rewarding yet pulls at many personal and professional challenges of new clinicians. Many of these challenges not only arise in one's professional work but also trigger unexpected areas in one's personal life as well.

Take, for example, a hospitalized patient who is diagnosed with end-stage renal failure, where their breathing capacity is extremely low. The family of the patient has been visiting and talking to the daughter, who is the primary healthcare power of attorney. Several family members have had disagreements about whether to transition the patient back to their home. The Medical family therapist (MedFT) is brought into an emergency family meeting in one of the corner rooms to consult with the family. With little knowledge or background about the case, the MedFT uses circular questioning, contextual interviewing, and shared language to help the family and therapist agree to the best possible option for the patient in a limited timeframe. This therapist balances these skills, all while facilitating a meeting where members must come to terms with the situation in the best way possible.

Where traditional psychotherapy offices generally provide a comfortable environment for providers and patients to meet, a healthcare setting can often present the therapist with unconventional practice situations. Family meetings may take place

M. Zubatsky (✉)
Department of Family and Community Medicine, Saint Louis University, St. Louis, MO, USA
e-mail: max.zubatsky@health.slu.edu

J. Williams-Reade
Department of Counseling and Family Sciences, Loma Linda University, Loma Linda, CA, USA

M. Zubatsky, J. Williams-Reade (eds.), *Self of the Therapist in Medical Settings*, AFTA SpringerBriefs in Family Therapy,
https://doi.org/10.1007/978-3-030-39271-0_1

in a hollow conference room, where overhead pages interrupt the flow of conversation. Brief consultations in the examination room force members to sit in crammed spaces and come near one another. Other providers needing a new room may disrupt the flow of an important conversation between the therapist and family. New interns, trainees, and students must adapt to a different way of providing counseling services. Patient care around certain mental and physical conditions can be just as effective during the 20-minute consultation as the traditional 50-minute psychotherapy appointment. Learning to provide care in shorter timeframes is thereby an important learning curve for trainees to traverse.

Behavioral health is on the cutting edge of providing key services to some of the most vulnerable and underserved populations in healthcare (Cummings, 2016; Doherty, McDaniel & Hepworth, 2014). This chapter will introduce a new world of medicine for beginning behavioral health providers, highlighting some necessary skills and areas to consider regardless of one's practice setting. The biopsychosocial–spiritual approach will be presented in a novel way, applying these aspects not just to patient and family care, but the parts of the "self" that impact the therapist's experience when working in these medical contexts. Specific suggestions on the "Do's and Don'ts" when working on a healthcare team will also be highlighted.

The Landscape of Therapists in Medicine

With the shortage of primary care physicians (PCPs) able to meet the service needs of patients in the United States, unattended mental health needs will be a continued challenge for many of these settings (Blount & Miller, 2009). Because primary care is often seen as the "de facto" setting for mental health screening and diagnosing (Kessler & Stafford, 2008), PCPs will increasingly be demanding the services of behavioral health providers to address this rise. Presently, behavioral health providers (BHPs) are uniquely positioned to address the ongoing health challenges in our system and identify effective opportunities to intervene with families in medicine. Increased areas of patients' social and familial lives that impact their health are primed for BHPs to provide additional services. The emergence of more social determinants of health factors, such as housing, employment, insurance, transportation, and healthcare resources, has also been a large area for BHPs to address. Primary care has acknowledged that these outside factors in patients' lives are affecting not just health outcomes, but the bottom-line revenue of these clinics.

Over the last two decades, both MedFTs and BHPs have provided care for families struggling with a myriad of these diseases in medical settings, such as anorexia nervosa (Cubic & Bluestein, 2008), asthma (Carr, 2009), cancer (Northouse, Katapodi, Song, Zhang, & Mood, 2010), chronic pain (Robinson & Reiter, 2007); Runyan, Schinamann, & O'Donohue, 2008) diabetes (Zubatsky & Mendenhall, 2018), and heart disease (Katon et al., 2010). Additionally, there are opportunities for therapists to work in medical specialties such as rehabilitation medicine, reproductive health, and geriatrics (Hodgson, Lamson, Mendenhall, & Crane, 2014).

Providers are even seeking areas to address community-based issues and needs via groups and action-based services.

The self-of-the-therapist work that professionals are encouraged to address in their graduate training and early career years is largely out of the traditional psychotherapy model of treatment. Certainly, topics such as transference, resistance, family of origin issues, and cultural factors still play a large role in the elements of the "self" in medicine. However, many operational, socioeconomic, political, and social areas of practice settings have been lightly discussed in the training of new behavioral health professionals. These areas are often the blind spots for not just new trainees, but experienced clinicians in practice who do not pick up these issues right away. As a white male (Max) who entered a medical setting in my graduate training for the first time, I had to learn how power, privilege, and cultural differences impacted not only interactions with patients, but my own sense of awareness when acclimating into a new care team. Thus, there are multiple areas in a BHP's training that should attend to the growth of one's "self" over time.

A Biopsychosocial–Spiritual View of the Self in Medicine

Many MedFTs have been trained in the biopsychosocial (BPSS) model of healthcare, which facilitates collaboration with medical professionals and interdisciplinary teams (Becvar & Becvar, 1999; Engel, 1977, 1980). The BPSS approach has been historically seen to view the context of the patient and family system in healthcare and taking a holistic view of a person's health. Clinicians must also attend to the spiritual aspects of a person's health regarding their beliefs on treatment and personal decisions of their healthcare (Wright, Watson & Bell, 1996). Yet, this same framework can be seen in the context of therapists' own reactions and situations when working in a new medical setting. The systemic principles that a patient might benefit from in their care could apply to the dimensions of the BHP working in these environments. Since this framework is the basis of many chapters in this book, it is important to acknowledge the different dimensions of the therapist's "system" that become activated when working with patients and families in these practice contexts (See Fig. 1).

Family therapists may have certain physiological responses to some of the procedures or materials in examination rooms or offices. Those who have significant germ or blood phobias may be challenged from going into rooms or procedural areas where equipment is present. Once must become familiar being around equipment and other medical supplies in rooms while speaking with patients and families. For example, a new trainee is staying in a hospital room while the patient is getting their medication injected. This therapist may have an aversion to needles or blood, which can affect how long they stay in the room or their mindset of continuing to interact with the patient moving forward. Additionally, any personal illnesses that the therapist has or is currently suffering from could impact their attitudes or motivation around particular patients. Often, personal illness may require one to

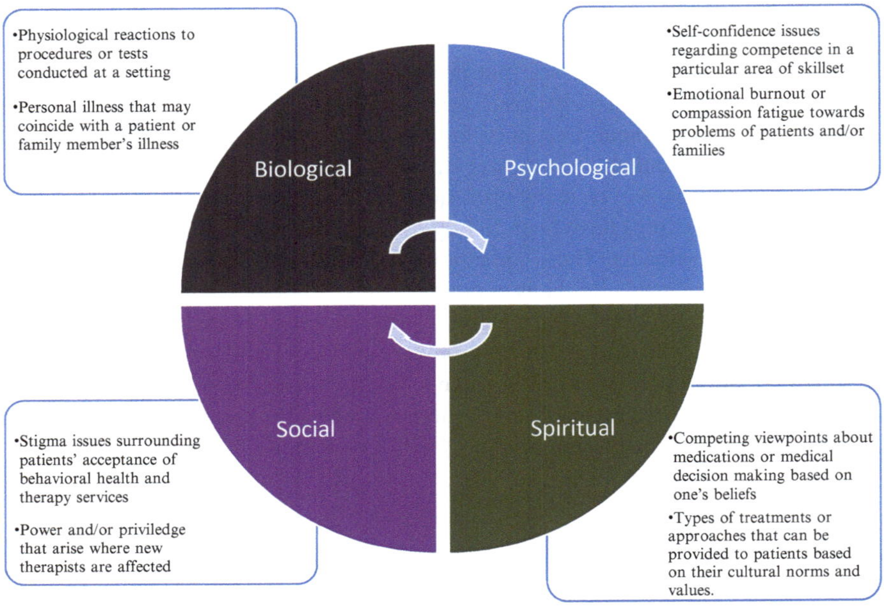

Fig. 1 The biopsychosocial–spiritual elements of the "self" in medical settings

monitor their own health during the day and maintain communication with the attending provider or the supervisor about any complications that might arise.

One might also experience psychological reactions and/or social experiences to issues or topics that arise during encounters in practice. Family of origin issues and/or personal illness (discussed in chapter "Personal Illness and Family of Origin") can often make a new student, intern, or professional feel vulnerable around any number of diagnoses that are either verbalized or charted in medical records. For instance, a MedFT trainee may not agree with a bipolar diagnosis of the patient in their chart, which may largely be due to a misdiagnosis of bipolar of their own family member. This perspective might impact the MedFT in how they interact with the physician who gave this diagnosis to the patient. New therapists may also have a mindset as being the "one-down" provider in a clinic, where the physician and other healthcare team members are playing a larger role. This type of mindset often happens when professionals enter "silo" types of practices (See Professional Identity Chapter), where each field operates in their own section of the clinic, setting, or hospital.

The provider's spirituality might even impact their views on areas such as medications, medical treatments, or family's perspectives on death and dying. Therapists also need to become aware to patients' varying belief systems around their philosophy of health change and health behaviors and learn to honor the patient's perspectives. These competing viewpoints can be difficult for even seasoned BHPs, where the incongruences around treatment options and follow-through of recommendations create frustrations for many. Examples may include herbal remedies to help treat depression instead of anti-depressant medications; resistance to follow-through with back surgery for religious reasons; a patient who wants to do something (e.g., birth control, a elective procedure), but is not "allowed" to by other family members; or decisions on end-of-life care in the hospital around renal kidney failure. The therapist must learn to first recognize these internal struggles around their own beliefs or biases regarding a patient's decision-making and find areas to work on this growth throughout training.

Strategies for New Therapists Entering Medical Settings

As the saying goes, "When you're getting your Bachelor's, you think you know everything. When you're getting your Master's, you think you know some things. When you're getting your doctorate, you realize you don't know anything." I (Max) was fairly intimidated the first week entering a new practicum position in a University-Based Eating Disorders Clinic. Despite previous master's courses in health topics, a year-long child and family internship, and several site visits to hospitals and clinics, being part of a healthcare team was now a reality. I immediately felt the need to prove my worth. My first medical note read more like a Robert Frost essay that was expanding on the patient's "Road Less Traveled." My introductions to new medical professionals turned into five-minute diatribes that was spanning my entire resume. Quickly, I realized the value of becoming an anthropologist in a new environment, studying the ways that I can and should assimilate into an existing group of providers. Joining a new team involves learning not just your role in the care of patients, but what other providers, staff, and administration need from you to strengthen the organization.

Beginning therapists in healthcare settings often have a mindset that several resources will already be in place. This is not only an unlikely scenario but hinders one's ability to pursue new collaborations in the clinical setting. New therapists should be proactive in their talks with other providers and budget their time to form these partnerships in their respective settings. Beginning therapists often learn about their system and organization through listening, observing, and shadowing providers at their site. Even emailing or "tasking" a provider through an electronic health record (EHR) will help other members know the presence of the provider and their willingness to collaborate. Despite using an EHR for continual communication, new therapists need to recognize the barriers that technology creates in establishing relationships with colleagues and providers.

Initiating Conversations with Providers

When mental health professionals think of the workflow of a doctor, they often assume several barriers that will get in the way of communication. Issues of time availability, scheduling longer psychotherapy appointments, consideration of mental health in the patient's care, and lack of knowledge about the therapist's role are often common challenges. A vital part of the early establishment of relationships is effective and intentional communication with medical providers. Without letting them know your role and information about certain patients, one becomes invisible at times in a clinic. For instance, a new BHP might be unfamiliar with the medical complications and treatment approaches of asthma. After receiving a "warm hand-off" from the physician to see the patient and his mother for behavioral health issues, the family asks several medically oriented questions to the BHP. After the consultation, the BHP and physician can arrange to either have a brief hallway consultation about the information shared, or the therapist can "task" the physician through electronic medical records.

Again, much of these initial conversations should be the BHP looking to offer help for patients and establish referral networks with these providers. It often takes several weeks or months for these initial collaborative efforts to pay off. It is easy for new BHPs to feel like they are forgotten or unwanted and begin to doubt themselves, but often persistence and patience will pay off in respectful and effective collaborations in the long run. As someone who learned to integrate into three different healthcare settings during my (Max's) graduate training, making these collaborations early and often with healthcare providers takes time. That is why supervision of new interns should place a greater emphasis on bumpability (Gunn et al., 2015), where a BHP's effectiveness relies on the number of times bumping into colleagues for consultations and regular communication.

A personal experience around this situation happened during the first couple of months of my (Max's) doctoral program in an eating disorders clinic. While the clinic had extremely supportive mental health professionals, nutritionists, and dieticians, I was often reluctant to initiate conversations about follow-up issues of patients. It may have been from my initial lack of confidence as a new therapist, but also to manage my own anxieties about bothering other colleagues in higher roles than myself. My supervisor quickly reminded me, "You have a role in this clinic that is highly important and recognized by others. They need your collaboration in order to facilitate better care." This experience made me realize the added value of team-based care, where an established plan for patients and families must incorporate multiple disciplines of health.

Access to Care Resources

Another difference between traditional psychotherapy services and medical settings pertains to insurance and third-party payer issues. Many patients from disadvantaged backgrounds and low socioeconomic status may be greatly impacted from not getting appropriate medical services. These financial barriers can also impact patients from seeking mental health treatment in primary care and other established care settings. BHPs and other providers need to be creative in how they can construct team visits with patients so that multiple services can be covered with affordable billing options for patients.

BHPs often advocate for patients and families regarding access to care issues, reminding medical team members of contextual factors that may limit patient's options for treatment. Taking on this role of patient advocate can be a very valued role in a care team. Even if one did not receive much graduate school training around billing and access to services, they can still serve as a liaison for the patient and family to seek resources and referral option for their health conditions. In primary care, a BHP may provide a 10-minute consultation for a patient struggling to pay for pain medications and follow-up doctor's appointments. A free consultation might be a way to connect the patient with services outside of the clinic and establish a communication line where the therapist can periodically call the patient about their progress.

Pace of Appointments and Scheduling

Mental health professionals embrace autonomy and flexibility in seeing patients that fit their practice preferences. Those in more minimally collaborative positions, such as private practice or consulting roles, must fully manage all components of their job, including scheduling, billing, paperwork, and costs of their practice. In medicine, many of these job components are out of the hands of the BHP, where adjusting to a faster paced schedule and quantity of consultations becomes a norm rather than an exception. Same-day appointments may appear in one's electronic health records, with minimal lead time to learn background information about the patient or family. Periodic conversations with front desk staff are often needed to coordinate time for either routine patients or open blocks for meetings, consultations, or other team tasks.

New therapists must learn to adjust to unanticipated situations or consultations, which forces one to establish clear boundaries in how they allocate their time. Physicians may ask the BHP for a quick 10-minute conversation to help address a patient in crisis. The nurse practitioner may have to interrupt a meeting you are in and require assistance on a question about a patient. The transition from the 50-minute psychotherapy appointment to a briefer consultation model may be difficult for new clinicians to embrace. Both setting a clear agenda and being clear about the patient's/family's goals become of greater importance in these instances.

Understanding Power and Privilege in Medicine

The history of medicine has long seen an established hierarchy of administrative power. Power and motivation are often interlinked in medical education and early training, where physicians and other medical providers must "prove their worth" through intense training during medical school and residency. Specific roles are also carried out by each rank in a medical setting, which can include medical directors, attending physicians, clinic coordinators, hospitalists, specialists, nurses, house staff, fellows, and administrative assistants.

New therapists must not only be aware of these power dynamics but also find ways to acclimate in this environment and offer a voice on the team. This can be a delicate balancing act that the BHP must follow, being aware that medical and administrative decisions need to be made by the appropriate people in the setting. This socialization process takes time and the BHP is encouraged to create gradual buy-in from other members. The new BHP must also realize that certain statements and directives towards them are not a sign of weakness, but rather of function of the strict time elements and efficiency in these settings.

Identifying Stigma in Patient Populations

What sets many medical settings apart from traditional psychotherapy is often the context for patients and families to seek behavioral health support. For a private practice therapist, a family will seek treatment for a particular provider for a specific psychiatric, emotional, or familial issue. The identified patient and family know the intent of the treatment and establishes goals to work on specific areas of their lives. In medicine, physicians will often "hand off" a referral in real time to a therapist, encouraging the patient to discuss a behavioral or medical issue on the spot. Patients may be unaware initially why they would see a behavioral health provider or what the end goal of that consultation would be. Terms that physicians and other medical providers should avoid when introducing the BHP would be terms that include the words "Psychologist," "Mental Health," or "Behavioral." Descriptions that include "Counselor," "Specialist," or "Team Member" are often better received from patients who may not understand the role that behavioral health serves in a medical setting.

The communication and language that is given to patients and families around the scope of a mental health provider is critical. Individuals from certain cultures, communities, and faith groups might have a negative connotation of using mental health services. A psychologist, social worker, licensed professional counselor, or marriage and family therapist might be seen to many as someone who is searching for any mental health diagnosis out there. It is very important that both the referring medical provider and behavioral health professional establish a level of trust and connection with the patient and/or family in this situation. BHPs play a key role in helping educate and mentor other providers around issues of stigma and negotiating the challenges of "selling" mental health to patients and families. The lexicon that physicians and other healthcare specialists use for behavioral health services in medicine is vital to help connect patients to appropriate services. BHPs will increasingly be in positions to coach other professionals on this topic.

The "Do's and Don'ts" of Working with a Care Team

Integrating into a new setting and care team can take time. The new therapist should consider several factors around the role they play in the team, while finding ways to get "buy-in" from physicians, administrators, providers, and staff. The following suggestions will help you develop your role integrate into the care team.

- *Do make yourself known to the staff early on and often.* Entering a new setting means establishing a new set of relationships with relatively unknown providers and staff. It is comfortable for a new trainee or intern to isolate themselves in their office or separate room. The concept of "shared space" becomes increasingly important not only for patient consultations, but to be also visible to other staff in your clinic. Forming 1:1 relationship with staff and providers will also give an opportunity to educate them on your clinical capacity and the conditions you can treat in practice.
- *Do make time to learn about the operations in your practice.* Outside of the clinical work that beginning therapists gear much of their focus towards, there are important operational and workflow aspects to consider. Understanding how the front desk operations connect to the rest of the clinic, practice, hospital, or setting is vital. The therapist should understand every space a patient may occupy in the practice setting. Knowing the room availability and workflow of the clinic or setting will also allow one to be more efficient in their role.
- *Do provide positive feedback to team members about their work.* Initial collaborations with healthcare providers often begin with getting "buy-in" about what you provide in that setting. Positive statements and validation to team members not only helps improve rapport, but also gets providers invested in your role of services to their patients and families. Even a simple statement such as, "Your collaboration with this patient around their depression treatment has really been beneficial," can go a long way towards building relationships with the care team.
- *Don't deny opportunities to learn more about medical terms, conditions, and knowledge from others.* Working in a medical environment enables a great deal of accessibility to other providers. Therapists have valuable opportunities to learn from physicians, nurses, medical assistants, and other skilled professionals about specific terms, conditions, labels, and treatments. It can be beneficial to ask colleagues to suggest information or resources to read on regarding certain medical topics. This shows motivation on the therapist's part and helps educate providers regarding the scope of conditions that BHPs can treat in practice.
- *Don't become isolated from the rest of the care team.* To assimilate in an integrated care type of practice, one must always be available to communicate with colleagues about patients. Some medical settings do not have the structure to foster hour-long psychotherapy appointments. Developing certain behavioral health skills (e.g., team visits, warm handoffs, huddle meetings, curbside consultations) can help BHPs encourage more team-based care and increase the presence of an integrated care culture in their setting. The more therapists become isolated into their own practice routine, the more distance they create from being a part of the care team.

- *Don't turn down working with patients with medical concerns.* A BHP in mental health is often equivalent to a primary care physician in the field of medicine. Both are the "jack of all trades" provider for their specific niche of practice. Referrals for patients to behavioral health should not be limited to just depression or anxiety. Physicians may want therapists to see a range of biomedical issues that need additional counseling help, such as diabetes, COPD, asthma, or smoking cessation. Therapists must be attuned to the psychosocial needs that may be underlying medical issues. A systems-based approach can help identify certain familial and social presenting issues. The BHP must continuously respond and attend to the needs of the family during any phase of the illness of the patient.
- *Don't think of yourself as "just a therapist."* To the new trainee, the role of a mental health therapist comes naturally; the therapist sees an individual, couple, or family for a presenting problem that needs psychotherapy treatment and interventions. In a medical setting, however, the BHP may have multiple hats that they must wear to attend to the immediate needs of patients and family members. One might serve as a health coach to provide psychoeducation tips for someone looking to quit smoking. In another instance, one might serve as a mediator or facilitator to handle a conflict that the patient had with a physician, nurse, or attending provider in the clinic. Therapists must be aware that they can get pulled into a variety of scenarios that demand both instinctual and straightforward skills.

Case Vignette

Maria is a third-year doctoral student who is starting a year-long internship in a diabetes clinic affiliated with her university. For three years prior to graduate school she worked in a mental health clinic that served patients and families in the Latino population. Maria was very comfortable in this setting, where clients not only appreciated a Spanish-speaking therapist, but also her strong therapeutic skills in traditional psychotherapy appointments. She had her own office and could easily refer patients to a medical clinic down the street that offered psychiatric and lab services. Transitioning into a new clinic with relatively unknown providers was now a little intimidating for Maria. Having to establish new relationships and learning a new system was something she knew would take some time.

When Maria was available to receive handoffs of patients from the two endocrinologists, she came across several families who were somewhat skeptical about mental health services. She was having trouble with patients following up for routine behavioral health consultations. Unlike her previous experience in which families with complex cultural and relational issues embraced her style of therapy, a couple referred for potential conflict around health management at this site was very skeptical of the word "therapist" or "counselor." The patient stated to Maria, "Not only does my doctor get mad at me around my diabetes, but now you both think I'm crazy? I didn't sign up for this." Maria did not anticipate the level of resistance from the patient, especially since they shared cultural backgrounds.

Adding to the complexity of Maria's transition into this clinic was her own family's history of diabetes. Maria had an interest of working with this population, given that her uncle recently passed away from complications of diabetic ketoacidosis (DKA) after a hospital admission. She remembers how her uncle struggled to regularly maintain his insulin injections and the frustrations his providers had over this. When one of the endocrinologists referred a couple with a patient with DKA, Maria jumped on the opportunity. The wife was frustrated with her husband's noncompliance with his insulin, having been hospitalized twice in the past year over dangerously high blood sugars. Maria was convinced that she could help solve some of the issues for the family. She developed a comprehensive treatment plan, put together several resources, and checked in with the wife three times over the next 2 weeks on the phone. Although Maria felt like she was making a big difference in their lives, it turned out that her several recommendations overwhelmed and frustrated the couple even more.

When the couple arrived at their next appointment with their doctor, the wife expressed some frustrations with Maria being "too intense in her recommendations and calling us to check in." When Maria was excited for the physician to make another same-day referral for behavioral health, she noticed that the couple left right after the doctor's appointment, and they were not scheduled on her list of patients. The physician spoke to Maria about the wife's hesitation to seek behavioral health services and made some recommendations to Maria about easing into the treatment with patients who have had DKA. When Maria brought up this case with her supervisor, she was noticeably upset. As they processed the details more, Maria quickly realized that she was trying to "save the couple," as a response to not being able to save her uncle who recently died of DKA. It was a hard but impactful learning opportunity for Maria, where she began to realize how her family of origin and personal issues around diabetes had a strong connection to her style of patient care with this couple.

The case of Maria's patient experience is a good illustration of several "self-of-the-therapist" areas that can impact a new professional in this type of setting. Maria was impacted by not only a cultural issue of the perspectives of behavioral health in practice, but a personal one that may have impacted some of her work with diabetes patients. Students such as Maria need supportive yet direct supervision to help process these feelings and find ways to work through challenges in training. Supervisors also can help by shadowing the provider-in-training on-site, where other team members will be encouraged to offer support to this student. For those in the early stages of their careers, finding peer mentoring or process groups will help normalize these challenges. We also advise that new professionals attend local and national conferences that address the financial, operational, collaborative care, and policy aspects of medical settings. The remaining chapters will help you get an overall sense of the different areas of the "self" that are important to keep in mind in these practice settings.

This is an exciting and opportune time for BHPs to be on the forefront of medicine and integrated care services. With the emergence of new roles, responsibilities, and treatment approaches comes a new territory that mental health professionals are occupying across disciplines and departments in healthcare. For early career professionals who are learning the basics of the medical world, the remaining chapters will introduce practice and personal areas that often challenge the morals, values, and confidence of BHPs.

References

Becvar, D. S., & Becvar, R. J. (1999). *Systems theory and family therapy: A primer*. Lanham, MD: University Press of America.

Blount, F. A., & Miller, B. F. (2009). Addressing the workforce crisis in integrated primary care. *Journal of Clinical Psychology in Medical Settings, 16*, 113–119. https://doi.org/10.1007/s10880-008-9142-7

Carr, A. (2009). The effectiveness of family therapy and systemic interventions for child-focused problems. *Journal of Family Therapy, 31*(1), 3–45. https://doi.org/10.1111/j.1467-6427.2008.00451.x

Cubic, B., & Bluestein, D. (2008). Preserving a life and a career: How a partnership between medicine and psychology saved a physician with anorexia nervosa. In R. Kessler & D. Stafford (Eds.) Collaborative medicine case studies (pp. 187–201). New York: Springer. https://doi.org/10.1007/978-0-387-76894-6

Cummings, N. A. (2016). Behavioral health in primary care: Dollars and sense. In *Psyche's Prophet* (pp. 141–155). Routledge, United Kingdom.

Doherty, W. J., McDaniel, S. H., & Hepworth, J. (2014). Contributions of medical family therapy to the changing health care system. *Family Process, 53*, 529–543. https://doi.org/10.1111/famp.12092

Engel, G. (1977). The need for a new medical model: A challenge for biomedicine. *Science, 196*, 129–136. https://doi.org/10.1126/science.847460

Engel, G. (1980). The clinical application of the biopsychosocial model. *American Journal of Psychiatry, 137*, 535–544. https://doi.org/10.1093/jmp/6.2.101.

Gunn, R., Davis, M. M., Hall, J., Heintzman, J., Muench, J., Smeds, B., … Brown, J. (2015). Designing clinical space for the delivery of integrated behavioral health and primary care. *The Journal of the American Board of Family Medicine, 28*(Supplement 1), S52–S62. https://doi.org/10.3122/jabfm.2015.S1.150053

Hodgson, J., Lamson, A., Mendenhall, T., & Crane, D. R. (2014). *Medical family therapy*. New York, NY: Springer.

Katon, W. J., Lin, E. H., Von Korff, M., Ciechanowski, P., Ludman, E. J., Young, B., ... McCulloch, D. (2010). Collaborative care for patients with depression and chronic illnesses. New England Journal of Medicine, 363(27), 2611–2620. https://doi.org/10.1056/NEJMoa1003955

Kessler, R., & Stafford, D. (2008). Primary care is the de facto mental health system. In *Collaborative medicine case studies* (pp. 9–21). New York, NY: Springer. https://doi.org/10.1007/978-0-387-76894-6_2

Northouse, L. L., Katapodi, M. C., Song, L., Zhang, L., & Mood, D. W. (2010). Interventions with family caregivers of cancer patients: meta-analysis of randomized trials. *CA: A Cancer Journal for Clinicians, 60*(5), 317–339. https://doi.org/10.3322/caac.20081

Robinson, P. J., & Reiter, J. T. (2007). Behavioral consultation and primary care: A guide to integrating services. New York: Springer. https://doi.org/10.1007/978-3-319-13954_8

Runyan, C. N., Schinaman, S. A., & O'Donohue, W. T. (2008). What goes up must come down: The complexity of managing chronic pain and bipolar disorder. In Collaborative medicine case studies (pp. 399–407). New York: Springer. https://doi.org/10.1007/978-0-387-76894-6_33
Wright, L. M., Watson, W. L., & Bell, J. M. (1996). *Beliefs: The heart of healing in families and illness*. Basic Books. New York, NY.
Zubatsky M., Mendenhall T. (2018). Medical family therapy in endocrinology. In: Mendenhall T., Lamson A., Hodgson J., Baird M. (eds.,) Clinical methods in medical family therapy. Focused issues in family therapy. Springer, Cham.

Personal Illness and Family of Origin

Jackie Williams-Reade and Max Zubatsky

As behavioral health professionals (BHPs) begin their work in the medical field, they face many new experiences for which they typically lack preparation and experience. They will be present for a patient as they receive a heart-breaking diagnosis; witness complex conflicts between patient, family, and/or medical team members; or see first-hand the impact of health disparities on patients and families. As discussed in chapter "Navigating the Culture and Context of Medicine", these tasks differ from previous experiences in traditional therapy and are not typically covered in the education content in school. These experiences can challenge us personally and it is important to attend to the unique self-of-therapist work required when we are working in the medical care system. In this chapter, we address how clinicians can engage in a personal exploration of individual and family aspects of illness and offer suggestions for how to integrate these personal experiences with the professional role.

Working in the medical field can elicit strong emotional responses to a variety of stressors unique to medical care. Many BHPs come to working in the medical setting influenced by personal stories of illness and are "wounded healers" (Nouwen, 1979), using personal experiences of suffering to fuel empathy and connection to the suffering in the lives of others. Empathy – alongside the quality of the relationships that therapists have with patients and families – is one of the most powerful predictors of positive care outcomes (Elliott, Bohart, Watson, & Greenberg, 2011; Norcross & Barnett, 2008; Norcross, Beutler, & Levant, 2005; Wampold, 2001).

J. Williams-Reade (✉)
Department of Counseling and Family Sciences, Loma Linda University,
Loma Linda, CA, USA
e-mail: jwilliamsreade@llu.edu

M. Zubatsky
Department of Family and Community Medicine, Saint Louis University,
St. Louis, MO, USA

M. Zubatsky, J. Williams-Reade (eds.), *Self of the Therapist in Medical Settings*, AFTA SpringerBriefs in Family Therapy,
https://doi.org/10.1007/978-3-030-39271-0_2

Empathy and other personal factors are referred to as "self-of-therapist." Being mindful to our self-of-therapist includes the ability to reflect on and be aware of how one's values, personality, beliefs, behaviors, and biases may influence clinical practice (Bean, Davis, & Davey, 2014).

Murray Bowen, a psychiatrist and one of the original pioneers of family therapy, believed that one's personal work with their family was the most important predictor of being able to conduct successful therapy (Bowen, 1978, Kerr & Bowen, 1988). Thus, it is essential for clinicians to understand how their individual, family, and sociocultural experiences of health and illness play a role in their ability to create positive and effective therapeutic relationships with patients and family members. Yet, despite the crucial role that therapists play in successful therapy outcomes (Blow, Sprenkle, & Davis, 2007), BHPs rarely receive training in how to address their interpersonal and intrapersonal processes as they relate to working in the medical settings. Behavioral health providers (BHPs) need to explore their family's intergenerational processes regarding illness that need to be resolved so they do not occlude therapeutic outcomes (Aponte et al., 2009). Understanding how these experiences may influence current reactions can help transform them into powerful tools to help facilitate patient change (Rolland, 2018).

For the behavioral health professional (BHP), this self-of-therapist work should extend to a focus on how illness in one's personal life, family of origin, and in the greater social context may influence their clinical work in both positive and negative ways. As a clinician and trainer, I (Jackie) am committed to addressing self-of-therapist dynamics for myself and my trainees. I work to acknowledge and address how my own lens is influenced by my experiences with personal and family illness and social locations. For instance, sometimes I am teaching a course while having recently experienced a positive medical encounter; while other times I have recently experienced a negative one. I may have recently felt my pain was minimized due to being female or witnessed how my privilege of being white allowed me the benefit of having my concern being taken seriously. In class, we may be reviewing an illness that one of my loved ones has lived with or died from. These personal realities influence my ability to be present to others – whether it's a patient or a student – and can also provide important insights into my teaching. As a clinician and trainer, I have a position of power that I also need to be accountable to in that I can pass on unexamined thoughts and feelings regarding the medical world to my patients and students. Using my experiences is an important part of my teaching; however, if my experiences lead me to emphasize the areas of deficit in medicine or overlook the experiences of those that are different from mine, these ideas can be transmitted to students, supervisees, and patients. Thus, it is a continual and careful dance for me to be mindful of how my experiences may be influencing my practice in both positive and negative ways.

Individual and Family Influences

Illness touches all families and, thus, clinicians working in medical settings typically have personally experienced an illness. These illness experiences often inspire BHPs to help others with the same illness or a similar illness experience. Many feel a desire to give back and this mission provides fuel and focus for their clinical work. However, it can also create blind spots or places where they may avoid challenging patients or family members.

Understanding the influence of individual and family illness narratives (Kleinman, 1988) is an important part of the self-of-therapist development when working in the medical culture. Clinicians often have increased empathy and insights for patients and families yet can also struggle with key clinical skills. They may over-empathize and not challenge patients and families, be blind to dynamics that are similar to their own, or harbor resentments towards the medical system. Being aware of one's experience and greatest strengths and struggles in our clinical work and attuning to these experiences can ultimately help us adjust our perspective which can result in more powerful clinical abilities. The following case examples provide insight into how individual, family, and socio-cultural influences can surface for BHPs and the effects they can have both personally and professionally. The following scenarios combine several stories and names and the identifying details have been changed to protect confidentiality.

Hermela

Hermela was an Ethiopian American female trainee who was diagnosed with fibromyalgia. She had years of experience of her pain and fatigue not being believed by friends, family, and the medical community. What emerged in her illness narrative was a strong emotional response to feeling dismissed and shamed by others for her challenges. Being from a culture in which respect for elders was tantamount, she found it difficult to speak up for her needs in her own family as well as with those in power such as her professors or supervisors at her clinical site. While she struggled, Hermela had done a lot of work to believe in her abilities and ask for the help she needed to succeed in classes.

In her clinical setting, being both a person of color and female gave her insight for patients who also experienced marginalization and discrimination and her work was culturally sensitive and successful. This confluence of social locations and experiences shaped her perspective and responses to patients, families, and colleagues in a beautiful and powerful way. She was often a fierce advocate for patients and created quick and strong relationships with colleagues at her site.

While Hermela's clinical skills were excellent, her performance at her site was greatly inhibited by the clash between her own sociocultural identity and the hierarchy of the medical setting. Hermela struggled in communicating with her colleagues and asking for referrals or support as she was influenced by her ethnicity, experiences, and gender to be hesitant in advocating for herself and sharing her needs. This was reinforced as when she did speak up she sometimes received the message that she was being too demanding or needy. In addition, Hermela would not share these concerns during supervision due to fear of not being believed, not wanting to be a problem, and feeling ashamed about her challenges.

Sociocultural identities of BHPs (which will be explored further in chapter "Making Sense of Socio-Cultural Context of Medicine and Identity Development") can play a significant role in successful and effective clinical work. When looking at Hermela, one can see how her personal experience with illness and her sociocultural identity both helped and hindered her work in the medical community. Sometimes a medical setting is not a good fit for a BHP and it can be due a variety of complex reasons such as personal experiences being triggered, being misunderstood or discriminated against in the medical setting, or a personality clash. Faced with this, it is a normal experience to find oneself feeling constrained and not able to show our best skills. In these instances, it is important to be able to acknowledge this for ourselves and find a way to bring out our best professional work which may mean additional supervision or a different clinical setting. For Hermela, this meant several conversations with the medical team and the supervisor to help work through the interpersonal challenges.

Arlene

Arlene was a female Caucasian student who was a dedicated learner and had insightful things to say about illness in class. After completing the illness genogram (see below) in class, she recounted her family illness story to fellow students and myself and primarily focused on her mother's diagnosis of Parkinson's being kept a secret for many years. She shared a significant level of frustration at her mother for her secrecy and felt it only caused her family and her mother additional suffering as they were cut off from social support leaving them unable to address the challenges head-on as a family. During her sharing, she also revealed that she was living with cognitive effects from a traumatic brain injury that she usually kept secret from even close friends (though she felt safe enough in our classroom to share.)

I was struck at the irony of her frustration with her mother for keeping her disease a secret while she was telling us her own diagnosis was being kept secret. I pointed out how her own secrecy towards illness sounded a lot like her mother's response. Her face portrayed a look of shock as she had not connected these patterns herself. This interaction, while uncomfortable to navigate in the classroom, brought an awakening to Arlene as it helped her more clearly see how responses to illness could be subconsciously transmitted through family interactions. This insight translated into her clinical work as she began to see and challenge the relational patterns in her patients. Being able to speak about what she saw happening with herself and her family brought about more instances of change in her client population. These insights also benefitted Arlene as she took more pride in her clinical work and began to speak up more for herself in her own family and personal life as well. Unlocking her own emotional response in her family opened her up in powerful ways to both her patients and in her personal life.

As a professor, I have found that when students share personal reflections, unknown patterns, blind spots, or biases that they had not previously recognized in their personal lives often surface. When this awareness emerges, I work to connect their experiences to their clinical work. This may include bringing their biases to light, challenging discrepancies in their work, or asking questions about clinical areas they seem to have a blind spot. When we can see our own personal reactions to illness and work through them, it can be a powerful experience both personally and professionally. While these insights are often disconcerting and working through them can be uncomfortable, their payoff is significant.

Self-of-Therapist Development Recommendations

Conversations regarding individual and family illness experiences embedded in the larger social context are important in clinical development. From an individual perspective, our personal experiences, can influence how we make sense of illness. From a family perspective, we may have had a loved one living with an illness and we learned values and beliefs that sometimes operate subsconsciously. Contextually, social factors, values, and expectations play into our meaning-making and how we are perceived. These varied experiences form our beliefs and values about what patients and families may need when facing illness. If left unexamined, we may perpetuate personal, family, or societal values and expectations listening to versus what the patient and family needs and wants. Thus, taking opportunities to address one's illness experiences is an important part of integration into medical culture and there are several ways to do so.

A practical way to begin exploring the influence that individual, family, and sociocultural factors have had on you is by constructing a health and illness genogram (McDaniel, Doherty, & Hepworth, 2014). I (Jackie) have participated in this assignment in both my master's and doctoral programs, and it is a common assignment in many medical family therapy courses. All the individuals have their own unique identities and experiences with illness; thus, the areas in which they may need to work on will vary. However, areas of growth are often found in those unexamined beliefs and patterns for which we hold little awareness. The challenge for most clinicians is to recognize their lack of awareness and commit to the additional work required to facilitate growth. Conducting a health and illness genogram can increase this aspect of self-awareness and knowledge (Rohrbaugh, Rogers, & McGoldrick, 1992; Schilson, Braun, & Hudson, 1993).

Illness genograms enable us to investigate personal and family illness histories and seek knowledge in terms of how sociocultural messages about illness may be influencing personal beliefs and professional clinical work. This activity includes both a personal narrative paper as well as an oral presentation in class or during supervision. The genogram serves a dual purpose as it helps practitioners reflect on their own experiences and can also be used to learn how to use a genogram as an assessment tool with patients and family members. The material in this activity should be considered confidential and participants are encouraged to share what is comfortable for them. Accessing supportive resources, such as counseling services, are encouraged in the event the activity results in strong reactions.

In this activity, participants review their family history for intergenerational patterns surrounding health and illness. Practitioners are asked to create a three-generation (or more) genogram which includes:

- Nodal medical or health-related experiences
- The general health, illnesses, hospitalizations, disabilities, injuries, and cause of death of all family members
- Family patterns around grieving and managing illness
- Family beliefs and rituals surrounding death and illness
- Cultural practices, socioeconomic issues, gender/power issues, and attitudes toward wellness, health, illness, and medical care (include alternative medicine, traditional practices, intersection of spirituality/religion with health, etc.)

This exercise is helpful only to the degree one takes for exploration of these influences and identities seriously. For instance, simply creating the genogram with medical illnesses and dates of diagnosis or death is informative yet it may not provide significant personal insights. However, exploring the generational influences, family patterns, sociocultural concerns, and relational dynamics offers a rich source of material regarding the meanings of these influences and identities. This exercise can promote a variety of important characteristics for BHPs, including:

- Recognize and articulate one's own values regarding illness and family and how these may differ from those of the other individuals and groups
- Identify the impact of their personal experiences on their emotions, strengths, limitations, and behavior
- Recognize how one's experiences can create biases and understand how these can affect their judgment and behavior
- Practice in analyzing and acting on feedback to help with self-awareness

To facilitate a reflective experience while conducting the health and illness genogram, the questions in Table 1 can be used to elicit meanings and spur further insights from the genogram. The questions can be completed individually in a written narrative and/or they can be used in a supervisory or classroom context to verbally explore the illness narrative. In the completion of this activity, a variety of reactions such as unexpected insight or emotions may surface. In this way, the personal illness narrative is significant as it can bring about a strong emotional response and reveal reactions and vulnerabilities that need attention.

Table 1 Questions for health and illness genogram assignment

How do your family members react when someone has an illness?
How does illness influence the relationships between family members?
How does your family talk about illness or going to the doctor?
Who in your family is most/least involved in caring for family members with an illness? Do you see any patterns in this related to family roles or rules?
How does your family communicate and make decisions about illness and treatments?
How is the lack of adherence to medical treatment addressed by your family?
What kind of conflicts or disagreements occur in your family regarding illness or health? How are these resolved or why are they left unresolved?
How do you think your and your family's social locations (e.g. race, class, gender, sexual orientation, abilities, etc.) have influenced your and your families' experiences with illness and healthcare systems?
How have values from your family's culture, religious/spiritual beliefs, personal ethics, etc., informed your family's views of illness? How have you been influenced by these?
What has been your and your family's experience interacting with medical professionals/the medical system?
How does your family respond when a loved one has died?
Are there others who have influenced you or your family in regard to illness (e.g., friends, teachers, or community members). How did they influence you?
How do you make sense of your family's response to illness? What are the positive and negative aspects of your family's response?
What insights have you gained after considering your family's response to illness?
How do you think you and your family's experience with illness might influence your work with patients and relationships with other medical professionals?
How has the illness experience shaped your biases and beliefs about illness, medicine, and the medical community? Describe how you might work with these reactions.
If a BHP had been involved, what would/could they have done? How might things have been different today?
How has your family's experience influenced you in terms of your areas of strength and weakness when working with illness?

Paying attention to our individual, family, and sociocultural experiences related to working with patients with illnesses can help increase meaning and effectiveness in our clinical interactions. Engaging in an illness genogram and the associated reflection questions is a good first step; however, we need to continually engage in the practice of self-awareness and pay attention to our mental, emotional, and physical reactions. Understanding these personal aspects in medical settings is important as it is a fast-paced, challenging practice environment and a BHP could encounter a variety of events that could trigger a strong reaction on any given day. From working with an angry patient, a demanding schedule, or challenges to one's competency, a BHP can encounter a variety of stressors. In these moments, we often respond in self-protective ways which could lead to adverse outcomes, such as an angry outburst at a client's lack of progress or shutting down in a meeting after a heated disagreement about patient care with a colleague. While these are normal responses to stress, it is important to be aware of them and work to respond in ways that can improve our overall care as well as take care of us personally and professionally (Gehart & McCollum, 2007).

Conclusion

Training BHPs to engage in self-of-therapist practices aids in achieving greater self-awareness into personal experiences as well as providing options to help manage the emotional reactions that may arise while working in the medical setting. The ability of clinicians to engage in self-reflection and take responsibility for the personal factors they may bring to the therapy process can help them improve therapeutic outcomes. Consequently, a central goal for those involved in behavioral health is to work on these self-of-therapist issues to be aware of their experiences and how they shape their responses in their professional work. As we engage in examining our personal reactions, we can become more mindful and conduct our work with our values leading the way.

References

Aponte, H. J., Powell, F. D., Brooks, S., Watson, M. F., Litzke, C., Lawless, J., & Johnson, E. (2009). Training the person of the therapist in an academic setting. *Journal of Marital and Family Therapy, 35*, 381–394. https://doi.org/10.1111/j.1752-0606.2009.00123.x

Bean, R. A., Davis, S. D., & Davey, M. P. (Eds.). (2014). *Clinical supervision activities for increasing competence and self-awareness*. Hoboken, NJ: Wiley.

Blow, A. J., Sprenkle, D. H., & Davis, S. D. (2007). Is who delivers the treatment more important than the treatment itself? The role of the therapist in common factors. *Journal of Marital and Family Therapy, 33*, 298–317. https://doi.org/10.1111/j.1752-0606.2007.00029.x

Bowen, M. (1978). *Family treatment in clinical practice*. New York, NY: Jason Aronson.

Elliott, R., Bohart, A. C., Watson, J. C., & Greenberg, L. S. (2011). Empathy. *Psychotherapy, 48*, 43–49. https://doi.org/10.1037/a0022187

Gehart, D., & McCollum, E. (2007). Engaging suffering: Towards a mindful re-visioning of marriage and family therapy practice. *Journal of Marital and Family Therapy, 33*, 214–226. https://doi.org/10.1111/j.1752-0606.2007.00017.x

Kerr, M. E., & Bowen, M. (1988). *Family evaluation*. New York, NY: WW Norton.

Kleinman, A. (1988). *The illness narratives: Suffering, healing, and the human condition*. New York, NY: Basic Books.

McDaniel, S. H., Doherty, W. J., & Hepworth, J. (2014). *Medical family therapy and integrated care* (2nd ed.). Washington, D.C.: American Psychological Association.

Norcross, J., Beutler, L., & Levant, R. (2005). *Evidence-based practices in mental health: Debate and dialogue on the fundamental questions*. Oxford, UK: Oxford University Press.

Norcross, J. C., & Barnett, J. E. (2008). Self-care as ethical imperative. *The Register Report, 34*, 20–27.

Nouwen, H. J. M. (1979). *The wounded healer*. Garden City, NJ: Image.

Rohrbaugh, M., Rogers, J. C., & McGoldrick, M. (1992). How do experts read family genograms? *Families, Systems & Health, 10*, 79–89. https://doi.org/10.1037/h0089325

Rolland, J. S. (2018). *Helping couples and families navigate illness and disability: An integrated approach*. Guilford Publications. New York, NY.

Schilson, E., Braun, K., & Hudson, A. (1993). Use of genograms in family medicine: A family physician/family therapist collaboration. *Families, Systems & Health, 11*, 201–208. https://doi.org/10.1037/h0089389

Wampold, B. E. (2001). Contextualizing psychotherapy as a healing practice: Culture, history, and methods. *Applied & Preventive Psychology, 10*, 69–86. https://doi.org/10.1017/S0962-1849(02)01001-6

Coping with Patients' Death and Dying

Jackie Williams-Reade and Max Zubatsky

During their careers, behavioral health professionals (BHPs) will experience the death of a patient or work with patients who face the potential outcome of death due to their illnesses. BHPs trained in the areas of death and bereavement can provide valuable assistance to patients, family members, and fellow healthcare team members. However, engaging with these issues requires self-reflection in order to engage sensitively and appropriately. This chapter will explore issues of grief, loss, death, and bereavement imperative for BHPs to consider in order to increase sensitivity and competence in their work with a diverse range of patients and families.

When working in a medical setting, physicians are often responsible for breaking bad news to patients regarding a diagnosis, prognosis, and pronouncements that bring with them the possibility of death. In these scenarios, BHPs may be called upon to provide support during or after a visit when an uncertain or terminal diagnosis is given or be present for grieving family members after a patient has died (Edwards & Patterson, 2006). A key skill that BHPs must develop is the ability to remain present during these difficult experiences and conversations and learn to recognize and address their personal reactions around issues related to death and dying (Schaffer & Norlander, 2009; Watts, 2007; Worden, 2018). As BHPs increase their ability to be present during the suffering and intense emotions associated with death and dying, they can provide better care (Gamino & Ritter Jr, 2012).

J. Williams-Reade (✉)
Department of Counseling and Family Sciences, Loma Linda University,
Loma Linda, CA, USA
e-mail: jwilliamsreade@llu.edu

M. Zubatsky
Department of Family and Community Medicine, Saint Louis University,
St. Louis, MO, USA

M. Zubatsky, J. Williams-Reade (eds.), *Self of the Therapist in Medical Settings*, AFTA SpringerBriefs in Family Therapy,
https://doi.org/10.1007/978-3-030-39271-0_3

Participating in the support of patients and families facing grief and loss can provide personal and professional fulfillment, as accompanying others during these times of suffering can be very meaningful. Working with grief and loss may also pose a threat to our abilities to remain empathic and engaged in meaningful work due to the emotional toll it can have on us. For instance, if we have experienced our own losses or worry about potential future losses, facing others' pain in similar situations can remind us of our own. When these emotions surface, they can pull us back into our sorrow or cause us to put up a tough exterior to prevent our pain from seeping back in. However, as we face these difficult emotions within ourselves, we are able to better help our patients. The following sections will aid in this endeavor.

Personal Experience

My (Jackie) own experience with the death and dying of loved ones made a profound shift in my personal and professional life. During college my grandfather was diagnosed with pancreatic cancer and was given 4 months to live. I moved in with my grandparents and witnessed his daily decline and death as well as my family's emotional response to the suffering. It was a difficult time as I saw cracks in my family relationships and witnessed conflict over how to communicate with my grandfather and other family members. It was a painful process and stayed with me for many months. After several months, I decided to volunteer at a camp for children with cancer. This choice opened up a new career path as I then interned with the cancer camp agency, moved away from my hometown to work in the oncology unit at the large children's hospital there, and then was a part of a small team that founded a nonprofit organization for families with children with serious illness. I spent most of my days interacting with families in hospital waiting rooms, sitting with a parent or sibling while we waited for a treatment, visiting young children while they lay in their hospital beds, or attending many memorial services of children. Being a part of these family's lives was meaningful, yet deeply sorrowful.

This consistent exposure to uncertainty, loss, and trauma took its toll on my work and personal life. At work, I became lethargic, not able to focus, and questioned my role in helping these families. In my personal life, I began to discount my own and friends' suffering as I compared it to what these families were going through and found it insignificant. My spiritual life was shaken as I questioned the existence and power of God as I witnessed so much injustice and prayers go unanswered. My supervisor noticed changes in me such as spacing out during meetings and a decline in passion for my work, and encouraged me to seek therapy.

In therapy, I had a safe space to process how the death of children was shaking my foundational beliefs about myself, my life, and the world. My therapist helped me adapt to a new belief system and a way of thinking about my role in these families' lives. I began to take less responsibility for helping make their suffering go away and learn to sit in the discomfort of profound grief and loss. I had to face the existence of unfairness in life and learn to take my own and my friends' suffering seriously even if it felt insignificant in the face of my daily work.

While seeking therapy helped me greatly, it did not protect me completely from moments of sadness or difficulty when working so closely to such deep suffering. I continually had to work to take care of myself so that I didn't overly identify with others' suffering or allow the pain to take away the joy and meaning in my own life. Having learned from this experience, my hope is that the rest of the chapter will help highlight and formulate ways to address the challenges BHPs will often face when working with the potential death and dying of patients.

BHPs, Self-of-the-Therapist, and Death and Dying

Our response to sensitive issues around death and dying is unique for each individual. One's personal response may be based on a number of factors, including personality characteristics, previous experiences, or cultural issues. The type of relationship with the patient and/or family members as well as the circumstances surrounding the death may also play a role in how it impacts us. For example, if a patient dies from breast cancer due to genetic factors, sadness and sympathy may follow in a relatively straightforward manner. However, if a patient dies from liver cancer due to drinking too much, responses of sadness and sympathy may be complicated by anger and sense of patient culpability.

Experiencing the death of a patient can be an isolating experience as typically a BHP may not be able to turn to friends for support due to confidentiality or, if sharing general details, may find that friends do not understand the depth of grieving for a patient. In addition, fellow colleagues who also experience the death of patients may not be open to these conversations. The medical culture tends to be reserved in terms of emotional expression and may not have resources to support employees in these challenges. Because of these factors, BHPs may question the appropriateness of their feelings and not share openly with supervisors or colleagues which can leave them with little support. In addition, they may also be called upon to provide grief counseling to other patients, family members, or colleagues while going through their own grief as well. The following case represents an example of a BHP intern encountering the death of a patient for the first time.

Case Example

Kendall, a female African-American student, began her internship in the trauma unit at a large medical center. She worked with many patients who had experienced traumatic injuries or illness complications, and often who were facing potential death. Upon the death of her first patient, Kendall was shocked and surprised at the impact that it had on her personally. She felt a strong connection to the patient, who was of a similar age to her parents (one of which was also in poor health). The day the patient died, she had not been able to see him due to a busy schedule. When she came to check on him the next day, a different patient was in the bed. Having not been able to say goodbye, Kendall felt she had failed the patient and family. She tried to put her emotions aside and focus on the tasks of caring for other patients, but over the next few weeks found herself feeling increasingly detached from patients, falling behind on charting, and experiencing her own feelings of depression. In supervision, she shared that she did not feel that she needed to discuss the death in supervision or engage in grieving activities, such as attending a funeral or taking time off work. Several months later, Kendall was able to reflect on her personal struggles and shared how she felt ashamed that she was having such a strong emotional reaction about a patient's death at the time. She felt it suggested that she was experiencing countertransference or had become too emotionally invested in her patient. This interpretation of her emotions led her to not share with those who could best support her, like her supervisor, or engage in appropriate grieving activities.

As this case illustrates, BHPs can be profoundly affected by the death of a patient, but uncertain as to how to cope with the experience. Had Kendall been trained to recognize her limitations and strong emotions as normal when caring for a patient who had died, she likely would have felt more comfortable discussing her reactions in supervision. Kendall's response also suggests that her work environment may not have provided resources for her when the death of a patient occurred. By understanding these emotions as being a part of professional experience and not simply her own personal feelings, Kendall may have also been more willing to engage in grieving activities that could have been beneficial to her both professionally and personally. Issues of countertransference, lack of time, diversity in grieving, and cultural and spiritual values and meanings are all aspects of working with death and dying and are all areas to consider when working with patients and families facing grief and loss.

Countertransference

The relationships that BHPs develop with patients are unique and can result in strong and complicated feelings if a patient dies. Strong feelings about the patients we work with can be stressful and require additional emotion management (Mann, 2004; Mann & Cowburn, 2005). While personal connections and compassion are often core values and sources of meaning for a BHP, these can also heighten the emotional responses that result from a patient's death. It can be difficult for BHPs to acknowledge these feelings as they may be perceived as countertransference and feel inappropriate in a professional context. Countertransference is especially salient when working with those anticipating or coping with death because we are working with patients and families during a very vulnerable experience: the end of life (Katz, 2006).

A therapist's personal beliefs, anxieties, and fears about death can easily leak into the therapeutic relationship. For instance, part of Kendall's emotional response may be connected to the similar age of the patient to her own parents, which would complicate her grieving process. This unaddressed countertransference could cause a therapist to avoid bringing up pertinent issues to the patient and family as they feel helpless or overwhelmed in the face of death-related concerns. Therapists are also at risk of taking on too much responsibility for the patient and family experience. BHPs may believe that they should be able to alleviate the suffering entirely to be successful. They may have their own insecurities such as not wanting to make a mistake or fail the patient and family. In these situations, it is important to remember that the goal is not to take away the pain, but rather to be present to the pain and help support meaning-making in the experience. Developing awareness of strong reactions and their influences is a key component of professional practice in grief, loss, and bereavement (ADEC, 2010). Recognizing these feelings in oneself can help BHPs make sense of their strong emotional reaction and facilitate working through them in order to provide an appropriate therapeutic response.

Time

Another clinical challenge when working with a patient who is dying is the factor of time. Time can feel extremely shortened when the time remaining for a patient's life is brief. Or time can feel like it's dragging on as we are aware that death will occur but unsure as to when. Issues of time can intensify the therapeutic process and relationship as it requires the BHP to determine priorities quickly and accept a more limited scope of outcomes. The patient's mental abilities or level of energy may also be limited, which can restrict the ability to make big changes. Further, a dying patient often has a variety of professionals involved and the increased coordination needs can also limit the time available.

The time limits of therapy when working with death and bereavement are a reality. For the case example above, Kendall's experience of not being able to see the patient before death can be a common experience due to the constraint of time in terms of a life-threatening illness. By normalizing that time is a significant factor in clinical care around these issues, Kendall may have been able to better understand this constraint as a common factor rather than blame herself for not being able to be present.

Workplace Culture

Kendall's experience in the case example also brings up questions about the work environment she is in and the kinds of resources it provides for employee grief support. Without organizational resources, one can begin to question one's effectiveness and become disillusioned with one's role, institution, or the world at large (de Jonge, Le Blanc, Peeters, & Noordam, 2008; Lee, Lovell, &

Brothridge, 2010; Yang & Chang, 2008). Work environments differ in the amount and types of resources they offer regarding the death of patients. Some may have no support or rely on an informal structure in which employees take care of one another, check-in about how they are doing, and overall provide an understanding and supportive environment to grieve and get support (Lima, Cavaliere, & Porensky, 2014). Other environments may have formal supports in place such as peer group debriefings, referrals to psychosocial support, or workplace rituals to acknowledge and honor patients' deaths (Stone, 2018). However, it is important to note that even in an environment that does provide support to staff for dealing with death, sometimes interns are not included in these activities. This could be due to the intern's limited availability on site or because they may be overlooked since they are not a formal staff member.

Another complication in workplace support is that BHPs are often seen as the ones who provide the emotional and/or supportive work. Since they are seen as the experts on issues of emotions and psychosocial experiences, they may be considered the main support for others but their own needs for support may be not be addressed. For the BHP, receiving professional support regarding issues of death and dying may require actively seeking it out. Options can include talking to a supportive colleague or supervisor, finding external support through professional development trainings, or talking with friends who can accept and support this kind of professional grief.

Diversity in Death and Dying

While illness and death are universal, the human experiences, meanings, and preferences we hold around illness and dying are very diverse and a cultural experience (Ho, Chan, Ma, & Field, 2013). A significant way in which people cope with death and dying is through finding meaning. This may include making sense of the death, finding benefit, and/or reorganizing one's identity (Neimeyer, Baldwin, & Gillies, 2006). Death and dying bring up a myriad of ideas about the meaning of life, how life can be unfair, questioning of deeply help spiritual values and beliefs, and more (Neimeyer, 2002). For many, this meaning-making is often directly connected to religious or spiritual beliefs (Sulmasy, 2006). To provide appropriate empathic response to those experiencing death and dying, BHPs must be able to empathize with others and recognize similarities and differences between their own cultural values and meanings and those of their patients.

Cultural dimensions such as ethnicity, gender, social class, family beliefs, religion, worldview, and other influences contribute to patient and family members' behaviors, beliefs, and values in relation to death and bereavement (Galanti, 2014). Western society often has a death-denying aspect such that it is common to fight death or hold out hope for a cure or healing until the very end. For Eastern cultures, death is often more accepted as a part of life and is not as much of an "end" as it is a transition or beginning of a new stage of life. Culture can influence the emotional expression around grief as some will grieve outwardly for long periods of time and others will respect a more restrained approach. While the United States values informing patients about their illness and if it becomes life-threatening (Lowey, Norton, Quinn, & Quill, 2013), other cultures may prefer that patients not be included in these conversations as it can be believed to only add suffering or perhaps hasten death. Keeping cultural context in mind with an attunement to how an individual may or may not align with cultural norms or generalizations is an important part of a BHPs practice.

Individuals from different cultures have different preferences regarding end-of-life choices, such as the location they would prefer to die in, drug treatments, and utilization of assisted breathing devices Rodriguez et al. (2007). These differences regarding preferences for care can be very difficult for the healthcare team, as some of these decisions may seem unethical from their own cultural standpoint. For instance, Jehovah's Witnesses do not typically approve of blood transfusions as they consider this an act that would be disobedient and disrespectful of God (Chand, Subramanya, & Rao, 2014). This belief and action can cause an ethical dilemma for providers who may be informed by Western medicine that values patient autonomy in decision-making and pursuing all possible treatments.

Working with patients and family members around issues of death and dying can raise a wide spectrum of meaning, beliefs, and values. This diversity in meaning can cause conflict between patients, families, and healthcare team members. In these instances of conflict, BHPs are often called on to advocate for their patients to other medical professionals and can share insights into the patient and family experience that influence their decision-making. Helping to bridge these relationships is a task of the BHP and is often undertaken while the BHP themselves experience value conflicts. Again showing the importance to be able to balance one's own reactions with those of others.

Self-Care When Working with Death and Dying

For BHPs working with death and dying, exposure to the suffering of others requires attention to self-care practice (Mendenhall & Trudeau-Hern, 2013). BHPs need to both help patients and family members cope with grief and loss, while also caring for themselves (Edwards & Patterson, 2006; Kumar, D'souza, & Sisodia, 2013). Recognizing and processing feelings of grief can be beneficial to both BHPs, patients, and families (Negash & Sahin, 2011; Sanchez-Reilly et al., 2013; Worden, 2018).

Self-care is a biopsychosocial–spiritual practice. Biologically, one must get adequate nutrition, exercise, and rest. Psychologically, attending to one's thoughts and emotions which includes gaining education and support in grief and loss is important. Socially, one needs to engage in close relationships and establish boundaries. Spiritually, practicing mindfulness or spending time engaging in important spiritual practices such as spending time in nature is important.

While the death of a patient is different from the death of a loved one, there are similarities that can be helpful to explore. The *Four Tasks of Grieving* were suggested by Worden (2018) as important stages that must be worked through when facing the death of a loved one. The model also provides a roadmap for professional grieving. Table 1 provides an outline of these four tasks adapted to a BHP. It is important to note that these tasks do not happen in order. They may overlap and need to be revisited over time.

Engaging in personal and professional self-care not only can protect against burnout, compassion fatigue, and moral distress, but can also promote one's engagement, compassion, and resilience. When one attends to their personal and professional self-care, increased job satisfaction and purpose can improve. Providing care for patients and families during the dying process can be a rewarding practice and can help cultivate a sense of meaning and purpose (Sinclair, 2011).

Table 1 Tasks around coping with death and dying

Task #1: *Accept the reality of the loss*	This task includes coming to terms with death. It is common to experience shock, denial, or disbelief after the death of a patient and it can feel surreal that they are no longer alive. Accepting the reality of the loss is working through this process and being able to acknowledge that the death has happened. It may be helpful to engage in grieving rituals such as attending the memorial service or sending a note to the family to help bring a sense of acceptance
Task #2: *Work through the pain and grief*	This task refers to the emotional work of grieving; this includes feelings of sadness, anger, confusion, anxiety, etc. This work is taxing emotionally but can also cause physical symptoms such as exhaustion, loss of appetite, difficulty with decisions, lack of mental focus, etc. It is also important to attend to self-care activities such as trying to get adequate sleep, nutrition, social activities, and exercise. You may need to take time away from work to grieve – sometimes this can mean taking a day off for an especially difficult experience or making time in your day-to-day life to grieve
Task #3: *Adjust to a new environment*	This task includes adjusting to a new awareness that the patient has died or perhaps the knowledge that patients die. This new awareness can make one feel as if their entire workplace or job has changed and one must make changes in order to adjust. This adjustment to a new environment can happen over an extended time period and can require personal and professional adjustments. Personal adjustments can be regarding your own sense of purpose or beliefs, while professional adjustments may include learning new skills or establishing additional support resources. This can include coming to a new awareness of your role as a grief counselor and a professional who experiences the death of patients. It may include additional personal self-care or a realignment of your feelings about your job
Task #4: *Find enduring connection with the deceased while moving forward with life*	This task includes finding connection in our emotional lives with the person who has died. For the BHP, this can mean allowing memories of patients or family members to peacefully exist within our minds or finding new activities that keep us connected to the meaning in our jobs. This task can be ongoing for the BHP as one copes with continued suffering and loss and connections to those people and their experiences may vary case by case. Consulting with team members, a therapist, or members of a spiritual community can be a helpful way to work through how this meaningful connection might appropriately look for each individual

Self-of-Therapist Activities

Training programs often fail to adequately prepare clinicians to treat those grappling with their patients' death or those affected by the death of a loved one. To help address this gap in trainees' experience, some potential teaching or supervision activities are provided below. Through these activities, clinicians can develop an awareness of personal beliefs and experiences and how these may influence their response and coping with the death of patients. See Williams-Reade and Trudeau (2018) for additional self-of-therapist activities related to death and dying.

Personal Reflection

One activity to promote personal insight and professional growth is personal reflection that engages one in further understanding and bringing a critical consciousness to their personal family experiences regarding death and dying. Through the following reflective questions, a BHP can trace how one's family responds to the issues of death and dying. The reflective questions to ask include:

(a) How has my family discussed and coped with death and loss?
(b) What beliefs and values do my family members hold regarding death and grief?
(c) As I look at my family experience with death and grief, what patterns of coping do I see?
(d) Considering my family's experiences, which grief, loss, and death experiences might be difficult for me?
(e) How can insights from looking at my family inform my clinical work?
(f) What do I know about how other cultures think about grief, loss, and death?
(g) What are my personal beliefs and values regarding death? What do I believe happens when we die? How do I think people should and should not grieve?
(h) Where do I get my ideas and values about death and dying from? How might the dimensions of my personal context and culture such as my age, ethnicity, social class, etc. influence my beliefs and responses?

Our beliefs and reactions to issues of grief and loss are often formed in our family of origin. Exploring and working through one's answers to these kinds of questions can help us better understand where our thoughts and feelings about death and dying come from. This awareness can help us better prepare to encounter death and dying in our clinical work as well as engage in self-care around these issues.

Advanced Directives Activity

Another activity that can be useful in helping us have discussions with patients and family members about death and dying is working through our own experience around this kind of conversation. One way to simulate this would be to fill out an advance directive document. There are several free or sample documents online that can be used. After completing an advance directive, respond to the following questions:

- What thoughts and feelings come up for you when thinking about your own mortality and future death?
- What experiences have you had regarding death, dying, and bereavement? How might those experiences influence your clinical work?
- What unfinished business would you want to address if you knew you were going to die soon?
- What are memorial/funeral service elements that you find most meaningful and would want included in your own?
- What are your feelings regarding organ donation?
- What are your views on assisted suicide and right-to-die legislation?

Thinking of one's own mortality is a challenge that often one doesn't need to face until a crisis occurs. For the BHP, it is important to understand their own reactions to this kind of conversation, and one way to do this is to engage in thinking about our own mortality. While this may sound dismal to some, it can be an important part of our professional work in that it can help us work through some of our emotional responses that may negatively influence therapeutic interventions with patients and family members. By engaging in these conversations, we come to more clearly see our sometimes latent values and beliefs and address them so as to provide a more empathic and therapeutic conversation with others.

Conclusion

For BHPs in medical settings, working with patients and families who are facing death or bereavement is a necessary area of therapeutic care. BHPs need to receive training to facilitate an increased understanding of the impact this has on their personal and professional experience. BHPs can be a key player in helping medical teams create team processes, facilitate team meetings, or help create learning opportunities around professional self-care in response to working with death and dying. Clinicians should be up to date on the literature on death and dying as well as their own experiences and plans for self-care strategies for when they encounter deep suffering in their work. By preparing and caring for ourselves in this way, we can continue to be present for patients, families, and colleagues in our work lives and for ourselves and our loved ones in our personal lives.

References

Association for Death Education and Counseling. (2010). *Code of ethics*. Retrieved from http://www.adec.org/about/ethics.cfm

Chand, N. K., Subramanya, H. B., & Rao, G. V. (2014). Management of patients who refuse blood transfusion. *Indian journal of anaesthesia, 58*, 658. https://doi.org/10.4103/0019-5049.144680

de Jonge, J., Le Blanc, P. M., Peeters, M. C. W., & Noordam, H. (2008). Emotional job demands and role of matching job resources: A cross-sectional survey among health care workers. *International Journal of Nursing Studies, 45*, 1460–1469. https://doi.org/10.1016/j.ijnurstu.2007.11.002

Edwards, T. M., & Patterson, J. E. (2006). Supervising family therapy trainees in primary care medical settings: Context matters. *Journal of Marital and Family Therapy, 32*(1), 33–43.

Galanti, G. A. (2014). *Caring for patients from different cultures*. University of Pennsylvania Press. Philadelphia: PA, https://doi.org/10.9783/9780812290271

Gamino, L. A., & Ritter, R. H., Jr. (2012). Death competence: An ethical imperative. *Death Studies, 36*, 23–40. https://doi.org/10.1080/07481187.2011.553503

Ho, S. M., Chan, I. S., Ma, E. P., & Field, N. P. (2013). Continuing bonds, attachment style, and adjustment in the conjugal bereavement among Hong Kong Chinese. *Death Studies, 37*, 248–268. https://doi.org/10.1080/07481187.2011.634086

Katz, R. S. (2006). When our personal selves influence our professional work: An introduction to emotions and countertransference in end-of-life care. In R. S. Katz & T. A. Johnson (Eds.), *When professionals weep: Emotional and countertransference responses in end-of-life care* (pp. 3–9). New York, NY: Routledge.

Kumar, S. P., D'Souza, M., & Sisodia, V. (2013). Healthcare professionals' fear of death and dying: Implications for palliative care. *Indian Journal of Palliative Care, 19*, 196. https://doi.org/10.4103/0973-1075.121544

Lee, R. T., Lovell, B. L., & Brothridge, C. M. (2010). Tenderness and steadiness: Relating job and Interpersonal Demands & Resources with burnout and physical symptoms of stress in Canadian physicians. *Journal of Applied Social Psychology, 40*, 2319–2342. https://doi.org/10.1111/j.1559-1816.2010.00658.x

Lima, J., Cavaliere, R., & Porensky, E. (2014). Ql-18closing the gap: Bereavement support for families, caregivers, and medical staff. *Neuro-Oncology, 16*, v182. https://doi.org/10.1093/neuonc/nou269.17

Lowey, S. E., Norton, S. A., Quinn, J. R., & Quill, T. E. (2013). Living with advanced heart failure or COPD: Experiences and goals of individuals nearing the end of life. *Research in Nursing & Health, 36*, 349–358. https://doi.org/10.1002/nur.21546

Mann, S. (2004). 'People- work': Emotion, management, stress and coping. *British Journal of Guidance & Counselling, 32*(2), 205–221. https://doi.org/10.1080/0369880410001692247

Mann, S., & Cowburn, J. (2005). Emotional labour and stress within mental health nursing. *Journal of Psychiatric and Mental Health Nursing, 12*(2), 154–162. https://doi.org/10.1111/j.1365-2850.2004.00807.x

Mendenhall, T., & Trudeau-Hern, S. (2013). *Developing self-awareness in clinicians who work in medical settings: A guide for using medical genograms in supervision. Increased self-awareness: Experiential exercises for dedicated clinicians and supervisors*. Thousand Oaks, CA: Sage Publications.

Negash, S., & Sahin, S. (2011). Compassion fatigue in marriage and family therapy: Implications for therapists and clients. *Journal of Marital and Family Therapy, 37*, 1–13. https://doi.org/10.1111/j.1752-0606.2009.00147.x

Neimeyer, R. A. (2002). Traumatic loss and the reconstruction of meaning. *Journal of Palliative Medicine, 5*(6), 935–942. https://doi.org/10.1089/10966210260499177

Neimeyer, R. A., Baldwin, S. A., & Gillies, J. (2006). Continuing bonds and reconstructing meaning: Mitigating complications in bereavement. *Death Studies, 30*, 715–738. https://doi.org/10.1080/07481180600848322

Rodriguez, K. L., Barnato, A. E., & Arnold, R. M. (2007). Perceptions and utilization of palliative care services in acute care hospitals. *Journal of Palliative Medicine, 10*, 99–110. https://doi.org/10.1089/jpm.2006.0155

Sanchez-Reilly, S., Morrison, L. J., Carey, E., Bernacki, R., O'Neill, L., Kapo, J., & deLima Thomas, J. (2013). Caring for oneself to care for others: Physicians and their self-care. *The Journal of Supportive Oncology, 11*, 75. https://doi.org/10.12788/j.suponc.0003

Schaffer, M., & Norlander, L. (2009). *Being present: A nurse's resource for end-of-life communication*. Indianapolis, IN: Sigma Theta Tau.

Sinclair, S. (2011). Impact of death and dying on the personal lives and practices of palliative and hospice care professionals. *CMAJ, 183*, 180–187. https://doi.org/10.1503/cmaj.100511

Sulmasy, D. P. (2006). Spiritual issues in the care of dying patients:"... it's okay between me and god". Jama, 296(11), 1385–1392.

Stone, R. S. B. (2018). Code lavender: A tool for staff support. *Nursing, 48*, 15–17. https://doi.org/10.1097/01.NURSE.0000531022.93707.08

Watts, J. H. (2007). Locating the "I" in the teaching of death and dying: Challenges of the open distance learning model. *Open Learning, 22*, 263–271. https://doi.org/10.1080/02680510701619968

Williams-Reade, J., & Trudeau, S. (2018). Medical family therapy in palliative and hospice care. In T. Mendenhall, A. Lamson, J. Hodgson, & M. Baird (Eds.), *Clinical methods in medical family therapy. Focused issues in family therapy*. Cham, Switzerland: Springer. https://doi.org/10.1007/978-3-319-68834-3_10

Worden, J. W. (2018). *Grief counseling and grief therapy: A handbook for the mental health practitioner*. New York, NY: Springer Publishing Company.

Yang, F. H., & Chang, C. C. (2008). Emotional labour, job satisfaction and organizational commitment amongst clinical nurses: A questionnaire survey. *International Journal of Nursing Studies, 45*, 879–887. https://doi.org/10.1016/j.ijnurstu.2007.02.001

Making Sense of Sociocultural Context of Medicine and Identity Development

Jackie Williams-Reade, Brittany Huelett, and Max Zubatsky

Medical settings represent unique cultural contexts wherein a variety of patients, disciplines, and staff are joined together. This chapter explores the sociocultural norms and values that can be present in such contexts, and how they can be challenging for behavioral health professionals (BHPs). Emphases on BHPs whose identity is of a historically marginalized group in the United States are also explored.

The Sociocultural Context of Medicine

The current U.S. healthcare system includes the constant mixing of societal values, patients' and families' unique cultural contexts, and the various perspectives of multiple disciplines all working together. These systems coexist and influence issues such as communication, beliefs about illness and health, and the conceptualization of treatment, goals, and outcomes for care. For the BHP, being aware of these differences and knowing how to navigate them are essential to successful clinical practice.

J. Williams-Reade (✉)
Department of Counseling and Family Sciences, Loma Linda University,
Loma Linda, CA, USA
e-mail: jwilliamsreade@llu.edu

B. Huelett
Department of Counseling and Family Sciences, Loma Linda University,
Loma Linda, CA, USA

M. Zubatsky
Department of Family and Community Medicine, Saint Louis University,
St. Louis, MO, USA

M. Zubatsky, J. Williams-Reade (eds.), *Self of the Therapist in Medical Settings*, AFTA SpringerBriefs in Family Therapy,
https://doi.org/10.1007/978-3-030-39271-0_4

Traditionally, training in this domain focuses on how to provide services to a spectrum of patients attending to unique needs related to class, race, gender identity, age, education, language competency, culture, illness beliefs, and more (Bean, Davis, & Davey, 2014; Caldwell & Galiardi, 2014). Addressing these issues consistently requires commitment from the individual clinician as well as the entire medical team and organization. An essential part of a BHP's work includes understanding these unique needs and adapting our practices to meet them. What is often not discussed is the social identity of the BHP and how the match between their own and the prominent characteristics valued in medical culture may influence their role and overall professional development.

BHP Professional Identity Development

A clinician's professional identity is developed through an understanding of their professional self within the field in which one is attempting to orient themselves (Brott & Myers, 1999). When BHPs do not match the "norm" of the medical culture, it can create challenges and discomfort regarding professional identity development that often go unaddressed in training or supervision. As clinicians navigate the environment of integrated care settings, an important aspect to consider is the power structure that exists within the healthcare environment (Janss, Rispens, Segers, & Jehn, 2012). Prior to the integrated care movement, physicians and therapists were viewed as competitors as healthcare relates to the perspective of understanding and provision of care (McDaniel, Doherty, & Hepworth, 2014). There has been a continued shift within the field in which healthcare providers are learning to share and conceptualize the perspectives and viewpoints of their behavioral oriented colleagues (Hodgson, Lamson, Mendenhall, & Crane, 2014; Interprofessional Education Collaborative Expert Panel, 2011). Despite this shift, BHPs are still tasked with acculturating to the healthcare context.

The U.S. medical system is a framework in which physicians typically hold a primary position within the workplace hierarchy. As BHPs work and attune to this hierarchical structure, they make connections to how they see, understand, and make sense of their professional identity. The hierarchy in medicine typically affords the physician a significant amount of power as leaders of the medical team. This privileged status may leave BHPs and other team members hesitant to question the provider or to voice their own unique concerns, conceptualizations, and/or perspective on patient cases. Due to differences in medical training, team members often speak differently about cases. Medical professionals may speak in an objective, linear manner in terms of treatment conceptualizations. BHPs, on the other hand, may conceptualize the patterns of interaction of multiple systems as leading to symptomology. These differences in conceptualization bring recognition to the inherent differences of professional position amongst the disciplines. The ways in which the BHP understands these differences and how their contributions are accepted (or not), incorporated, and utilized in the medical setting will influence how they make sense of their developing professional identity.

Medical Culture and BHP Professional Identity

Each workplace culture has certain norms and expectations for how emotions should be handled (Hochschild, 1983). An aspect of professional identity development for the BHP is the practice of emotionally demanding tasks inherent in working with patients and families in a medical setting. Medical culture has been long studied in terms of emotional experiences and expression at work (McQueen, 2004; Parsons, 1951). Being a professional in a medical context includes working with patients who are ill, which can elicit strong emotional responses from both patients and family members as well as medical team members.

This emotional work on the job can be understood through emotion management theory (Hochschild 1979, 1983). Emotion management theory suggests that individuals engage in surface and deep acting as forms of emotional labor. Surface acting involves adapting your expression of emotion, such as laughing when you are sad, in order to present a certain emotion to others. Deep acting includes the work done to try to make your internal feelings match the expected emotional norm of a situation, such as trying to make yourself feel happy when you are sad. This acting is shaped by social context as we are informed by culture as to how we should respond emotionally and we typically will act in order to adhere to this standard.

In healthcare settings, emotional labor is shaped by the culture of the healthcare system as one that is embedded in economic, political, and social contexts. This emotional management includes maintaining one's professional image; emotions in reaction to illness; reactions to challenging patient/family encounters; and reactions to the medical system, colleagues, and culture at large. Not being able to manage these emotions may have serious consequences both personally (e.g., depression, interpersonal conflict) and professionally (e.g., making errors, inability to accomplish one's responsibilities, or difficulty working as a team). For example, a lead on the medical team may have an emotional response to a patient's complications with an illness, which is seen by various team members as an inability to maintain composure in a stressful work environment. Our inability to handle our emotional responses in accordance with the cultural norms can tarnish our professional image that may create doubts regarding our role and ability as a leader.

Social Identities and BHP Professional Identity

Beyond the hierarchy of the medical system, another area that has the potential to impact the professional identity of clinicians is the intersectionality of one's societal standing as it relates to race, gender, sexual orientation, and cultural background.

While each context has its own rules for emotion management, each individual is also held to different emotion norms and, thus, the amount of emotional labor we must perform in our jobs varies (Lovell, Lee, & Brotheridge, 2009). A clinician who is a member of a minoritized group often engages in additional emotional management compared to those who are more privileged or closely align with the cultural values and norms. This additional emotional management is often found in managing how they are being perceived by others.

Social identity theory (Tajfel & Turner, 1986; Ten Hoeve, Jansen, & Roodbol, 2014) suggests that the self-concept of an individual or a group is derived from the perceived image of the group by society. Thus, the way individuals view and understand themselves may be influenced by the way society perceives, understands, and accepts an individual's social location. For the BHP, the ways in which they are perceived, understood, and accepted by patients and other medical team members may have an impact on the development of their professional identity, the way they feel they should present themselves in the medical setting, and how they perform their role.

Gender and Race and the BHP Professional Identity

Gender and race are two primary identities that we will explore in how they may challenge a BHP's professional identity development in medical settings. The following are examples of how these different identities may be perceived by BHPs, and how a BHP's identity can be influenced by these social identities. The discussion of these issues is not to suggest that all medical contexts and settings value the same norms or treat BHPs of minoritized groups the same way. The authors acknowledge that many BHPs of various social identities are in supportive medical contexts that are addressing these challenges head-on and creating a new kind of medical culture. These ideas are meant to engage in a conversation that is often unaddressed in order to help prepare BHPs and trainers/supervisors to speak candidly about these issues.

In regard to gender, the medical field has been criticized as a heteronormative setting in which participants – including patients and medical team members – can experience stigmatization (Eliason, Dibble, & Robertson, 2011; Zimmerman & Hill, 2006). For those who are of the stigmatized group, they may be hindered in being valued or obtaining roles of leadership in professional environments due to gendered norms and expectations (Henderson, Simon, & Henicheck, 2018). Psychotherapy is often perceived as a more female profession due to its emphasis on addressing emotions, and most mental health professionals are women (Erickson & Ritter, 2001; Simon & Nath, 2004). For those who identify as male in a BHP position, they may have to navigate ideas regarding their masculinity in response to being in a profession that primarily consists of women and works with emotions (U.S. Department of Health and Human Services, 2017). For those who identify as female, being a BHP in a medical setting may come with challenges related to issues of power. The following is a reflection from one of the authors (Jackie) regarding their experience of navigating identity development as a woman in a medical setting.

As a clinician, my experiences working in the medical setting have been mostly positive. Working with a diverse team has taught me a lot about collaboration and I've been lucky to make several deep and productive connections with colleagues. However, as I reflect on my experiences through the lens of gender, I am reminded of many instances and feelings in which my being female caused additional work for me or made me feel less-than others. One instance involved my work at an integrated care site in which my caseload was dependent on referrals from the doctors. One doctor, specifically, had many patients – but did not work closely with behavioral health. I worked hard to build a relationship with him to improve referrals, and it resulted in me able to have a busy caseload working with his patients. However, an additional aspect of this relationship included enduring his sexist remarks typically regarding patients but sometimes directed at me. Some mornings, when I would check in with him, he would look me up and down and make remarks about how I was dressed that day, often repeating that I was a "tall drink of water." (I am of above average height.)

I tolerated these comments and didn't tell fellow colleagues or supervisors because I didn't want to rock the boat. I didn't want to put my relationship with this doctor at risk as I needed client hours. Also, I had been socialized as a female to ignore these kinds of comments and behavior from men in order to achieve success in professional settings. I have many stories of inappropriate remarks and touching from men in professional contexts, and have had mixed results in terms of speaking up about these acts. Sometimes I was believed, but removed from further career opportunities. Sometimes I was not believed, and felt I was seen as a liability and untrustworthy. While I like to think I would no longer put up with this treatment, I continue to deal with sexism in the workplace.

Though what I experience now is not as overt as in the past, it continues to be difficult to navigate professional life as a female. For example, I once worked with a doctor who did not seem to like answering questions I had regarding technical aspects of medical treatment. I was trying to gain a better understanding so as to help my patients, but it was clear he did not want to take time sharing this with me. I accepted that as him being busy and found other ways to get this knowledge. Later, a new male BHP began working in our clinic and I noticed that he had similar questions to mine, and the doctor would gush about how great his questions were and would excitedly tell him about many of the technical aspects of treatment. This brought a realization that the doctor's hesitancy to talk to me about technical aspects of treatment was potentially personal and related to my gender. Suddenly, I became very watchful of the ways my fellow male BHP was treated in comparison to myself. While my awareness of this dynamic helped me better understand my professional context, I then had more emotional load in my job as I worked to reconcile my gender and how it influenced my professional work.

Over time I have learned to counteract these issues in many ways. In these instances, it's important to find support from others who understand and can help mentor you in ways to address and cope with the discrimination you are experiencing. However, I continue to find sexism to be wearing on me and causes additional emotional energy to be used to process through these interactions.

As seen from the example above, the status of being a woman can create additional emotional management in a medical context (Lewis, 2005). The same ideas apply to a person of color as medicine often privileges ideas of whiteness. So a professional who is a person of color may be marginalized or oppressed by feeling that they need to fit into white culture. Furthermore, those of a racial minority group may have different experiences and be perceived differently in the clinical environment than that of their peers of the racial majority (Harlow, 2003). Identity Theory poses the argument that an individual's behavior is developed as a result of their conception of self and influenced by the responses of others that are obtained through interaction (Stryker, 1992). Similarly, an individual's identity as it relates to race is impacted by the information an individual receives from their professional peers and/or patients based on the perceptions they hold about their behavior. The conceptualization of an individual's behavior can be perceived differently based on an individual's race.

For example, an individual of color standing firm on a particular opinion may be perceived as combative or argumentative in comparison to their majority counterpart who may be perceived as a confident leader. Persons of color who are entering the medical field are not only positioned from a point of inexperience of which they are trying to overcome, they are also carrying the weight of cultural alienation and possibility the responsibility of creating institutional changes as it relates to the perception of their race. They may take on an added layer of responsibility to prove to others with whom they interact that they do not adhere to negative stereotypes of their race/culture (Cropper, 2000; Granados & Lopez, 1999; Robinson, 1999; Watts-Jones, Ali, Alfaro, & Frederick, 2007). The following is a reflection from one of the authors (Brittany) regarding their experience of navigating identity development as a woman of color in the medical setting.

As a female clinician of color, I am often reminded of my social location and the intersection of my position with those whom I work with. My social location has the potential to positively impact clinical outcomes as I am sensitive to and compelled to attend to the diversity of patients. However, the attention that I often receive reminds me of this country's history of marginalization, discrimination, and racism toward African American people. I regularly experience both colleague's and client's perceptions regarding African Americans as an unexpected topic of discussion in the clinical setting.

One case specifically, I was called in by a resident physician to speak with a woman in her mid-sixties about challenges in her life which were impacting her health. I walked into the room and as I sat down and introduced myself, she interrupted me. The patient began to assure me that my presence in the medical exam room was OK with her and that she was not a racist. She continued to talk about how she takes pride in the Confederate Flag and all that it means for her, her family, and those who live in the southern United States. She explained how this pride should not threaten me as a person of color, as she was okay with working with me.

As I gathered my thoughts, I was left wondering: "If she was okay with me seeing her, why did she feel the need to assure me of this? Why did she defend her stance on the Confederate Flag and her Southern Heritage? What expectations did she have of me that she felt it was necessary to make me aware of her position?" Without answers to any of these questions I proceeded. I chose to do nothing more than acknowledge her sharing and continue providing the brief intervention that was interrupted.

While instances such as these have not occurred with every client that I meet, this in some form or fashion has been my reality in providing clinical care in the medical setting. It has taken me a while to come to terms with my experience of such comments as I'm often left questioning the motivation of clients who say these things. I find myself continuously questioning what my responsibility is to the client, to myself, and to other clinicians of color in these moments. Should I reassure the client, critique them, or further explore their thoughts and feelings in the room? I have not determined a stance with which I am most comfortable. These situations remind me that no matter how far I move up in educational obtainment, or socioeconomic status my race will always have a position in the room, and often speak louder than other points of my social location.

Experiences such as the one previously described continues to make me aware of the implicit biases and assumptions that have been deeply ingrained by the dominant narrative that cannot be escaped and are often a point of discomfort for me. I often strive to have those whom I work with (client, physician, supervisor, etc.*) see me as a competent clinician of color who rises above the dominant culture's stereotypes of African American women.*

While this internal work can be taxing, I can say that I am fortunate to have a team of faculty, mentors, and supervisors who are sensitive to issues surrounding diversity and intersectionality. These individuals work to provided support as I navigate experiences such as those previously mentioned. While I am not sure what my response or position will be in future situations. I have learned to utilize supervision as well as collaboration with colleges to find useful ways to navigate the clinical environment when situations such as these arise.

These are just some examples of how one's social location may influence their professional role and identity development in a medical context. As these examples describe, clinicians of a marginalized group are often tasked with the additional responsibility of being aware of their social identity and how they do not align with the dominant culture. They put extra effort into tolerating unwanted attention or treatment, may experience intrusions or blocks to their clinical work, and must manage how they perceived so as to hopefully be regarded fairly. In these ways, a BHP's performance is expressed through their ability to manage their own internal emotions while maintaining an outward image that is congruent with what they believe others desire to see of them (Goffman, 1978).

Lack of continuity of an individual's social identity in relation to what is viewed as socially acceptable to a larger social context can be a challenge for those in any type of minoritized group. While there is typically an additional level of self-management associated with being a minority, this identity may also provide positive aspects to the professional role. For instance, individuals may utilize their minority status as a resource to distinguish themselves as individuals who could offer a unique perspective in a clinical setting (Henderson et al., 2018).

Those whose social location sets them apart from what is more socially acceptable may find themselves having a more difficult time integrating and utilizing these parts of their identity into having a functional role in their clinical work. Appearance, for example, has been well documented in its power to impact perceptions of an individual's competence, intelligence, trustworthiness, and perceived work performance (Rosette & Dumas, 2007). For women of color, the appearance of hair has been a topic of discussion of social acceptance in professional environments for some time. Individuals with textured or Afrocentric hair styles are often asked to tame or present their hair in a Eurocentric manner. Clinicians of color who have this part of their racial identity challenged have the difficult decision of how to portray themselves within the professional environment. This creates implications for how they will choose to relate to their work environment or carry out discussions of identity with other clients of color who face similar difficulties.

The perceptions that one has of their own identity has implications for professional identity development. If an individual is uncomfortable with their identity it will impact their perceptions of how they are being viewed by others. Thus this insecurity could, in turn, cause them to question their decision-making ability or cause hesitation to provide input on case conceptualization. A clinician's comfort with their own identity coupled with an encouragement to utilize their unique perspective in the context of interactions with patients can be of great benefit to the healthcare environment. BHPs who come from minoritized backgrounds have a noteworthy perspective and contribution to therapy and case conceptualization. A clinician of a particular minority group may be more sensitive and bring an awareness to how racial identity or felt marginalization can impact the way in which a patient's understands or aligns with their illness experience or attending medical staff.

Implication for Supervision

As clinicians of diverse identities exercise their unique perspectives, it is important that supervisors are available and willing to address areas of diversity and their intersections with illness experiences. Clinicians of minoritized groups, as well as clinicians who utilize cultural awareness and sensitivity to issues of diversity, have the opportunity to utilize this facet of their identity to better orient themselves to the perspectives of their patients. Supervisors should be prepared to assist developing clinicians in navigating the hierarchy of the medical system from the vantage points of their social location. This would require that the supervisor be comfortable discussing the social identity of the therapist within their specific medical context and corresponding assumptions and biases that may accompany this identity. Supervisors should also be prepared to discuss the intersection between the development of professional identity in relation to the clinician's social location. Helping facilitate an understanding regarding how it may impact clinical work in terms of how they present themselves to colleagues and relate to their patients is important.

Some bodies of literature suggest that supervisors leave discussions regarding multicultural issues up to the supervisee (Bernard & Goodyear, 2009). There may be some benefit to supervisees feeling empowered to bring these discussions to supervision. Supervisors should be ready to engage in these discussions to help the BHP understand and face the challenges that these realities may bring. While other bodies of literature suggest that supervisors who initiate discussions of diversity and power within the context of supervision foster a supportive environment for supervisees which enhance learning outcomes, increase satisfaction in supervision, and promote positive clinical outcomes (Green & Dekkers, 2010). By addressing these points of diversity, intersectionality, and social location in the context of supervision, BHPs will be equipped to navigate the dynamics of the medical setting while also feeling normalized, affirmed, and validated in their skills, role, and experiences (Green & Dekkers, 2010).

As supervisors engage their students in addressing these areas in the medical environment, they should also keep in mind the power and social dynamics that may be at work within the context of the supervisor supervisee relationship. Writings from Cook, McKibben, and Wind (2018) found in looking at the power dynamics of the supervisory relationship, supervisees see the supervisors as the person of power as it relates to setting goals for supervision and providing feedback and support that is geared toward enhancing their clinical skills. This would suggest that it is the responsibility of the supervisor to make the discussion of diversity and the resulting navigation of the medical environment a goal of supervision and provide opportunities for feedback and discussion. Despite social location differences between supervisor and supervisee, conversations around these issues and their implications have the potential to deconstruct stereotypes and normalize interactions that are often difficult to navigate in isolation: To create awareness of intersectionality, social identity, and how they may impact the work of the BHP as they work with their supervisor and/or patients. The following activity will serve as a point of exploration clinician can use to assess their positions on the areas of discussion held within this chapter.

Self-of-Therapist Activity: Oppression or Privileged Narrative

Whether one is a member of a minoritized group or not, it can be helpful to take time to reflect on the social identities that may offer one privilege or oppression in the medical culture. The following questions can be used to help facilitate this awareness:

1. What are your social identities that may offer privilege and/or oppression?
2. How do your different identities offer you privilege and/or oppression?

3. How did you come to understand that you are oppressed and/or privileged? What are some specific experiences related to oppression/privilege that have influenced your professional identity?
4. In what ways does the medical setting influence your identities? In what ways does it contribute to oppression and/or privilege?
5. How do these identities and experiences contribute to your professional identity development?

Once this exploration has begun, it is important to find trusted people to discuss these issues within one's work or academic setting. Whether that is a colleague, supervisor, or friend, better understanding identities and experiences of oppression and privilege, and brainstorming what to do to address them, are essential toward continued professional growth.

Conclusion

Being attentive to the ways in which our current medical system, country, and world may marginalize certain people and populations applies to patients and family members as well as to ourselves as members of the healthcare team. While providing appropriate patient care is one of the primary responsibilities for BHPs, there is merit to discussing how the BHP perceives and understands the intersectionality of their identity in relation to the work environment and its impact on their role. A BHP who identifies as a member of a marginalized group can offer a much needed perspective and provide contributions to the healthcare system at large. Helping to address inequities for the BHP can be a step toward creating a medical environment that sees and respects differences for all.

References

Bean, R. A., Davis, S. D., & Davey, M. P. (Eds.). (2014). *Clinical supervision activities for increasing competence and self awareness*. Wiley: Hoboken, NJ.

Bernard, J. M., & Goodyear, R. K. (2009). *Fundamentals of clinical supervision* (4th ed.). Upper Saddle River, NJ: Merrill.

Brott, P. E., & Myers, J. E. (1999). Development of professional school counselor identity. *Professional School Counseling, 2*, 339–348.

Caldwell, K. L., & Galiardi, S. (2014). Increasing awareness of multicultural issues in therapy and supervision. In R. A. Bean, S. D. Davis, & M. P. Davey (Eds.), *Clinical supervision activities for increasing competence and self-awareness* (pp. 151–157). Hoboken, NJ: Wiley.

Cook, R. M., McKibben, W. B., & Wind, S. A. (2018). Supervisee perception of power in clinical supervision: The power dynamics in supervision scale. *Training and Education in Professional Psychology, 12*, 188–195. https://doi.org/10.1037/tep0000201

Cropper, A. (2000). Mentoring as an inclusive device for the excluded: Black students' experience of a mentoring scheme. *Social Work Education, 19*, 597–607. https://doi.org/10.1080/02615470020002326

Eliason, M., Dibble, S., & Robertson, P. (2011). Lesbian, gay, bisexual, and transgender (LGBT) physicians' experiences in the workplace. *Journal of Homosexuality, 58*, 1355–1371. https://doi.org/10.1080/00918369.2011.614902

Erickson, R. J., & Ritter, C. (2001). Emotional labor, burnout, and inauthenticity: Does gender matter?. *Social Psychology Quarterly*, 146–163.

Goffman, E. (1978). The presentation of self in everyday life (p. 56). London: Harmondsworth.

Granados, R., & Lopez, J. (1999). Student-run support organizations for under-represented graduate students: Goals, creation, implementation, and assessment. *Peabody Journal of Education, 74*, 135–149. https://doi.org/10.1207/s15327930pje7402_11

Green, M., & Dekkers, T. (2010). Attending to power and diversity in supervision: An exploration of supervisee learning outcomes and satisfaction with supervision. *Journal of Feminist Family Therapy, 22*, 293–312. https://doi.org/10.1080/08952833.2010.528703

Harlow, R. (2003). "Race doesn't matter, but": The effect of race on professors' experiences and emotion management in the undergraduate college classroom. *Social Psychology Quarterly, 66*, 348–363. https://doi.org/10.2307/151983

Henderson, M. M., Simon, K. A., & Henicheck, J. (2018). The relationship between sexuality–professional identity integration and leadership in the workplace. *Psychology of Sexual Orientation and Gender Diversity, 5*, 338–351. https://doi.org/10.1037/sgd0000277

Hochschild, A. R. (1979). Emotion work, feeling rules, and social structure. *American journal of sociology, 85*(3), 551–575.

Hochschild, A. (1983). *The managed heart*. Berkeley, CA: University of California.

Hodgson, J., Lamson, A., Mendenhall, T., & Crane, D. R. (Eds.). (2014). *Medical family therapy: Advanced applications*. New York, NY: Springer.

Interprofessional Education Collaborative Expert Panel. (2011). *Core competencies for interprofessional collaborative practice: Report of an expert panel*. Washington, D.C.: Interprofessional Education Collaborative.

Janss, R., Rispens, S., Segers, M., & Jehn, K. A. (2012). What is happening under the surface? Power, conflict and the performance of medical teams. *Medical Education, 46*, 838–849. https://doi.org/10.1111/j.1365-2923.2012.04322

Lewis, P. (2005). Suppression or expression: An exploration of emotion management in a special care baby unit. *Work, Employment, and Society, 19*, 565–581. https://doi.org/10.1177/0950017005055673

Lovell, B., Lee, R. T., & Brotheridge, C. M. (2009). Gender differences in the application of communication skills, emotional labor, stress-coping and well-being among physicians. *Archives: The International Journal of Medicine, 2*(3), 273–279.

Mcdaniel, S. H., Doherty, W. J., & Hepworth, J. (2014). *Medical family therapy and integrated care* (2nd ed.). Washington, D.C.: American Psychological Association.

McQueen, A. C. (2004). Emotional intelligence in nursing work. *Journal of Advanced Nursing, 47*, 101–108. https://doi.org/10.1111/j.1365-2648.2004.03069.x

Parsons, T. (1951). Illness and the role of the physician: a sociological perspective. *American Journal of orthopsychiatry, 21*(3), 452.

Robinson, C. (1999). Developing a mentoring program: A graduate student's reflection of change. *Peabody Journal of Education, 74*, 119–134. https://doi.org/10.1207/s15327930pje7402_10

Rosette, A. S., & Dumas, T. L. (2007). The hair dilemma: Conform to mainstream expectations or emphasize racial identity. *Duke Journal of Gender Law & Policy, 14*(1), 407–421. Retrieved from http://search.ebscohost.com.catalog.llu.edu/login.aspx?direct=true&db=sih&AN=24495718&site=ehost-live&scope=site

Simon, R. W., & Nath, L. E. (2004). Gender and emotion in the United States: Do men and women differ in self-reports of feelings and expressive behavior? *American journal of sociology, 109*(5), 1137–1176.

Stryker, S. (1992). Identity theory. In E. Borgatta & M. Borgatta (Eds.), *Encyclopedia of sociology* (pp. 871–876). New York, NY: Macmillan.

Tajfel, H., & Turner, J. C. (1986). The social identity theory of intergroup behavior. In S. Worchel & L. W. Austin (Eds.), *Psychology of intergroup relations* (pp. 7–24). Chicago: Nelson-Hall.

Ten Hoeve, Y., Jansen, G., & Roodbol, P. (2014). The nursing profession: Public image, self-concept and professional identity a discussion paper. *Journal of Advanced Nursing, 70*, 295–309. https://doi.org/10.1111/jan.12177
US Department of Health and Human Services. (2017). Sex, Race, and Ethnic Diversity of US, Health Occupations (2011–2015). Rockville, MD: National Center for Health Workforce Analysis.
Watts-Jones, D., Ali, R., Alfaro, J., & Frederick, A. (2007). The role of a mentoring group for family therapy trainees and therapists of color. *Family Process, 46*, 437–450. https://doi.org/10.1111/j.1545-5300.2007.00224.x
Zimmerman, M., & Hill, S. (2006). Health care as a gendered system. In J. Chafetz (Ed.), *Handbook of the sociology of gender* (pp. 483–518). Boston, MA: Kluwer Academic.

Resources

AHRQ Health Literacy Universal Precautions Toolkit. https://www.ahrq.gov/professionals/quality-patient-safety/quality-resources/tools/literacy-toolkit/index.html
Behavioral Health Equity. https://www.samhsa.gov/behavioral-health-equity
Cultural Competency assessments/quizzes. https://guides.lib.uiowa.edu/c.php?g=131924&p=864758
Culturally Effective Care Toolkit. https://www.aap.org/en-us/professional-resources/practice-transformation/managingpatients/Pages/effective-care.aspx
Georgetown University National Center for Cultural Competence Self-Assessments. https://nccc.georgetown.edu/assessments/
Glossary of Terms Related to Gender. https://www.hrc.org/resources/glossary-of-terms

Burnout and Fatigue

Max Zubatsky and Jackie Williams-Reade

Burnout is described as a condition based on the protracted depletion of an individual's energies (Shirom, 1989) and is characterized by emotional exhaustion, lower personal accomplishment, and feelings of insufficiency and depersonalization at work (Houkes, Winants, Twellaar, & Verdonk, 2011). Although there is no unified definition of burnout in either the International Classification of Diseases (ICD) or Diagnostic and Statistical Manual of Mental Disorders (DSM-5), many consider burnout to be a mental health impairment (Korczak, Huber & Kister, 2010). Work-related stress has been recognized as one of the largest predictors of mental health and family conflict issues in Western society (Rosa, 2014). Approximately 21%–67% of mental health professionals experience high levels of burnout in their current work environment (Morse, Salyers, Rollins, Monroe-DeVita, & Pfahler, 2012). BHPs working in medical settings are starting to experience these same rates of burnout and compassion fatigue in their services provided to patients (Dyrbye et al., 2017; O'Connor, Neff, & Pitman, 2018).

The concept of burnout can be viewed differently from those who experience compassion fatigue in their work (Canfield, 2005; Dunkley & Whelan, 2006). Both terms overlap in that the professional has emotional burdens and exhaustion as a result from patient-related issues. However, burnout often stems from a lack of personalization for patients and staff while compassion fatigue is usually a residue of exposure to working with high-risk situations or health conditions that burden the provider over time. For new therapists entering these training settings, supervisors

M. Zubatsky (✉)
Department of Family and Community Medicine, Saint Louis University,
St. Louis, MO, USA
e-mail: max.zubatsky@health.slu.edu

J. Williams-Reade
Department of Counseling and Family Sciences, Loma Linda University,
Loma Linda, CA, USA

M. Zubatsky, J. Williams-Reade (eds.), *Self of the Therapist in Medical Settings*, AFTA SpringerBriefs in Family Therapy,
https://doi.org/10.1007/978-3-030-39271-0_5

should consistently be aware of the risks that both situations may pose. Signs of burnout might be seen as low motivation levels or signs of apathy toward the value that the job provides (Morse, Salyers, Rollins, Monroe-DeVita, & Pfahler, 2012) whereas compassion fatigue might be an indication of a provider lacking appropriate support and connection for the patients, families, and cultures in their practice.

Burnout can affect new trainees who are entering medical settings and environments for this first time. Those new to the helping professions may be especially vulnerable to the risks of burnout as they may not understand the emotional and professional demands a healthcare position entails. Career choice satisfaction may be a large contributor to how students perceive potential burnout in future healthcare positions. Thus, a larger mental health workforce in medicine may be stalled due to the perceived stress and job burnout that students possess (Kovach Clark, Murdock, & Koetting, 2009).

Perspectives of Burnout in Healthcare

Certain instruments and frameworks have viewed how burnout should be measured in healthcare. The Maslach Burnout Inventory (MBI) is perhaps the most recognized and widely used scale to determine burnout areas of mental health professionals (Maslach, Jackson, & Leiter, 1996); Maslach and Leiter (2008). Aspects of depersonalization, personal accomplishment, and emotional exhaustion are conceptualized as low, moderate, or high levels of burnout in one's work environment. One shortcoming of the MBI is that the validation of the scales comes from several organizations outside of the healthcare field. Additionally, there are current demands in healthcare that were not fully present 20 years ago, such as increased managed care challenges, operational pressures of work productivity and increased committee roles for BHPs in care settings.

A widely used questionnaire that measures compassion fatigue and professional satisfaction is the Professional Quality of Life Scale (Stamm, 2009). Supervisors and administrators can use this evaluation to determine the positive and negative qualities that trainees and providers feel about the quality of their work. The questionnaire has been used extensively in the nursing field (Lauvrud, Nonstad, & Palmstierna, 2009; Lee, Dai, Park, & McCreary, 2013) where large patient caseloads and the psychological impact of impatient settings cause significant burnout and compassion fatigue over time.

Others have applied social exchange theory to burnout (Schaufeli, 2006), where people who invest in relationships should gain a proportional return. Sometimes, the time and resource investment does not pay in certain rewards. The lack of this reciprocity or unbalanced relationship often drains a professional's emotional resources, which can lead to emotional exhaustion. For healthcare professionals, many offer their services, skills, and personal time to improve the health and well-being for patients. When many of these efforts at work are not appreciated or taken for granted, an increased sense of hopelessness, depression, or personal accomplishment can set in. Administrators are starting to take note of these reciprocal processes, where healthcare employee burnout is rising due largely to the lack of support for

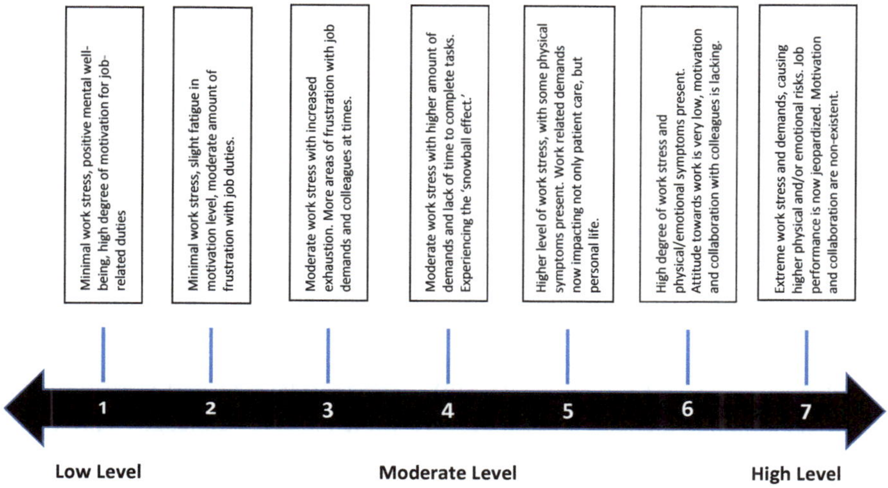

Fig. 1 A spectrum of burnout for behavioral health providers

the job and professional demands they face (Morse et al., 2012; Shah, Kapoor, Cole, & Steiner, 2016)

We view burnout as a spectrum of levels and combination of personal elements (see Fig. 1) rather than a binary construct, where someone is either (burned out or not burned out) based on a total score. Providers can still function effectively at low levels of stress or burnout without major impact on work productivity, patient care or team rapport. In fact, some low-level burnout is expected during times of intense rotations or clinical demands. For instance, a therapist supervising students or residents on a hospital rotation may encounter several high crisis cases. The challenges of patient care, coordination with medical departments, documentation, and finding resources for several patients would be exhausting even for experienced BHPs. Although this provider may have a lower level of burnout, this job stress does not necessarily warrant mentorship, remediation, or possible counseling. When providers start to climb up the ladder of higher burnout, one may look into peer consultation groups or other forms of mentorship to curb these emotional and physical risks. Supervisors should routinely explore 'self–of-the-therapist' areas of the supervisee, processing personal characteristics that might be challenged in a medical environment. (Such as confidence, rapport, competency in medical terminology, and reactions to patient's stories and narratives).

Cultural Factors Related to Burnout

The concept of healthcare burnout crosses over to several cultures in the world. Where research has normally focused on physician burnout (Dugani et al., 2018; Salyers et al., 2017), other healthcare providers are starting to report similar rates of work burnout and work-related stress. Family history and cultural backgrounds can largely shape how one handles the stresses and demands of high workloads. As behavioral health providers are assuming more healthcare positions across the globe, the increased time pressures, caseloads, and job demands appear regardless of the geographic location of the organization (Bria, Baban, & Dumitrascu, 2012; Lo, Wu, Chan, Chu, & Li, 2018).

My (Max's) experience of determining burnout around work boundaries was greatly influenced during my primary care training in my doctoral program. During this internship period, I had diverse colleagues who were also training students from different programs. A Hmong colleague of mine made sure to prioritize her work schedule only within the clinic hours during the week. She placed a high precedence on family life and family rituals during the week, where the balance in other job duties and requirements would get addressed on her terms. She also needed to make sure that her emotional and physical well-being were adequate as she was caretaking for an ill family member at the time. As a white male, my colleague's priorities made me reassess the boundary setting that is needed for a professional to set where family and cultural perspectives of work can serve as a buffer to potential burnout. At that time, I was an overworked therapy intern where my background taught me to commit fully to your job no matter what it takes. My obsession to gain clinical hours and overextend my job duties took away from other personal areas of my life. By scaling back these commitments, I learned that my self-care and work–life balance made a significant difference in the outcomes of the patients.

The following case examples depict another way in which cultural values and norms can influence professional boundaries and the potential for compassion fatigue of patients.

Case Scenarios

Salima, a 37-year-old female from Pakistan, attends a rural university for her doctoral program. She is interning at a rural primary care practice in the Midwestern United States and has a special interest in refugee and immigrant populations. Her graduate courses and additional trainings have made her a very competent provider in this field. One of the physicians in her practice wants Salima to get referrals for patients with abuse histories related to chronic pain. The first two patients that she saw around trauma issues were able to effectively process their grief experiences in sessions and felt comfortable in the room with a therapist. However, several subsequent patients began to refuse treatment from Salima, many claiming that they did not want to see a therapist for their problems. Salima heard through a few providers that patients shared their fears of seeing a Muslim woman in the clinic. In a predominantly Caucasian town, Salima was not only stigmatized by patients, but also the community that she lived in. Salima realized that wearing her hijab in the clinic might be making some patients feel uncomfortable. She started to question not only her work, but how effective she would be as a therapist in general. She became more isolated at work and tended not to show her face to patients in the lobby. The staff noticed this and began to be concerned about Salima's perception of the clinic and her role in the practice.

Over the next couple of months, Salima continued to struggle with comments that patients would say about her. She began to show frustrations with a few patients, where even their curiosity and questions about Salima's culture would aggravate her. Midway through her internship, she started to notice more apathy and depersonalization toward patients in the practice. She now internalized her frustrations that most patients would not accept her cultural differences. It took Salima several supervision meetings to process her "self-of-the-therapist" issues and feelings around her worth in the clinic. Her supervisor made sure that Salima could attend team meetings and more social outings to be part of the team and feel a greater acceptance in the community.

This situation presents a cultural dilemma for the intern that can be very challenging to navigate. In many training sites and geographic locations, aspects of cultural and religious biases unfortunately arise. Salima would benefit from increased supervision from both her site supervisor and current graduate program. The graduate program and site might need to talk and discuss options for Salima to feel comfortable in her work environment and feel supported by the clinic staff. Physicians, nurses, and other providers should be made aware of the comments from patients and where their communication with patients during handoffs and consults could increase awareness and support. If the situation were to continually remain problematic, the graduate program may look at either relocating Salima to a different training site or shift the role for her services in the clinic. Examples of this shift in roles may include having Salima serve as a liaison for families, shadowing physicians during encounters for additional training or handling crisis calls that come to the clinic.

Diego is a 44-year-old Latino male who identifies as gay. He is a newly licensed therapist and assumed a position in a community mental health clinic. He has taken on multiple responsibilities in his clinical and supervisory work and has been asked to serve on the healthcare board of their organization. Diego has had a difficult time saying "no" to certain bosses and administrators, since they know how hard he has been working so far. After months of overcommitting his schedule, several things start to get ignored. The most glaring issue is that patients have complained about his missed appointments or not being able to reach Diego. Diego was so alarmed by this news, that he started to book after hours appointments three days per week to make up these clinical times. As a result of overscheduling his weekday appointments and meetings, Diego's sleep and health have been affected greatly. He was hospitalized six months into his job for dehydration and extremely low potassium levels. Even after being discharged, he felt a sense of disappointing his staff and colleagues for not doing enough in his work to meet demands in the clinic

His clinical supervisor made it a priority that Diego creates a wellness plan transitioning back to work. Diego was very surprised in the support that he received from the care team. He did not realize that others in the clinic were somewhat concerned from his overcommitment to tasks and how much burnout he was experiencing. As the year went along, Diego took part in more wellness workshops, as well as creating a quarterly workshop for medical assistants, nurses and front desk staff.

The hospitalization was a wakeup call for Diego that he had to make boundary setting a key priority in his scheduling and professional work.

Burnout can often arise when a provider feels that they need to prove their skills and worth above-and-beyond the call. In this case, Diego has placed himself in a role of continually trying to please colleagues and staff by taking on every role and volunteer position. The lack of boundaries around trying to protect one's self-care can lead to increased risks of emotional, physical and family problems. Diego needs to feel comfortable saying "no" to several commitments at his work with support from a supervisor or administrator. Additionally, someone at his work may need to mentor Diego around his boundary setting with some close monitoring of his balance of job responsibilities moving forward.

John is a 63-year-old that has been a Behavioral Science faculty member for 17 years in a residency program. Recently, his wife of almost 35 years passed away from breast cancer. John continues to work in the residency because it is close to his brother and a good friend. He has been getting good support from colleagues and mentors. One of John's responsibilities is to educate and supervise residents on their behavioral health rotations. A few of them have taken an interest in families with a cancer diagnosis and using psychotherapy skills with this population. After a few weeks of shadowing residents on this rotation, John has become very affected by the cases that he has seen through his supervising. He began going home emotionally exhausted and crying at times when remembering his wife. As John began to work with more chronic illness cases the next several weeks, the flooding of emotions from the loss of his wife continued. He has become more distant from educating and teaching residents on this rotation as a result of the personal issues that come up in his work.

In this case, the therapist is experiencing self-of-the-therapist issues that is affecting both his personal and professional life. Burnout and personal struggles can happen not just with beginning therapists but in advanced careers as well. With seniority in the job, it is sometimes common for supervisors to operate their self-care issues alone. Although John is receiving support and comfort from colleagues, there are clear grief issues that are triggered by some of the clinical rotations that he is working on. The residency program might want to support some time off for John, getting away from the stresses of work. His supervisor or boss may also want to support John seeking help for his grief and put supports in place so that the program could help him with any work-related issues that may trigger his grief reactions.

Strategies to Combat Burnout for BHPs

Resiliency strategies for burnout and burnout prevention should ideally come from all levels of a healthcare setting. Without support and systems in place to help the BHP through their work, the therapist is forced to operate on an island regarding their personal self-care and validation for their work. The following are strategies at three levels of healthcare roles that can help mitigate some of the burnout and fatigue factors that often arise in early career professionals.

Behavioral Health Providers

- *Consider self-care activities.* BHPs should have a range of self-care strategies that help them get away from the weekly demands of the job. Activities should ideally be non-related to work and help professionals find areas to help improve overall wellness.
- *Target motivational and intrinsic goals.* Whether one is an intern or a long-time therapist in a healthcare setting, setting up motivational goals and aims is a way to stay engaged in their work. Goals should also be intrinsic in nature where the work achievements are gratifying for the purpose of the job itself.
- *Interprofessional skill development.* Therapists can learn ways to interact more with their team and get support from colleagues about their skills. Often, burnout can lead to increased isolation from colleagues and the treatment team.
- *Personal retreats/mental health days.* BHPs can benefit from taking mini retreats whether for self-care or creating more of a life balance outside of work. Therapists should reward their hard work with these periodic retreats to re-charge their motivation and interest levels in their work duties.

Support from Supervisors and Mentors

- *Increased emphasis on evaluation of self-care.* Supervisors would benefit from incorporating self-care strategies in their periodic evaluations of trainees or staff. Making this a priority in the evaluation process allows for new therapists to develop self-care skills during their training period.
- *Involvement of more care team activities.* One way to increase confidence and support for trainees and supervisees is to engage them in more team-based activities or meetings. A colleague or provider could have the trainee shadow or sit in certain clinical huddles or patient rounds to get increased exposure to the team and greater support.
- *Strength-focused feedback.* Often, supervisors are quick to notice the deficits in trainees and new healthcare interns. Increasing the number of strengths for trainees is a way to build one's confidence and highlight hidden areas of work that have been productive.
- *Preventing overcommitment from interns.* Sometimes, a new clinician who is burning out from the medical environment will need periodic breaks. Supervisors and mentors should also monitor that new professionals do not overcommit to committees, groups or other outside tasks from their clinical roles. The supervi-

sor should continually monitor which clinical activities and rotations might be too heavy on the intern during periods of burnout.

Support from Administrators and Organizations

- *Greater appreciation of job accomplishment.* Providing employees with periodic emails or letters about job work and accomplishment can help curb some self-doubt of providers.
- *Safeguards to address burnout in the workplace.* Administrators need to consider ways to reduce overworking and outside demands for BHPs. Clinics, hospitals and other settings would benefit from having process groups or in-service talks about work satisfaction and areas of burnout.
- *Increased resources and support systems.* For all providers (including BHPs), having multiple resources or supports in place when burnout arises is essential. BHPs should feel like they have a work environment that supports time to seek therapy, groups, or other community forums that help combat work fatigue or personal issues.
- *Wellness days for clinical teams and staff.* Healthcare settings that create wellness days or retreats allow employees to bond with colleagues on a deeper level. This also shows the organization's commitment for looking out for the well-being of providers and emphasizing a team-oriented environment.

With more healthcare providers required to meet professional demands in the context of their work, burnout and compassion fatigue will be an ongoing challenge for organizations and clinics to address in future generations (Lamson, Meadors, & Mendenhall, 2014). While the development of process groups, support systems, and scheduled work activities has helped curb some of this trend, the unpredictable nature of both workload and patient hours in medical settings impacts work–life balance. New trainees and students would benefit from practicing wellness habits and boundary setting during their rotations and internship years. Learning these skills early in training can help protect individuals' time for family, cultural rituals, hobbies, and other life necessities. Without these safeguards in place for the next workforce of BH providers, fewer incentives will be offered for aspiring therapists to enter work in the medical field.

References

Bria, M., Baban, A., & Dumitrascu, D. L. (2012). Systematic review of burnout risk factors among European healthcare professionals. *Cognition, Brain, Behavior: An Interdisciplinary Journal, 16*, 423–452.

Canfield, J. (2005). Secondary traumatization, burnout, and vicarious traumatization: A review of the literature as it relates to therapists who treat trauma. *Smith College Studies in Social Work, 75*, 81–101. https://doi.org/10.1300/J497v75n02_06

Dugani, S., Afari, H., Hirschhorn, L. R., Ratcliffe, H., Veillard, J., Martin, G., … Bitton, A. (2018). Prevalence and factors associated with burnout among frontline primary health care providers in low-and middle-income countries: A systematic review. *Gates open research, 2*. https://doi.org/10.12688/gatesopenres.12779.3

Dunkley, J., & Whelan, T. A. (2006). Vicarious traumatisation: Current status and future directions. *British Journal of Guidance & Counselling, 34*(1), 107–116.

Dyrbye, L., Shanafelt, T., Sinsky, C., Cipriano, P. F., Bhatt, J., Ommaya, A., & Meyers, D. (2017). *Burnout among health care professionals. A call to explore and address this underrecognized threat to safe, high-quality care*. Washington, D.C.: National Academy of Medicine.

Houkes, I., Winants, Y., Twellaar, M., & Verdonk, P. (2011). Development of burnout over time and the causal order of the three dimensions of burnout among male and female GPs. A three wave panel study. *BMC Public Health, 11*, 240. https://doi.org/10.1186/1471-2458-11-240

Korczak, D., Huber, B., & Kister, C. (2010). Differential diagnostic of the burnout syndrome. GMS health technology assessment, 6, Doc09. https://doi.org/10.3205/hta000087

Kovach Clark, H., Murdock, N. L., & Koetting, K. (2009). Predicting burnout and career choice satisfaction in counseling psychology graduate students. *The Counseling Psychologist, 37*, 580–606. https://doi.org/10.1177/0011000008319985

Lamson, A., Meadors, P., & Mendenhall, T. (2014). Working with providers and healthcare systems experiencing compassion fatigue and burnout. In *Medical family therapy* (pp. 107–123). New York, NY: Springer. https://doi.org/10.1007/978-3-319-03482-9_7

Lauvrud, C., Nonstad, K., & Palmstierna, T. (2009). Occurrence of post traumatic stress symptoms and their relationship to professional quality of life (ProQoL) in nursing staff at a forensic psychiatric security unit: A cross-sectional study. *Health and Quality of Life Outcomes, 7*, 31. https://doi.org/10.1186/1477-7525-7-31

Lee, Y. W., Dai, Y. T., Park, C. G., & McCreary, L. L. (2013). Predicting quality of work life on nurses' intention to leave. *Journal of Nursing Scholarship, 45*, 160–168. https://doi.org/10.1111/jnu.12017

Lo, D., Wu, F., Chan, M., Chu, R., & Li, D. (2018). A systematic review of burnout among doctors in China: A cultural perspective. *Asia Pacific Family Medicine, 17*, 3. https://doi.org/10.1186/s12930-018-0040-3

Maslach, C., & Jackson, S. E. (1981). The measurement of experienced burnout. *Journal of Occupational Behaviour, 2*, 99–113.

Maslach, C., Jackson, S. E., & Leiter, M. P. (1996). MBI: Maslach burnout inventory. Sunnyvale (CA): CPP, Incorporated.

Maslach, C., & Leiter, M. P. (2008). Early predictors of job burnout and engagement. *Journal of Applied Psychology, 93*, 498–512. https://doi.org/10.1002/job.4030020205

Melamed, S., Shirom, A., Toker, S., & Shapira, I. (2006). Burnout and risk of type 2 diabetes: A prospective study of apparently healthy employed persons. *Psychosomatic Medicine, 86*, 863–869. https://doi.org/10.1097/01.psy.0000242860.24009.f0

Morse, G., Salyers, M. P., Rollins, A. L., Monroe-DeVita, M., & Pfahler, C. (2012). Burnout in mental health services: A review of the problem and its remediation. *Administration and Policy in Mental Health and Mental Health Services Research, 39*, 341–352. https://doi.org/10.1037/a0026534

Myers, S. B., Sweeney, A. C., Popick, V., Wesley, K., Bordfeld, A., & Fingerhut, R. (2012). Self-care practices and perceived stress levels among psychology graduate students. *Training and Education in Professional Psychology, 6*, 55. https://doi.org/10.1037/a0026534

O'Connor, K., Neff, D. M., & Pitman, S. (2018). Burnout in mental health professionals: A systematic review and meta-analysis of prevalence and determinants. *European Psychiatry, 53*, 74–99. https://doi.org/10.1016/j.eurpsy.2018.06.003

Rosa, H. (2014). From work-life to work-age balance? Acceleration, alienation, and appropriation at the workplace. In *The impact of ICT on quality of working life* (pp. 43–61). Dordrecht, Netherlands: Springer.

Salyers, M. P., Bonfils, K. A., Luther, L., Firmin, R. L., White, D. A., Adams, E. L., & Rollins, A. L. (2017). The relationship between professional burnout and quality and safety in healthcare: A meta-analysis. *Journal of General Internal Medicine, 32*, 475–482. https://doi.org/10.1007/s11606-016-3886-9

Schaufeli, W. (2006). The balance of give and take: Toward a social exchange model of burnout. *International Review of Social Psychology, 19*, 87–131.

Shah, J. L., Kapoor, R., Cole, R., & Steiner, J. L. (2016). Employee health in the mental health workplace: Clinical, administrative, and organizational perspectives. *The Journal of Behavioral Health Services & Research, 43*, 330–338. https://doi.org/10.1007/s11414-014-9428-5

Shirom, A. (1989). Burnout in work organizations. In C. L. Cooper & I. T. Robertson (Eds.), International review of industrial and organizational psychology 1989 (p. 25–48). John Wiley & Sons. Hoboken, NJ.

Stamm, B. H. (2009). *Professional quality of life: Compassion satisfaction and fatigue version 5 (ProQOL)*. 2011-03-20. http://www.isu.edu/bhstamm.

Practice Challenges and Ethical Decision-Making

Max Zubatsky and Jackie Williams-Reade

During my (Max's) doctoral training, I came across a situation where a chief resident was describing a patient in a very unprofessional manner. The resident was clearly frustrated with the patient's lack of motivation around their health, shaming the patient's weight in front of his colleagues. As I was hearing the conversation in the huddle room next door, my anger rose very quickly. The resident then proceeded to mock the family's weight, joking about their health habits. A challenge for confronting this resident that day was that there were two encounters that demanded this person either be consulted on or part of the team visit. I was advised to wait until the following week to process these feelings with the resident. Although the conversation was not easy to initiate, I learned that there were deeper issues present that impacted the resident's views of the patient. Through a few more follow-up conversations, there were some cultural aspects of the patient that I brought to the attention of the resident. These were blind spots in the resident's training that were not indicative of his clinical competencies but rather lack of cultural awareness of the population he was serving.

When working in the healthcare field, one will always come across several practice and ethical challenges that tests one's moral compass. These situations not only pertain to patient issues but to colleagues and the entire organization (Bazerman & Tenbrunsel, 2012). A new therapist often does not recognize or anticipate these challenges that will arise during their training, largely due to entering a new context

M. Zubatsky
Department of Family and Community Medicine, Saint Louis University, St. Louis, MO, USA

J. Williams-Reade (✉)
Department of Counseling and Family Sciences, Loma Linda University, Loma Linda, CA, USA
e-mail: jwilliamsreade@llu.edu

M. Zubatsky, J. Williams-Reade (eds.), *Self of the Therapist in Medical Settings*, AFTA SpringerBriefs in Family Therapy,
https://doi.org/10.1007/978-3-030-39271-0_6

with unknown roles and responsibilities (Curtis & Christian, 2012; Hall et al., 2015). Although most ethical issues can be largely avoided, BHPs face a tougher challenge when the ethical conduct applies to a work partner or friend in the workplace. What is described in this chapter are real-life ethical dilemmas and practice situations that pertain specifically to therapists working in medical and healthcare settings. These issues not only affect how the therapist responds to patient care, but how one handles internal conflicts that push their decision-making and morals to different places. As a White male, I have increasingly focused on the areas of power and privilege within the context of care in medicine. I also have worked on how my personal ethics, morals, and beliefs might contradict other colleagues' perspectives, where learning to navigate and negotiate this terrain is always an evolving process.

Ethical decision-making is often seen as gray area for professionals working in medical settings. Whereas providers know the appropriate legal steps after a patient states a plan for suicide, navigating through challenges such as power and privilege, cultural sensitivity, and best clinical practices become less concrete (Thompson et al., 2016). Ethical decisions in healthcare require that BHPs consistently make sound decisions that help protect themselves, their care team, and the patient. Training programs often lack the necessary preparation for new training interns and students for situations that require immediate decision-making in medical settings or appropriate times to consult around a clinic issue (Bischoff, Springer, Reisbig, Lyons, Likcani, 2012; Hall et al., 2015). When BHPs get thrown into these tenuous situations, many often struggle with navigating the appropriate action or steps in a new setting.

Common Ethical Dilemmas for Therapists in Practice

Those who chose to practice in healthcare settings must anticipate potential ethical dilemmas. Some of these situations are inherent challenges within the medical system, whereas others test the moral compass of therapists in their everyday practice. Practitioners always need to be aware of adhering to their code of ethics in a given discipline (Bazerman & Tenbrunsel, 2012). Often, there are gray areas of practice and professional work that place therapists in tough spots to make confident decisions. Unlike many traditional psychotherapy practices where a therapist may operate as a solo provider, addressing practice challenges on collaborative teams requires skillful navigation on the part of the BHC (Curtis & Christian, 2012; Robinson & Reiter, 2016). The following are some ethical issues that often come up for clinicians and present both moral and ethical dilemmas.

Informed Consent

Just like in routine psychotherapy services, medical clinics and organizations have protocols for informed consent of services for patients (Patterson, Peek, Heinrich, Bischoff, & Scherger, 2002). Hospitals have become so efficient at collecting consent that a "blanket" consent will often cover the communication and information provided from multiple providers in the patient's care. Consent becomes a trickier process when the BHP provides quick consults or warm handoffs from physicians where the conversation may not warrant a patient encounter (Hodgson, Mendenhall, & Lamson, 2013). However, do patients know the scope of your work and goals of your services even in these brief conversations? Do patients know the scope of psychotherapy services even if they are not established patients? These areas should not be glossed over in appointments even if patients may be seen for a one-time consultation or encounter.

Therapist may need to revise their policies for how their clinics and practice settings manage informed consent around all types of mental health services. The patient needs to be aware of their control of the treatment process and their rights of not having to see a BHP if requested. BHPs should also make it a routine practice of explaining their role to patients and their understanding that they might be engaging in a behavioral treatment or intervention. Providing verbal consent to patients and families may be necessary in times where sensitive issues or topics may have to be addressed in appointments. Any safety or risk issues such as self-harm, partner violence, or previous traumas often warrant permission from the patient to speak on these issues in front of family or other friends.

Addressing Medical Errors

One of the most challenging and humbling experiences of new providers of any discipline is to admit your mistakes to patients and/or family members. The admission of a medical error not only takes a certain amount of humility but a willingness to use the patient's frustrations as a learning experience (Khoo et al., 2012; Mazor, Roblin, Greene, Fouayzi, & Gallagher, 2016). Therapists often do not realize that they may be brought into these conversations, especially during work in hospital or inpatient settings. Families may direct their frustrations to behavioral health providers on physician errors around failure to report test results, missed diagnoses, or medication errors. The BHP must decide how to not only bring this information back to the provider, but how the care team will negotiate this error with patient and/or family.

If you are in a situation where a mistake happened, showing a clear sense of compassion and forgiveness of the situation is a top priority. This should be the case regardless if the BHP was part of the initial error. BHPs are a part of the team in which patients may view the scope of a problem as the fault of the entire set of providers involved. The therapist's interpersonal skills can help repair and find resolve for the patient or family during these conversations. Nevertheless, the medical team, specifically the provider at fault for the error, has a legal responsibility to discuss this error with the patient and/or member in charge of their health decisions (Khoo et al., 2012; Rosser et al., 2005).

Secret Keeping

Medicine can be a very vulnerable place for patients to disclose their information about personal health, emotional, or family issues. Often, there is an internal script that patients carry regarding what their providers might judge them by as a result of a medical issue, lifestyle choice, or healthcare decision (Rolfe, Cash-Gibson, Car, Sheikh, & McKinstry, 2014). Although BHPs are trained to be open about discussing a range of clinical and personal patient topics, situations get complicated when the BHP is requested to hold secrets. Patients might triangulate therapists into making sure that their doctor or specialist does not know about a confidential issue or situation in their lives.

For instance, a patient may have multiple sexual partners and recently contracted an STI. This patient confides in you not to tell their physician, in hopes that the physician will not think badly of them or shame them for not adhering to safer sex practices. As the therapist, it is important to explore the patient's hesitation to keep this issue a secret from the physician and, possibly, other care providers. Also, BHPs have the responsibility not to withhold important health information from their care team. The aspect of secret keeping needs to be highlighted to the patient in this appointment and outlining the risks of withholding this information for more time (Richards, 2009).

Boundaries Around Scope of Practice

All mental health professionals adhere to a scope of practice as part of their code of ethics. This parameter allows therapists to work within the bounds of areas such as diagnosis, assessment, treatment interventions, and types of services that can be provided. In health care, therapists often work with patients where overlapping medical and medication concerns are present (Bischoff et al., 2012; Edwards & Elwyn, 2009). BHPs ride a fine line between therapeutic conversations of medical and pharmacological issues and giving straightforward medical advice of decision-making of one's condition or illness (Hall et al., 2015).

It is important for therapists to be consciously aware of their questions, curiosities, and treatment recommendations for patients around health and medication issues. Therapists might be put on the spot to give advice about a particular antidepressant medication or decision about getting a particular procedure done. A new therapist should not feel insecure about their lack of knowledge of a topic or condition but rather refer the patient's questions to their current physician or specialist in that area. For example, patients who have a history of failed response for antidepressant medications are recently prescribed a new SSRI for depression. Although a BHP cannot give direct advice about stopping or readjusting medications for depression, they can provide elements of psychoeducation of the risks of withdrawing their medication early. Additionally, the patient can receive some behavioral strategies to help improve their mood while deciding how dedicated they are to take their medication.

Reporting Unethical Behavior

Unethical behaviors and situations can range on a large spectrum in healthcare settings. Some situations may involve a colleague talking bad about a patient or colleague in public. Extreme situations may involve provider–patient relationships, falsifying documentation in charts, or overcharging for procedures and codes that add to large amounts. Whatever the case, therapists can often be placed in the uncomfortable role of reporting inappropriate behaviors of colleagues and other staff. These situations place a high degree of anxiety and vulnerability on the part of the BHP, where the risk of fracturing close relationships with a care team is a possibility.

Several factors can go into one reporting or bring up an unethical issue in their practice setting. New BHPs should have a decision-making process for how one would go about addressing this issue and to which providers. Therapists in training should also have a conversation with their supervisors about how to go about a situation in their practice setting, should something arise. More experienced clinicians can benefit from having good rapport with their administrative staff in case of any unethical conduct that needs to be communicated or processed.

Family Decision-Making/Power of Attorney

In certain medical situations, families will have to make very difficult choices around their loved one's health. For end-of-life patients, family members not only reorganize their priorities around the person's care but also honor the wishes of the patient during hard circumstances (Yadav et al., 2017). In hospital settings, a family without a designated power of attorney (POA) may have to choose who will assume this responsibility and decide whether the member gets a "full code" for procedures to be continued to keep the patient alive. Some families not only lack a POA for their loved one but have trouble understanding the definition and responsibilities of this role. The BHP and healthcare team have a responsibility to not only educate the family about a healthcare POA, but process any cultural, spiritual, or familial areas that impact the family's decision to determine their loved one's health.

Therapists must navigate a difficult path with families concerning end-of-life issues and scenarios. These conversations may take the form of family meetings in a consult room in the hospital or in a larger conference room in a primary care clinic (Curtis & Christian, 2012). Often, the BHP will gather all members' perspectives of the POA issue and help families best negotiate what is best for the patient (Milte et al., 2015). Despite who takes the legal responsibility to be the executor of healthcare decisions of the patient, the therapist can skillfully find ways for the family to be involved in the care moving forward.

Access of Services by Minority Populations

Patients from underserved or underrepresented populations are often challenged to get adequate healthcare services and coverage. This population not only underutilizes mental health care services (Wilson & Schild, 2014) but often has strong cultural or personal values that go against the use of these services. Additionally, the power dynamics of a doctor or other health specialist to request mental health services may place minority groups in a submissive role when making decisions about their care. Therapists should consider the culturally sensitive nature of minority populations in practice. BHPs have to be sensitive in offering services at an affordable, cost-effective rate for patients and families, all this while administration and operations may put increased pressures on productivity and revenue generation of their job. Certain social determinants of health should routinely be assessed in healthcare settings to gain a fuller scope of the patient's barriers to care (Cunningham, 2009). Areas such as housing, transportation, access to medication refills, and family supports make a significant difference in how often patients follow-up with their care team.

Case Study

Jasmine is an African American female in her late 20s and started practicing in a primary care clinic for her doctoral fellowship. Because she is the only behavioral health provider on the staff, she has garnered lots of referrals and consultations around the clinic. Her director has already seen the impact she has made in improving patient care and coordination with other colleagues. Dorothy, one of the nurses on her team, has been going through some difficult personal struggles in her life. She recently lost her husband to cancer and is currently living with her mother due to financial problems in the family. Others in the office have noticed a considerable change in mood in the last three months. Although her director has suggested that she take a leave of absence, Dorothy is insistent on continuing to work because it takes her mind off of the stressful events in her personal life.

One day, Dorothy knocks on Jasmine's office door and needs to talk to someone. Dorothy confesses to Jasmine that she is really going through a difficult time and needs to borrow some money. She promises to pay back Jasmine and to honor her word. Jasmine says that she would need to think about the situation first before making any rash decisions. Later that week, Jasmine gets an email from her director at the clinic. The director feels that Dorothy would benefit from seeing Jasmine on a periodic basis to talk about her mental health issues. The director would also be open to Jasmine touching base with him about any updates from Dorothy from these consultations. Jasmine now feels like she is in a bind, wanting to help Dorothy without making their professional relationship compromised.

After a few consultations with her supervisor, Jasmine decided to have a brief meeting with Dorothy in a separate office in the clinic. Jasmine expressed her wor-

ries about seeing Dorothy as her therapist and exchanging money where these issues would present a boundary issue for Jasmine. Jasmine also expressed that she did not want either situation to affect their professional relationship, considering that they work collaboratively on many of the same patients. Jasmine encouraged Dorothy to talk with her boss about the financial issue to see what other resources or supports could help. Jasmine's supervisor had a follow-up conversation with the clinical director to clarify Jasmine's decision not to be Dorothy's therapist and how this role could pose a dual relationship problem going forward.

This dual relationship dilemma is becoming increasingly common in health care settings. It is commonplace for physicians to treat staff and other providers as part of routine medical care. The ethics are different, however, for behavioral health services provided to professionals in the same clinic. Jasmine was caught with the dilemma of wanting to help a colleague but without jeopardizing the ethics of a dual relationship with someone in her same practice. The merging of medical and behavioral health fields in integrated care practice has been one of the biggest challenges in regards to confidentiality of the care team. Jasmine should realize that although her director feels that Dorothy would benefit from periodic consultations for her emotional issues, this would blur the work boundaries even further. Additionally, Jasmine must navigate the hierarchical structure and gender issue of confronting her director about this dilemma. Her conversation with the director should not only take Jasmine's perspective into account but an opportunity to educate the director about the ethical differences between medical providers and behavioral health providers. For a new intern, this can be a very difficult position to face, given the need for Jasmine to gain trust and connection with her care team at the start of her rotation.

Practice Challenges in Routine Care

In addition to ethical concerns and dilemmas that happen within the scope of medical practice, there are practice challenges that BHPs need to consider in their settings. These challenges can often deal with space, communication with the patient, and/or understanding of health concerns and cultural considerations in clinical encounters.

- *Office space and practice locations.* In many clinics, the BHP will not always see the patient or family in a therapy office. Sessions can be conducted in an exam room, conference room or common room that is shared by other providers. Anticipating interruptions and overhead pages are a common distraction in sessions. Additionally, these settings may not have the most comfortable seating options for patients and/or members to have during a longer session. When the BHP does not have the resources of a traditional office, he or she must adjust their style of therapy to align with the presenting problems of the patient or family.
- *Gender issues that may arise during an encounter.* Patients often have challenges disclosing certain personal information due to the gender of the physician

(Bertakis, 2009). BHPs may be brought in for consultations to help alleviate these concerns of patients and/or family members. In the hospital settings, BHPs routinely encounter such examples, where the pace of the conversation, sensitivity to the gender-specific issues and volume of speech needs to be altered to adjust to the patient's situation. Some examples of sensitive gender issues may include partner violence, sexual dysfunction issues, or previous trauma-related conditions.

- *Confidentiality in the hospital setting.* Another challenge on inpatient services is the lack of true confidentiality when speaking with patients. The patient might be sharing a room with another patient or have an exposed room where those in the hall might be able to hear (Hodgson et al., 2013). Nurses, medical assistants, specialists, and other providers will frequently enter the room at unexpected times and unintentionally interrupt the conversations. Therapists should remind the patient about the possibility of the conversation being open for others to hear and handling ongoing disruptions in rooms.
- *Health literacy and health education.* A major shortcoming that health care providers continue to overlook is the literacy and education of patients surrounding their healthcare decisions (McCune, Lee & Pohl, 2016). Aspects such as socio-economic status, race, ethnicity, age, and educational level can make a large impact on how patients manage their health issues. Many patients struggle with knowing how to organize medications, read labels and information, understand complex medical terms, and complying with a long-term treatment from a provider. When BHPs offer an intervention, skill, or technique for the patient to consider, one should also assess for the patient's level of understanding this recommendation and what supports could help with the follow-though of the plan of care.
- *Using interpreters for sessions.* Some patients, for whom English is a second language, may need an interpreter (in-person or phone) to help translate sessions. Therapists should consider ways to adjust their conversations in these types of sessions (Jacobs, Ryan, Henricks, & Weiss, 2018; Kalina, 2015). The pacing of questions and time allowed for translation to be communicated back to the therapist is a learning curve for many new therapists. BHPs must also be sensitive to any cultural issues in how questions are answered and how the interpreter constructs the information going two ways.

- One specific case stands out for me (Max) around the issue of interpreters and health education.

This example occurred when I was rounding with a family medicine team in a hospital. A Puerto Rican patient and her mother were in the room with five providers on the family medicine team (one BHP, one physician, one medical resident, one pharmacist, and one case manager). The physician was Spanish-speaking and willing to interpret the conversation for the patient, mother, and medical team. When the doctor began to ask questions, the patient's mother became increasingly frustrated. The mother interrupted the physician and said, "You are speaking the wrong kind of Spanish." The patient asked the physician if she could call the interpreter to finish the conversation. Although the physician was respectful and supportive of their decision, the encounter extended an extra 15 minutes because of locating an interpreter, allowing translation time, and processing all the patient's concerns. The patient also reiterated to the physician and team that her mother does not understand all of the medical terms and medications that the other doctors have discussed. The physician was very brief with the mother and left the room to attend to other patients on the floor. The pharmacist and resident spent an additional 10 minutes going over the list of medications and what they are used for.

After the team finished rounding, both the therapist and team went back to the room to process any concerns or questions they had. The patient said that she was appreciative that they heard her concerns and did not like the tone of the previous physician. This also became a learning experience for the residency team where they had to admit as a group that they did not hear the family's concerns effectively. Respecting the culture and language of patients and family members in the hospital setting is a very important competency for all health care providers. BHPs often have this role of listening to patients' frustrations, concerns, or opinions as a result of decisions made by the care team.

Conclusion

Legal and ethical considerations will always exist for mental health professionals who work in interdisciplinary settings. While each professional discipline has their own code of ethics to follow, many ethical challenges in medicine are considered new territory for beginning therapists in their training or career. Even more unknown ethical decisions and challenges exist for BHPs in secondary and tertiary care settings (Bazerman & Tenbrunsel, 2012). As the roles of therapists expand in an ever-changing United States health care system, the work tasks, scope of practice and autonomy of decisions will continue to be an evolving issue moving forward.

References

Bazerman, M. H., & Tenbrunsel, A. E. (2012). *Blind spots: Why we fail to do what's right and what to do about it*. Princeton University Press, Princeton, NJ.

Bertakis, K. D. (2009). The influence of gender on the doctor–patient interaction. *Patient Education and Counseling, 76*, 356–360. https://doi.org/10.1016/j.pec.2009.07.022

Bischoff, R. J., Springer, P. R., Reisbig, A. M., Lyons, S., & Likcani, A. (2012). Training for collaboration: Collaborative practice skills for mental health professionals. *Journal of Marital and Family Therapy, 38*, 199–210. https://doi.org/10.1111/j.1752-0606.2012.00299.x

Cunningham, P. J. (2009). Beyond parity: Primary care physicians' perspectives on access to mental health care. *Health Affairs, 28*, w490–w501. https://doi.org/10.1377/hlthaff.28.3.w490

Curtis, R., & Christian, E. (Eds.). (2012). *Integrated care: Applying theory to practice*. Taylor & Francis, New York, NY.

Edwards, A., & Elwyn, G. (Eds.). (2009). *Shared decision-making in health care: Achieving evidence-based patient choice*. Oxford University Press, Oxford.
Hall, J., Cohen, D. J., Davis, M., Gunn, R., Blount, A., Pollack, D. A., … Miller, B. F. (2015). Preparing the workforce for behavioral health and primary care integration. *Journal of the American Board of Family Medicine, 28*(Supplement 1), S41–S51. https://doi.org/10.3122/jabfm.2015.S1.150054
Hodgson, J., Mendenhall, T., & Lamson, A. (2013). Patient and provider relationships: Consent, confidentiality, and managing mistakes in integrated primary care settings. *Families, Systems & Health, 31*, 28–40. https://doi.org/10.1037/a0031771
Jacobs, B., Ryan, A. M., Henrichs, K. S., & Weiss, B. D. (2018). Medical interpreters in outpatient practice. *Annals of Family Medicine, 16*, 70–76. https://doi.org/10.1370/afm.2154
Kalina, S. (2015). Ethical challenges in different interpreting settings. *Universitat Jaume I, Special Issue 2*, 63. https://doi.org/10.6035/MonTI.2015.ne2.2
Khoo, E. M., Lee, W. K., Sararaks, S., Samad, A. A., Liew, S. M., Cheong, A. T., … Ismail, R. (2012). Medical errors in primary care clinics–a cross sectional study. *BMC Family Practice, 13*, 127. https://doi.org/10.1186/1471-2296-13-127
Mazor, K., Roblin, D. W., Greene, S. M., Fouayzi, H., & Gallagher, T. H. (2016). Primary care physicians' willingness to disclose oncology errors involving multiple providers to patients. *BMJ Quality Safety, 25*, 787–795. https://doi.org/10.1136/bmjqs-2015-004353
McCune, R. L., Lee, H., & Pohl, J. M. (2016). Assessing health literacy in safety net primary care practices. *Applied Nursing Research, 29*, 188–194. https://doi.org/10.1016/j.apnr.2015.04.004
Milte, C. M., Ratcliffe, J., Davies, O., Whitehead, C., Masters, S., & Crotty, M. (2015). Family meetings for older adults in intermediate care settings: The impact of patient cognitive impairment and other characteristics on shared decision making. *Health Expectations, 18*, 1030–1040. https://doi.org/10.1111/hex.12076
Patterson, J., Peek, C. J., Heinrich, R. L., Bischoff, R. J., & Scherger, J. (2002). *Mental health professionals in medical settings: A primer*. New York, NY: Springer.
Richards, M. M. (2009). Electronic medical records: Confidentiality issues in the time of HIPAA. *Professional Psychology: Research and Practice, 40*, 550.
Robinson, P. J., & Reiter, J. T. (2016). Behavioral consultation and primary care: The "why now?" and "how?". In *Behavioral consultation and primary care*. New York, NY: Springer. https://doi.org/10.1007/978-3-319-13954-8_1
Rolfe, A., Cash-Gibson, L., Car, J., Sheikh, A., & McKinstry, B. (2014). Interventions for improving patients' trust in doctors and groups of doctors. *Cochrane Database of Systematic Reviews*, (3). https://doi.org/10.1002/14651858.CD004134.pub3
Rosser, W., Dovey, S., Bordman, R., White, D., Crighton, E., & Drummond, N. (2005). Medical errors in primary care: Results of an international study of family practice. *Canadian Family Physician, 51*, 386–387.
Thompson, A. E., Anisimowicz, Y., Miedema, B., Hogg, W., Wodchis, W. P., & Aubrey-Bassler, K. (2016). The influence of gender and other patient characteristics on health care-seeking behaviour: A QUALICOPC study. *BMC Family Practice, 17*, 38. https://doi.org/10.1186/s12875-016-0440-0
Wilson, J. A., & Schild, S. (2014). Provision of mental health care services to deaf individuals using telehealth. *Professional Psychology: Research and Practice, 45*(5), 324. https://doi.org/10.1037/a0036811
Yadav, K. N., Gabler, N. B., Cooney, E., Kent, S., Kim, J., Herbst, N., … Courtright, K. R. (2017). Approximately one in three US adults completes any type of advance directive for end-of-life care. *Health Affairs, 36*, 1244–1251. https://doi.org/10.1377/hlthaff.2017.0175

Professional Perspectives of the 'Self' in Their Journey Through Medicine

Max Zubatsky, Jackie Williams-Reade, Jose Bayona, Tai J. Mendenhall, Stacy Ogbeide, and Alison G. Wong

The value of mentorship and collegial support for beginning interns, therapists, and graduate students in medical and integrated care settings cannot be understated. When challenges or unexpected encounters arise, having strong supports from faculty supervisors, directors, and colleagues can help one manage these hurdles more effectively. The mentoring process often parallels the process of therapy where both parties learn to feel comfortable with the quality of conversations while strengthening trust in the relationship over time. Mentors are not just supervisors, but educators, models, and confidants to learners in new training contexts

M. Zubatsky (✉)
Department of Family and Community Medicine, Saint Louis University, St. Louis, MO, USA
e-mail: max.zubatsky@health.slu.edu

J. Williams-Reade (✉)
Department of Counseling and Family Sciences, Loma Linda University, Loma Linda, CA, USA
e-mail: jwilliamsreade@llu.edu

J. Bayona
Rundberg Health Center, CommUnityCare Health Centers, Austin, TX, USA

T. J. Mendenhall
Department of Family Social Science, College of Education and Human Development, University of Minnesota, Minneapolis, MN, USA

S. Ogbeide
Department of Family and Community Medicine, UT Health San Antonio, San Antonio, TX, USA

A. G. Wong
Department of Marriage and Family Therapy, School of Psychology, Fuller Theological Seminary, Pasadena, CA, USA

M. Zubatsky, J. Williams-Reade (eds.), *Self of the Therapist in Medical Settings*, AFTA SpringerBriefs in Family Therapy,
https://doi.org/10.1007/978-3-030-39271-0_7

(Prouty, Helmeke, & Fischer, 2016; Prouty & Storm, 2014). Effective mentors also introduce the professional culture of medicine to new professionals while providing a buffer to some of the common operational and structural challenges in a clinic or organization (Paris & Hoge, 2010).

Each of us (Max and Jackie) learned the value of acknowledging "self" in our training through many professional experiences. Unexpected clinical situations and difficult patient encounters made us attune to how our family of origin background affects our perceptions of certain mental health and medical conditions. These encounters also reminded us of how critical power and privilege comes into play from the provider side, stressing how we must continually check on this social status in our work. Different styles of supervision and mentoring allowed us to gain unique perspectives of not just patient care but how to function effectively in a new medical environment. We both arrived at helpful self-care strategies during times of rising burnout, lack of personal hobbies and family time that created the necessary life balance outside of our work. Regardless of the path that each professional takes to work in the medical field, we all create a journey that is unique to our own and make personal discoveries that are often never found in a textbook or the classroom.

The following are personal narratives presented from four professionals in the field who have worked in a variety of health care settings. Their reflections highlight specific personal and professional topics that have impacted their growth as a clinician and demonstrate how their own "self of the therapist" issues were processed during these experiences. These professionals offer sound advice to future learners and new professionals as they embark in new practice and training settings.

Knowing the Story Is Not the Same as Knowing the "St-o-o-o-ry"

Jose Bayona Rundberg Health Center, CommUnityCare Health Centers, Austin, TX, USA

The stories we tell when ill and their meaning have gained my attention and curiosity since I was a young boy as my parents both worked in hospitals. My father was the director of the physical therapy section in the only local public hospital dedicated to people who had work-related injuries and my mother was a social worker in a public adult and pediatric hospital. They took me to their respective workplaces during the summer school break from ages 8 to 12. I was in the occupational therapy unit when I went to the hospital with my father and was assigned to do small building projects with my hands, like the ones that patients were doing. The difference in purpose between the patients and me was that I was doing the projects for fun and they were doing theirs as part of their injury's rehabilitation.

Initially, I was a curiosity in the unit. Patients were in the rehabilitation unit because they had a work-related injury frequently causing to lose a body part or a neuromuscular impairment, whereas I had no injuries. Their building projects were designed to help them rehabilitate and my projects were for fun. However, despite our differences, the patients embraced my presence in the unit and I gained enough confidence to ask them about their injuries. Usually, I began with a simple question, "How were you injured?" The patients not only told their stories about how they were injured, but about their lives, families, hopes from rehabilitation, regrets, pain, challenges, and how they were coping. I remember listening with curiosity to their stories the whole day. These experiences, without me knowing at that time, led me to develop fundamental empathy for a person experiencing adverse health problems. I gained an interest in knowing more about the person by deeply listening to their stories, which revealed the fundamental meaning making of their worlds and style of coping during adverse situations.

Going to the hospital with my mother provided a different experience. Here, I listened to physicians talking to my mother about noncompliant patients that did not show up to their appointments or follow up with treatment recommendations. One core task of my mother's job was to contact the patients and encourage them to come to the hospital outpatient clinic and or assist them with any social or medical barrier affecting their treatment. Most of the time my mother scheduled a home visit, especially if the patient did not have a phone or did not respond to a letter sent by the hospital.

I enjoyed home visits that allowed me to travel outside the city. Most patients lived in rural areas, which I rarely visited before. Quickly, I was educated on the impact and role of poverty in health. I thought that everybody lived like me, in a house, with running clean water and electricity. Sadly, I realized this was not the case. I visited homes where families slept in the dirt with no beds, no running water, and no electricity. This extreme poverty was totally unknown to me, but by this young age, I learned that the hospital and the physician were not aware of social and economic situation of their patients. Lacking transportation, money, and physical living environment placed their health at higher risk. Visiting their physician or following treatment instructions had lower priorities compared to their daily life struggles with subsistence.

From interactions like these, I learned two meaningful personal and professional life lessons. First, that addressing poverty and social determinants of health are fundamental to improving the health of the indigent population and addressing them has greater health impact than working only from the local biomedical oriented clinic-based care. Second, the gap between my life experiences, both personally and professionally, is wide and deep with those from my patients. I need to be mindful of these gaps to avoid bias thinking and my characterization of patient conditions and behaviors.

Advice for Professionals in the Field

- All behaviors are contextual. Understanding the context though the patient's eyes and meaning making through their stories are fundamental tasks to effectively help our patients.

- We need to be mindful of our upbringing, values, and culture as we join with our patients to be understood as they see themselves through their meaning making stories.
- There is a lot that is unknown in health care, and every piece of knowledge is tentative. We must learn to feel comfortable with not knowing and be eager to learn from our patients and others, including team members.
- Participating in an interdisciplinary, collaborative, and reflective healthcare team helps all team members become more connected to their patients as fellow humans, thereby taking the fundamental step toward developing trust and healing.
- To avoid the tendency of using mechanistic efforts to fix health problems (e.g., rigid templates, catalog of algorithms, questioners, templates for history taking) we must extend ourselves even further to the domain of the human by not only listening to our patients' stories but by being touched by them.

Practicing-What-We-Preach: Recognizing and Responding to Our Own Humanness as Healthcare Providers

Tai J. Mendenhall Department of Family Social Science, College of Education and Human Development, University of Minnesota, Minneapolis, MN, USA

My journey into medical family therapy was more of a process than it was an event. It represented a culmination of professional and personal experiences – arguably spanning from early childhood to about halfway through graduate school – that led me to understand how the fast-paced, unpredictable, and clinically intense nature of medicine is where I am most comfortable. Some say it is because I came from a "medical family." Some say it is because I am an adrenaline junkie at-heart. Others maintain that my tendencies to be a workaholic are a perfect fit with the 80-hour work weeks of residency training. Any or all of these experiences may fuel my empathic struggles vis-à-vis students or colleagues who complain about being tired after they have only seen six or seven patients/families in a single day.

Medical practices – hospitals, clinics, trauma response teams, etc. – are usually more intense than the conventional private-practice therapy jobs for which most graduate programs train young professionals. And while some gravitate toward medicine (like I do), I have found that these care contexts will chew-you-up and spit-you-out if you are not careful. What about all of that warm-and-fuzzy "self-care" stuff that they talk about during the last two minutes of conference presentations or within the comfort and safety of practicum/supervision groups? I learned the hard way that you cannot just offer lip-service to taking care of the person who you are with 24 hours-per-day (i.e., one's self).

I had an epiphany several years ago after working "call" for a large medical system. Having been awake for almost 30 hours, I was ready to go home. It had been a relatively "normal" shift, with some nonemergency presentations (e.g., depression, chronic pain), some urgent situations (e.g., stroke, suicide ideation), and some more heartbreaking things (e.g., a positive HIV diagnosis, a lost pregnancy, an unexpected and tragic death of a loved one). While driving home, I began thinking about how I, as a healer, was giving all of myself to my patients and their families. I was helping them to cope and/or reclaim their mental and physical health. But at the same time, my well-being was deteriorating. I was depressed. I was overweight. I was not following any of the sleep hygiene strategies that I am so good at teaching others to do. I was going to an empty house as a divorcee because I could not hold my own personal relationships together (despite being good at helping others with theirs).

We know that depression, anxiety, alcohol abuse and dependence, burnout and compassion fatigue, relationship dissolutions, and a variety of other sequelae are more common – ironically – within groups of people whose job it is to allay others' suffering. I recall pulling over on that drive home, finally falling apart in tears because I knew – or was least beginning to admit what I had already known for some time – that I was becoming a statistic. I would like to say that this was a turning-point with a "happily ever after" ending – that I immediately changed everything around with my diet, my physical activity, my relationships, and my work–life balance. This is how things would have gone in an inspiring movie or engaging self-help book. Instead, and in a similar way to my process (not event) in choosing MedFT, I began taking steps to practice what I preach. I started walking – and eventually jogging – around a nearby lake. I began going to the grocery store for food instead of various drive-throughs on my ways to-and-from work. I started seeing my own therapist. I rekindled friendships and resumed a social life. I stopped working so much (and do not think that anybody noticed). I lost 50 pounds. I met an amazing woman who I am blessed now to call my wife, confidant, teammate and friend.

My success with all of this – working hard, playing hard, balancing personal and professional pursuits – is dynamic. It has gone up and down over the years, and I have learned that, at least for me, constant vigilance to self-care is essential. I gained back (and lost again) that 50 pounds a few times before I finally figured out how to eternally keep my own self on my to-do list. I still take on too much sometimes, only to then recover and resume the ability to say "no" and set limits. Nowadays, I am more consistent with all of this than I have ever been – but I know to never take any of it for granted. Never, ever.

Professionally, my attention to self-care has translated into sensible work hours (I average about 50 hours-per-week nowadays). But my clinical and teaching efforts are more rewarding and effective than they have ever been. My "products" as an academic (e.g., publications, grants) are better in both quality and volume compared to my 80 hours-per-week days. Personally, my attention to self-care has translated to things – in terms of my own mind, my own body, and my own relationships – that are even more important. I am thereby glad for my struggles; they taught me that there is more to life than work. And my realization regarding this has made all the difference.

Advice for Professionals in the Field

- There is more to life than work. If you are not engaging in things outside of your hospital or clinic – for your own health, your friendships, your marriage, your family, etc. – you may lose all of them. And often times by working less, we accomplish more.
- Your hospital or clinic was doing fine before you joined them. They will do fine without you someday, too. Be careful about presuming that it is only you who can effectively respond to a clinical emergency, advance an educational or training sequence, or cover for a particular colleague. Learn how to say "no," and to internalize the notion that you are not as indispensable as you sometimes think you are.
- Remember the "rocks, gravel, sand" metaphor as you prioritize your day (and your life). Like filling up a jar without running out of space, you must attend to the big things first. Make sure that you – the only person who you are with 24 hours per day – are one of the rocks. This way exercising, date-nights with your partner, time with your family, etc., are not crowded-out because you "do not have time." If it is important, you have time. And there will always be time later for the less important things (gravel, sand) like getting your car's oil changed, mowing the lawn or checking Facebook.
- It is better to do 10 things well than it is to do 11 things poorly.
- If you are hurting, seek help. Healers are often reluctant to seek out other healers, but we are just as human as any of our patients. Do not be afraid to ask your physician or a trusted colleague for a referral to see a therapist. Participate in a support group, seek peer-supervision or talk with your faith mentor or advisor.
- Do not catastrophize backsliding. If (or when) you notice that you are not practicing what you preach to your own patients, students, etc., work to reclaim what you have let go. Self-care requires consistent and everyday attention.

"I Need Who?"

Stacy Ogbeide Department of Family and Community Medicine,
UT Health San Antonio, San Antonio, TX, USA

Mentorship has always been a fascinating topic to me. I have experienced mentorship at different levels throughout my academic experience – from working with a guidance counselor in high school to being assigned an advisor in college that shaped the formative years of my life. There are many definitions of mentorship, but the one I have found most impactful is a mentor is someone who serves as a guide, who even though they have seen what lies ahead, is willing to walk beside you – leading but never leaving you behind on your journey. With my personal experience with informal and formal variations of mentorship, one could assume that I would naturally continue this process into my professional life, but that has not exactly been the case.

I have always wanted to work in a health care setting. When I was exposed to health psychology as an undergraduate, I could combine my interests of health and clinical psychology in a concrete way. In graduate school, I received additional training in medical settings, specifically working in primary care and specialty pain clinics. I was also given many opportunities to teach undergraduates and graduate psychology students, which further refined my interest to work in an academic health center or medical school setting. At the time, I did not know exactly how to prepare myself for this position, but I was fortunate to have advisors throughout my graduate training who provided guidance on the steps to take to work in an academic health care setting. However, due to the intricacies of dealing with the ebbs and flows of academic life – I was not quite sure how I would navigate this new territory.

During my fellowship training, I learned about a group mentoring program which was part of a national association. Side note: I fashioned myself as a professional stalker – not what you are thinking. I was (and still am) really good at finding out information about researchers and authors whom I had a strong appreciation for their work and wanted to find a way to meet them in person – either at a future conference or, in a mentoring program. When I discovered a particular academician in medicine I very much admired who could be a potential mentor in this program, I jumped at the chance and submitted my application. I was fortunate to be matched to this individual to receive a year's worth of valuable advice and encouragement not only from the mentor but also from my peers in the mentoring group.

As the mentoring program was ending, the mentor offered to continue to mentor me – if it was something I wanted. Of course! I was ecstatic and humbled at the same time. To this day, this individual continues to mentor me through monthly phone calls filled with encouragement, honesty, and critical conversations along the way. I have even added a few more mentors along the way but this initial mentoring relationship has truly shaped my career trajectory. It helped me step out in faith and take risks, understand that the grass is not always greener on the other side, encouraged true self-care, and taught me that failure is okay and when I can learn and grow from it, it is a bonus. Having this perspective shift has helped me understand and come to enjoy the ebbs and flows of being a psychologist with multiple and sometimes conflicting roles in a medical setting.

Advice for Professionals in the Field

- If you do not have a mentor, consider getting one! You do not have to be an academician to benefit from having a mentor.
- Do not forget your peers! They can serve as great mentors too – especially on the fly. Peers may be experiencing some of the same joys and struggles that you are – shared experience can be a powerful experience.
- Mentors can serve different roles: coach, cheerleader/encourager, sponsorship, career guidance, just to name a few. Sometimes one person can fill all these roles,

but it is okay (and probably desirable) for you to have different mentors fill different roles. You may have a mentor that focuses on your role as a clinician. You may have another mentor that focuses on your role as an administrator or researcher. Having multiple mentors can be a great benefit.

- You may want to consider having a mentor who is not in your discipline. It can give you a different perspective/worldview. Is not expanding your perspective what it is really all about anyway?
- Our professional lives can be challenging. We are pulled in many different directions with competing demands. Mentorship can truly help you refocus and determine what the most important elements of your career are and then tend to those areas more often than getting lost in the weeds. How do you get started? The first step is to take the risk and ask someone that you admire. I promise – the risk is worth it.

Finding Your Place

Alison G. Wong Department of Marriage and Family Therapy, School of Psychology, Fuller Theological Seminary, Pasadena, CA, USA

Collaboration was the concept that drew me to Medical Family Therapy. The idea that I could work with physicians to provide holistic care excited me about integrative healthcare. During my internship at a family medicine center, I was the only MedFT intern and was introduced to a family physician that was interested in mental health treatment. We were paired to conduct co-therapy and I was tasked with teaching the physician basic therapy skills. At a time when I should have jumped at the opportunity to partner with a physician, I instead cowered inside because all I could see were our roles in the medical system hierarchy and our differences in social status. This hierarchy is based on factors such as education level, scope of practice, prestige, and money earned. I was a young, inexperienced, unpaid Asian-American female therapist-in-training, and the physician was a confident, middle-aged Caucasian male who was knowledgeable and held degrees in many fields. He was nothing but respectful, collegial, and eager to learn, but I was filled with internalized prejudices that resulted in a lack of confidence, fear, and frustration.

As I reflect on the experience, I realize how much pressure I had put on myself to positively represent the minority groups with which I identified. I was given a position of power to teach this physician basic therapy skills, but I was plagued by my perception of being at the bottom of the hierarchy. Despite being in a learning environment where mistakes are assumed to happen, I felt as if any mistake I made would reinforce stereotypes, such as being immature, meek, or weak, that were associated with my identity groups. My fear of the self-fulfilling prophecy obstructed my sense of self, and I lost sight of all I had to offer our co-therapy team. I doubted myself and my ability to help patients. Then we met "Marisol."

Marisol was a middle-aged Puerto Rican woman from a low socioeconomic status with numerous health issues, including a traumatic history and symptoms of major depression with hallucinations. She and I met alone for her first therapy session where she shared that she had never before sought mental health treatment. She was courageous yet hesitant, and I was hopeful that therapy would help. Marisol reported that her medications were not working, and with her trust and permission, I invited my physician co-therapist to join us. Marisol extended her trust to my colleague because she could see that I trusted him, and all future sessions were conducted as a team. This approach allowed Marisol to safely process her trauma, gain agency over her medical care, and increase awareness of the relationship between physical and mental health. In our work together, Marisol's hallucinations diminished, her ability to cope and engage social support increased, and her health issues resolved.

In our final session together, we asked Marisol if she could identify what was most helpful about our time together. She shared that she felt cared for in a way she never had in the past. She felt that we had truly seen her as a whole person and treated her as an equal. I realized that while we each brought different perspectives, social statuses, and roles, treatment was successful because we connected as humans who trusted and valued one another. We each had knowledge, care, and motivation to offer each other. Though this experience I learned that collaboration is not just a treatment approach, it is a humble posture.

Advice for Professionals in the Field

- Although the medical system can be hierarchical, therapists bring valuable skills and perspective to the treatment team. Have confidence in what you have to offer.
- Find your champions. There will be some who do not understand what a therapist does, so find those who value integrative care and are willing to advocate for you.
- Remember that you cannot do it all. You are one of many members on a team. Identify, appreciate, and rely on others' strengths.
- Take time to reflect and gain awareness of your internal biases and prejudices and how they may impact your ability to work in a system with roles often distinguished by power and status. Are your internal biases hindering you, a colleague, or a patient in some way?

Conclusion

These narratives from the field highlight several important themes when navigating the waters of the medical world. The concept of self-care and awareness of burnout was a common thread across many of the stories and advice given by these professionals. While some stressed the importance mentorship plays in advocating for self-care, others had to find their own path to establish personal/professional boundaries in their lives. The importance of being part of a team and seeking help when needed from colleagues was very beneficial for these professionals. How one enters a new setting or health care system reiterates the role that the behavioral healthcare provider (BHP) plays as a "beginning anthropologist" in this new environment.

While the need for mental health services in medicine will continue to grow in coming years, there is a looming shortage of BHPs and mental health providers in these settings (Blount & Miller, 2009; Hall et al., 2015). Graduate mental health programs and internship sites would benefit from increased curriculum and community experiences to get new professionals exposed to the world of medicine earlier in their training (Newton, Woodruff-Borden, & Stetson, 2006). Supervisors should also be mindful that first-time trainees or new professionals are likely to encounter personal issues in a medical environment that warrant ongoing attention and support.

Through this book, our hope is that clinicians can grasp the importance of how practicing in medicine impacts one's "self" in many areas, including family of origin, faith, culture, professional competencies, power status as providers, and ethical decision making. We also encourage readers to use the ideas in this book to help expand opportunities to effectively treat patients, couples, and families with emotional and physical concerns in the broader health care system. Even after several years of clinical and supervisory roles at medical sites, Jackie and Max continue to discover new areas where our 'self-of-the-therapist' work continues to arise. We invite you to keep attending to how your growth evolves not just as a professional but as a human being. After all, you can't heal effectively if you do not understand and comfort yourself.

References

Blount, F. A., & Miller, B. F. (2009). Addressing the workforce crisis in integrated primary care. *Journal of Clinical Psychology in Medical Settings, 16*, 113. https://doi.org/10.1007/s10880-008-9142-7

Hall, J., Cohen, D. J., Davis, M., Gunn, R., Blount, A., Pollack, D. A., … Miller, B. F. (2015). Preparing the workforce for behavioral health and primary care integration. *Journal of the American Board of Family Medicine, 28*(Supplement 1), S41–S51. https://doi.org/10.3122/jabfm.2015.S1.150054

Newton, T. L., Woodruff-Borden, J., & Stetson, B. A. (2006). Integrating mind and body: Graduate psychology education in primary behavioral health care. *Journal of Clinical Psychology in Medical Settings, 13*, 3–11. https://doi.org/10.1007/s10880-006-9037-4

Paris, M., & Hoge, M. A. (2010). Burnout in the mental health workforce: A review. *The Journal of Behavioral Health Services & Research, 37*, 519–528. https://doi.org/10.1007/s11414-009-9202-2

Prouty, A. M., Helmeke, K. B., & Fischer, J. (2016). Mentorship in family therapy training programs: Students' and new graduates' perspectives. *Journal of Family Psychotherapy, 27*, 35–56. https://doi.org/10.1080/08975353.2016.1136546

Prouty, A. M., & Storm, C. L. (2014). Training the next generation of supervisors. In T. C. Todd & C. L. Storm (Eds.), *The complete systemic supervisor: Context, philosophy, and pragmatics* (2nd ed., pp. 399–416). London, UK: Wiley-Blackwell.

Index

M. Zubatsky, J. Williams-Reade (eds.), *Self of the Therapist in Medical Settings*, AFTA SpringerBriefs in Family Therapy,
https://doi.org/10.1007/978-3-030-39271-0

MIX
Papier aus verantwortungsvollen Quellen
Paper from responsible sources
FSC® C105338

FSC
www.fsc.org

If you have any concerns about our products,
you can contact us on
ProductSafety@springernature.com

In case Publisher is established outside the EU,
the EU authorized representative is:
Springer Nature Customer Service Center GmbH
Europaplatz 3, 69115 Heidelberg, Germany

Printed by Libri Plureos GmbH
in Hamburg, Germany

LEGAL COMMUNICATION OF CHINESE JUDICIARY

ZHENGRUI HAN

LEGAL COMMUNICATION OF CHINESE JUDICIARY

— A DISCOURSE-BASED VIEW —

PETER LANG
Bern · Berlin · Bruxelles · Frankfurt am Main · New York · Oxford · Wien

Bibliographic information published by die Deutsche Nationalbibliothek
Die Deutsche Nationalbibliothek lists this publication in the Deutsche Nationalbibliografie; detailed bibliographic data is available on the Internet at ‹http://dnb.d-nb.de›.

British Library Cataloguing-in-Publication Data:
A catalogue record for this book is available from The British Library, Great Britain

Library of Congress Cataloging-in-Publication Data

Han, Zhengrui,
Legal communication of Chinese judiciary : a discourse-based view / Zhengrui Han.
p. cm.
Includes bibliographical references and index.
ISBN 978-3-0343-1199-1
1. Judicial process–China. 2. Judgments–China. 3. Judges–China.
4. Procedure (Law)–China. 5. Justice, Administration of–China.
6. Law reform–China. I. Title.
KNQ1679.H36 2012
347.510501'4–dc23

2012026111

Cover illustration: from iStockphoto.com © by Blai B Mestrich & Paulo Ribau
Cover Design: Didier Studer, Peter Lang AG

ISBN 978-3-0343-1199-1 pb. ISBN 978-3-0351-0452-3 eBook

Hochfeldstrasse 32, CH-3012 Bern, Switzerland
info@peterlang.com, www.peterlang.com

Preface

This research attempts to analyze empirically judges' writing of civil judgments in Mainland China, where the judges' writing is traditionally considered structured, conventional and free from rhetorical variations. The writing of civil judgements in Mainland China requires that judges strictly adhere to a number of rules and conventions, the contravention of which deleteriously affects the generic integrity of civil judgements and the perceived professionalism of judges' writing. While rules and conventions are fixed, society is ever changing. It is therefore common for judges to manipulate rules and conventions legitimately or illegitimately to solve contemporary situation-specific problems. This research conducts a multidimensional and multi-perspective analysis of Mainland Chinese civil judgments to demonstrate some of these rules and conventions and, more importantly, show how judges manipulate them in specific cases.

The research data constitutes a comprehensive medium-sized corpus of civil judgments (100 cases), interviews with ten legal specialists (seven lawyers and three judges), intertextual data of related written laws and news reports, and other law-related documents rendered by provincial courts and authorities. Research findings are divided into three groups based on move analysis, lexico-grammar and discourse coherence.

Move analysis in this research identifies the required and optional moves/steps in civil judgments and macro rhetorical patterns. Since civil judgments are publicly accessible and enable laypersons to study litigation practices, there are two groups of target readers: specialists and non-specialists. Specialist readers refer to judges, lawyers, law professors, and other legal professionals. Non-specialist readers refer to laypersons who may lack legal knowledge but are interested to learn about legal affairs. The distinction between the two is important when interpreting the readability and accessibility of civil judgments. The analysis identifies several important findings. For example, Mainland Chinese litigants seldom engage lawyers when undertaking complicated litigation proceedings. More commonly, individual parties seek assistance from relatives and friends, while corporate parties are usually represented in court by non-legal staff. This is explained by a traditional distrust of lawyers in Mainland China, and by the parties' intentions to avoid costly lawyer fees.

The lexico-grammatical analysis in the present research investigates the use of numerical expressions and the occurrence of metadiscourse in civil judgments. Numerical expressions are widely used by judges in the moves *Parties' Arguments* and *Judges' Arguments*. Some are used to describe a particular time when a specific event occurred, and others report specific sums of money claimed as compensation by the plaintiffs. The analysis reveals that these numerical expressions do not appear in isolation. Temporal expressions in the move *Parties' Arguments* always correspond closely with more exact ones used in the move *Judges' Arguments*. The interview and intertextual data verify that this correspondence demonstrates that the primary intention of Mainland Chinese judges' written civil judgments is to report the working of their results in litigation, not to provide a faithful recontextualization of parties' arguments. The occurrence of metadiscourse suggests that Mainland Chinese judges make considerable rhetorical and legal effort when resolving the tension between parties' views and when they interpret the law to build legal bases for litigation.

Coherence analysis in this research concentrates on how specialist and non-specialist readers can acquire a coherent reading of Mainland Chinese civil judgments. Non-specialist readers face two levels of reading difficulty: the linguistic level and the discursive level. A civil judgment is the final textual artefact of the specialized litigation practice and employs many legalized terms and expressions to report court proceedings. A preliminary understanding of these terms and expressions is required for a coherent reading of civil judgments. However, familiarity with legalized words and expressions does not guarantee a thorough understanding of the judges' writing in civil judgments. For example, everyday language might carry specialized meanings in a legal field, the connection among specific arguments might be mediated by quoted texts, and the actual litigation practices might be intentionally or unintentionally simplified. Judges who write civil judgments presuppose that their readers will have considerable social and legal knowledge. A reconstruction of this presupposed knowledge is therefore necessary for specialist and non-specialist readers to understand civil judgments at the discursive level, which only specialist readers may achieve.

This research has both academic and pedagogic significance. Few empirical studies of Chinese professional discourses exist and there are fewer still of legal discourse. This research makes a preliminary attempt to examine the genre of Chinese civil judgments from an empirical perspective and attempts to understand how judges write rules and conventions and how they manipulate them in specific cases. The research findings suggest that the impression that Chinese civil judgments primarily consist of standardized jargon and conventional syntax is inaccurate. Rather, rules and conventions are principles that are constantly manipulated by experienced judges to solve a number of situation-specific problems. The findings revealed in this research can be utilized to produce several pedagogic tasks suitable for use in legal education and training. Such tasks will help law students critically read civil judgements and raise their awareness of litigation practices embedded in this genre.

Acknowledgements

This book is based on my research conducted at the Department of English, City University of Hong Kong. I would like to thank my PhD supervisors, Professor Vijay Kumar Bhatia and Dr. Stephen Bremner, for their continuing help and encouragement when I tried to complete this study. Professor Bhatia's knowledge and expertise in genre and legal discourse made my study a happy experience. I have greatly benefitted from the systematic training in discourse analysis provided in his lectures. He gave me an opportunity to join his international project on arbitration discourse and kindly urged me to do research at an early stage. Whenever I had difficulty conducting research and felt depressed, he would be available by email. I have always found him a great source of confidence and courage for my study and research. Dr. Stephen Bremner read my book draft with great care and patience, and gave me detailed advice on various drafts and the final outcome. It is with his advice and comments that I was able to make the book more coherent and reader-friendly.

Another person I want to thank is Dr. Becky Kwan Siu Chu, who read my qualifying report and suggested appropriate ways of using academic language. My sincere thanks go to Dr. Deng Liming, Mr. Hu Kang, Miss Li Xiaoyu, and Mr. Zhang Zhanyu who gave me ideas and thoughts for analysis in various discussions. The Department of English at City University of Hong Kong has supplied generous financial and academic support for my study and research. Lastly, I want to thank my wife, Fuxue, and my son, HAN Fujia, for their everlasting companionship in my life and research.

Table of Contents

Chapter 1
Introduction

1.1 Introduction

Genre studies has become an established field in applied linguistics over the past two decades and proved itself to be a useful approach for analyzing academic and professional discourse. There are a number of studies of academic/disciplinary discourse (Swales, 1981, 1990a, 1998, 2004; Johns, 1997; Berkenkotter & Huckin, 1995; Bazerman & Paradis, 1991; Hyland, 2000; Flowerdew, 2002), business discourse (Bargiela-Chiappini, & Nickerson, 1999; Bargiela-Chiappini, Nickerson, & Planken, 2007), and legal discourse (Bhatia, 1993, 2004; Bhatia, Candlin, Engberg, & Trosborg, 2003a; Bhatia, Candlin, & Sharma, 2009). Academic discourse remains a strong research focus in the literature within which researchers have studied a variety of professional discourses in their research agendas, including legislation, administration, teaching, business, advertising, etc. However, most of these studies have been conducted in English contexts, and few attempts have been made to study Chinese professional genres, especially legal ones.

Following the research in Bhatia (1983a, 1993, 2004), Swales (1990a, 1998), Bazerman (1988), Bazerman & Paradis (1991), and Miller (1984, 1994), the present research intends to expand the territory of genre studies by applying it to a non-English language (Chinese), a different profession (Chinese judges), and a different text (civil judgments). This research examines civil judgments, which refers to Mainland Chinese civil judgments (not criminal judgments), from the perspective of applied genre analysis, aiming to understand its roles, textual features, and contextual interpretations. In addition, this study is intended to introduce the multidimensional and multi-perspective framework of genre analysis to Mainland China, where discourse analysts have traditionally focused only on the linguistic level.

Compared to legal genres in legislation and courtroom trials (Atkinson, & Drew, 1979; Levi, & Walker, 1990), little attention has been given to civil judgments. Some practical reasons make civil judgments less accessible to genre analysts than other academic and professional genres. Firstly, civil judgments are neither easy nor interesting to read because of the complex syntax and specialized vocabulary used. Secondly, civil judgments can appear more intimidating than other genres like business letters and book blurbs because they cover tens of pages. Thirdly, some analysts reasonably assume that civil judgments are formal and institutionalized such that few significant generic variations occur. Finally, limited access to legal specialists in China and the difficulty of understanding basic content knowledge pose practical difficulties for genre analysts.

It is a fact that institutional genres seem conventional and free from variation because they are often de-contextualised because they are separated from the people who routinely produce, interpret, and consume them. Freedman & Medway argue that

> to analyze [...] writing in the light of the recent reconception of genre is a demystifying move, in that it, for instance, affords explanations of conventional forms that previously appeared arcane or arbitrary (1994b, p. 12).

This is also true for legal settings where much specialized knowledge and information is hidden from non-specialist readers. This research aims to demystify some of the 'backstage work' (Goffman, 1959) that gives appropriate meanings to civil judgments and thus uncover the true dynamic nature of this genre.

1.2 Context of the research

This discursive research is designed to explore the ongoing judicial reform (Jiang, 1997; Hu, 2007) being conducted in Mainland China and also the influence of this judicial reform on aspects of Chinese litigation practices. Chinese society, in particular its economy and technology, has been developing remarkably fast over the past three decades; however, its judicial system has remained fairly static when compared to China's fast-developing social and economic situation. Chinese judges must today handle a variety of disputes in new areas that were never handled by their predecessors, like contract, patent, computer, internet, and international trade. The challenge of these new areas is magnified by some judges' lack of professional experience and skills (Gechilk, 2005, p. 123). In order to upgrade the judicial system and improve the judges' professional competence, China officially launched its ongoing judicial reform in 1997 (Jiang, 1997). This comprehensively conducted judicial reform programme has influenced several aspects of Chinese litigation practices, including judges' writing of civil judgments, as examined in this research.

China follows a civil law tradition, like countries such as Japan and Germany. Although China shares many legal practices with these countries, the Chinese legal system differs in a number of areas. As illustrated in Stevenson (2003), legal texts in the U.S. and other common law countries are mainly addressed to 'the state itself, or more specifically, a set of state actors – courts, agency officials, and enforcement officers' (p. 108). Laypersons, as non-specialists, are not usually the target audience in judges' and lawyers' professional writing; rather, the lay reader accesses legal texts through lawyers' and other legal specialists' explanations and interpretations. The major function of civil judgments (judicial opinion) in common law countries is to establish authority for the judicial system and for future adjudication (White, 1995, p. 1368).

However, Fu convincingly pointed out that China stresses both the legal and social function of civil judgment as a legal genre (2000, p. 123).

Civil judgment in China is not only an authoritative text which carries the judges' legal opinions and settles the parties' dispute but also an important textual artifact which illustrates and popularizes law for the public (Article 134, *the Civil Procedural Law of PRC, 1991*; Article 13, 38, *Five-year Reform Outline of People's Courts, 1999*). The situation in China now is that civil judgments are mostly required by the Supreme People's Court to be made accessible to the public through either the internet or printed volumes. Consequently, in addition to their legal function, the generic analysis of Chinese civil judgments has to consider the social function of this legal genre and their readability for both specialist readers and non-specialist readers.

The primary concerns in analyzing Chinese civil judgments and civil judgments in common law countries are also significantly different. Firstly, because judges in common law countries enjoy professional judicial independence in litigation, their writing is usually personal and furnished with legal reasoning and rhetorical considerations (Carroll, 1995; Hafner, 2006; Posner, 1995; Solan, 2004, 2005; Tiersma, 2001). However, Chinese judges, as pointed out by Su, do not have the power to establish judicial precedents or even to interpret the written laws flexibly (2001a, p. 12). Chinese judges' writing of civil judgments is dominated not by individuality but by standardized rules and conventions. So, most research findings revealed in the above studies of judges' writing in common law countries are not found in the present study of Chinese civil judgment. A primary concern of practising Chinese judges is how they can conduct the judicial reform that requires they break some of the over-standardized rules and conventions while also disclosing relatively sufficient information about the background litigation practices. The Chinese judicial reform process has yet to reach a stage where civil judgments cease to be a legal genre dominated by the collective voice of the court, and where judges have adequate power to demonstrate their individual voices. Secondly, because of the judges' considerable lack of professional independence (Su, 2000, 2001b) and their closer connection with the government, a strict observation of government policies is always important when judges write civil judgments. In cases where policies and law are not completely in agreement, the judges will give priority to government policies. This point is also reported in Lin (2003), Pan (2003), and Peerenboom (2003). Accordingly, the interpretation of the judges' discursive practices in this research needs to take into account these concerns of the judges, who sometimes produce significantly different interpretations and findings from those found in studies conducted in common law systems.

1.3 Aims of the research

The major aim of this research is to investigate the generic features of civil judgments, their writing rules and conventions, and manipulations made by judges and lawyers. Generic features in this research refer to both text-internal features and text-external ones (Johns, 1997, p. 93). Through studying textual data of judgments, indictments, statements of defence, legal news reports, etc., the researcher analyzes text-internal features including the move structure of judgments, their discipline-specific vocabulary, lexico-grammatical patterns, rhetorical strategies, and textual coherence. Moreover, identified textual characteristics are interpreted with reference to analysts' insights, specialist informants' intuition, and with reference to the Chinese judicial context and its ongoing reform.

Text-external factors include intertexts, readers/writers, the social function of genres, and the discursive/social practices of which civil judgments are a part. As in the case of text-internal resources, the research findings are verified against specialists' accounts. The text-external factors include the litigation context of civil judgments and the broad socio-political contextual elements, such as professional practices and cultures in professions, institutions, political parties and social lives as a whole. Verification of the research findings is conducted through discourse-based interviews based on preliminary textual analysis, the purpose of which is to invite specialists to crosscheck the findings and give comments on them.

1.4 Research questions

This research is intended to answer the following research questions:

- What are the status, role, and function of civil judgments in litigation practice? Who drafts them and who reads them? What are the roles of judges?
- How are civil judgments structured? Are there any typical structural patterns? What are the specific moves typically used in this genre? Which moves are required and which are optional?
- What are the typical lexico-grammatical features of civil judgments? How are these features textualized?
- What are the typical rhetorical strategies used in civil judgments? How do judges justify using these strategies?

1.5 Research methodology

The writing of civil judgments requires judges to follow a number of legal and rhetorical conventions and rules, although they may sometimes be manipulated by experienced judges. In order to acquire a comprehensive understanding of these conventions and manipulations, the research method adopts the multi-perspective and multi-dimensional model of Bhatia (1993, 2004) and includes textual analysis of judgments, intertextual analysis of quoted/referred texts in judgments, and analysis of specialists' accounts, Furthermore, drawing on the analysis of disciplinary discourse in Hyland (2000), this research analyzes civil judgments in three steps. Firstly, the judgments in the corpus are read carefully. For example, in order to get a general understanding of the texts, the crucial textual features are explicitly marked, which includes identifying signpost sentences, section boundaries, parts in bold type, frequently repeated sentences/

phrases, and highly legalized expressions. From this preliminary analysis, attempts are made to identify the move structures of civil judgments. Secondly, typical uses of lexico-grammar are identified and interpreted, including nouns, verbs, adjectives, sentence types (declarative/interrogative), and others which are relevant. The purpose is not only to understand their meanings at sentence level but to place them in the context of the broader litigation practice and judicial culture. Thirdly, effort is made to examine in what ways civil judgments can be read coherently, and what knowledge is necessary for a coherent reading of this genre.

1.6 Structure of the book

This book consists of seven chapters. Chapter one introduces the general background of the study, the methodology used, and the research significance. Chapter two highlights a number of conceptions of genre accepted in different research traditions to lay the theoretical ground for the analysis of civil judgments. Chapter three explains the methodological framework by drawing on the dimensions of genre analysis reviewed in Chapter two. The research results are reported in Chapters four, five and six. Chapter four reports the move pattern of civil judgments, including required moves, optional moves, and their conventional textualization. Chapter five reports and explains the typical lexico-grammatical patterns in civil judgments from the multiple perspectives of texts, analysts and specialists. Chapter six examines judges' construction of coherence in civil judgments and the ways readers can understand this construction. Chapter seven summarizes this research and discusses directions for further research.

1.7 Significance of the research

This study of civil judgments as a Chinese professional genre expands the territory of genre studies. Furthermore, genre analysis adds an empirical and grounded dimension to the study of Chinese professional genres. This study of civil judgments can be drawn on in other studies of Chinese legal or political genres. Law in Mainland China is closely related to sensitive political issues. A detailed and insightful interpretation of civil judgments therefore needs to incorporate some discussion of the background judicial and political issues. Since Mainland China conventionally holds a conservative attitude towards any kind of critical analysis of political power and structure, this problematizes discursive studies of Chinese legal and political issues. The analysis and investigation conducted in this research concentrate on the description and explanation of judges' professional practices, rather than on the analysis of power relationships between judges and readers of civil judgments. Interview questions in the appendix are sensitively structured so that lawyers and judges may feel appreciation and respect rather than critical evaluation. This strategy can be repeated in other similar discursive studies conducted by discourse research in Mainland China.

The research also has practical pedagogic significance because the study tries to reveal the hidden lexico-grammatical features, move patterns, and judges' practical considerations in writing civil judgments. The research findings can guide junior judges when writing similar texts. They may also be used to design discussion topics, writing tasks, or reading materials in other legal education and training settings. Since linguistic features and underlying rhetorical motivations are explored, instructions can be supplied so that the legal awareness of students and trainees can be raised in relation to civil judgments on issues like textual conventions, discursive strategies, legal professional practices, and socio-legal cultures. This may enable legal students to develop enhanced competence and expertise in handling civil judgments and improved reading and writing abilities.

Chapter 2
Literature Review

2.1 Introduction

This chapter reviews the literature on genre conceptions and legal discourse in order to place this research into an appropriate context, and also highlights and discusses a variety of dimensions in analyzing genres in preparation for the construction of the methodological framework in the next chapter. Hyon (1996) discusses three distinctive traditions of analyzing genre in the field of applied linguistics: the North American School, the Sydney School and the British ESP School. Each has common interests in the study of textual and contextual factors but takes different perspectives.

These different perspectives are understandable because they differ in their theoretical considerations, pedagogical aims and surrounding academic contexts. The Sydney School is concerned with teaching literacy to secondary school students, whose focus is the study of general 'generic values' (Bhatia, 2004, p. 60), like arguments, narratives, and descriptions of specific grammatical devices realizing these values. The North American School studies academic and professional genres and attempts to interpret the dynamic relationship between text and context. The ESP school initially took the teaching of academic genres to non-native English speakers as its primary task, and has gradually become more concerned with context-based interpretations of academic and professional genres.

The distinctions between these Schools are not greatly significant. Bhatia and Swales' work (Bhatia 1993, Swales 1990a) in the ESP School is frequently cited by scholars of the North American School; Miller and Bazerman (Miller 1984, Bazerman 1988, 2000) are also often referred to in the publications of ESP scholars. They discuss a number of different yet related issues such as intertextuality, the ethnographic study of genre, the dynamic nature of genre, the tension between convention and creativity, and the conflict between generic integrity and genre mixing/bending (Berkenkotter & Huckin, 1995; Bhatia, 2004). Since the ESP and North American schools share more common ground, the following section discusses the distinguishing elements of the Sydney School and considers its useful perspectives that can be utilised in the present research.

2.2 Genre and the Sydney School

The Sydney School is closely affiliated with Systemic Functional Linguistics (SFL) developed by M.A.K. Halliday. SFL scholars argue that genres 'are not simply a set of formal structures into which meanings are poured' (Martin, Christie, & Rothery, 1987, p. 64), and that genres are the medium through which meanings are negotiated. However, the meaning discussed is word meaning, sentence meaning, and textual meaning. Social-cultural meaning is occasionally discussed (Martin & White, 2005), but the discussion focuses primarily on abstract social values like power and ideology and the analyzing effort is on textual practices. Freedman and Medway observe that 'there is far greater emphasis by the Sydney School scholars on explicating textual features, using Hallidayan schemes of linguistic analysis, while North American work has focused on unpacking complex relations between text and context' (1994, p. 9).

Sydney School scholars demonstrate a strong interest in establishing a systemic genre theory at the socio-semiotic level. Martin builds a close-ended social semiotic theory of context (Martin, 1992, p. 493). He holds that context consists of three abstraction levels: register, genre and ideology; text consists of another three levels: semantics, grammar and phonology. This complicated theoretical construct makes it challenging to do research of the type done by Bhatia (2004) and Bazerman & Paradis (1991) that explores the relationship between textual practice and social practice.

The focus on quantity and statistics relating to grammatical items suggests that the Sydney School has less common ground with the other two schools. The Sydney School ignores intertextual analysis and contextual/social investigation, although it does produce comprehensive and systematic studies of various lexico-grammatical features, such as patterns in subject choices, action verbs, cohesive tools, etc. The present research draws on this aspect of the Sydney School's studies and attends to the calculation and analysis of subjects, predicative verbs, and cohesive devices (Halliday, & Hasan, 1976).

2.3 Genre and the North American School

2.3.1 Genre as social action

Traditional rhetoric focuses on analyzing textual features, text types, and disciplinary registers. However, New Rhetoric studies (Miller, 1984) show a new theoretical concern with context and social practice. The conception of genre is not only confined to the interpretation of text as product. It also incorporates a consideration of social and contextual information, aiming to interpret the text as process and as an embedded artefact of social practice. Miller writes:

> since 'rhetorical forms that establish genres are stylistic and substantive responses to perceived situational demands', a genre becomes a complex of formal and substantive features that create a particular effect in a given situation. Genre, in this way, becomes more than a formal entity; it becomes pragmatic, fully rhetorical, a point a connection between intention and effect, an effect of social action [...]. [W]e understand genres as typified rhetorical actions based on recurrent situations. (Miller, 1984, p. 153)

Miller's understanding suggests a social constructionist interpretation of genre which cannot be defined based solely on an analysis of linguistic features, and that effort must be taken to investigate the context and situation. One important aspect of the contextual investigation is the relationship between genre and readers/writers. Although writers in specific settings have to follow typified conventions to achieve their communicative purposes, they may also have situation-specific intentions. In order to realize these intentions, writers need to address both the social setting and their own needs. The genre thus constructed is not only a formal entity, but also a rhetorical artefact instantiating the writers' intentions.

The interactive relationship between genre and writer/reader is discussed in Miller (1984), Biesecker (1989), and Berkenkotter & Huckin (1995). Berkenkotter and Huckin also supply a comprehensive review of some of the important dimensions of analyzing genre, including dynamism, situatedness, form and content, duality of structure, and community ownership. The following section examines some of the dimensions which can be exploited in the analysis of civil judgments. Further discussion of genre in this School can be found in Bitzer (1968) and Biesecker (1989).

2.3.2 The analytical dimensions

The North American scholars have adopted a number of analytical dimensions to examine the complex social context of academic and professional genres. Firstly, although not strictly following the practice of ethnographic studies, these scholars draw on observation, interviewing and historical document analysis to illustrate the intertwined relationships between texts and situated contexts. For example, through analyzing diachronic textual data including the early 'Philosophical Transactions' and 'Physical Review', Bazerman (1988) traces the development of specific scientific genres and explains how the changing social situations have shaped genres to the way we see them today. To provide a rich description of textual organisation, he suggests that 'Questions of textual interaction with cognition (schema, story grammars), social interaction (ethnomethodological approaches), and social history (genre approaches) currently seem more promising in understanding textual organization' (Bazerman, 1988, p. 229). Studies that take an ethnographic approach by carrying out longitudinal fieldwork include Beaufort (1999) and Smart (2006, 2008).

Secondly, new rhetorical studies discuss the issue of reflexive agents and writing creativity/individuality. Miller (1984) refutes the materialistic, not dynamic, view of context held by Bitzer (1968) and stresses writer/reader's creativity in exploiting existing generic conventions. Seeing genre as both social conventions and individual selves has produced a number of insightful studies such as Connor & Johns (1990) and Bazerman (2004). The common concern of these studies is to see how individuals claim their personal identities in socially conventionalized communications and how they exploit established discursive patterns to realize private purposes. The mature members of academic or professional communities understand the situational context and kairos (timing) so well that they know how to manipulate the rules in accepted manners to reach their specific ends. Reflexive agency and individuality are a common phenomenon in any genre, even highly institutionalized and conventionalized ones like contracts, legal statements, and judgments.

Thirdly, intertextuality is frequently discussed and analyzed in New Rhetoric studies, and a theoretical classification is proposed in Devitt (1991). Devitt identifies three kinds of intertextuality: generic, referential and functional. Generic intertextuality comes close to Miller's 'genre as social action', or Bitzer's 'controlling power of rhetorical situation', which means whenever a person writes a text, he is bound by generic conventions mutually agreed by discourse community members. Referential intertextuality defines the concept in a narrower sense, e. g. one text is quoted or referred to by another. Functional intertextuality is related to genre set or genre chains (Swales, 2004, p. 18). For example, the job application letter gets a reply, the request for a book in a library receives a collection notice, and the submission of a research article leads to a review report, etc. This classification of intertextuality produces a solid framework for studying the intertwined texts and genre of civil judgments.

2.4 Genre and the ESP School

2.4.1 The conception of genre

ESP scholars are concerned with teaching various academic genres to non-native college students and have recently focussed on professional genres. In order to raise students' awareness of academic literacies (Swales, 1981, 1990a), generic purposes and textual patterns are valued and analyzed. John Swales writes:

> A genre comprises a class of communicative events, the member of which share some set of communicative purposes. These purposes are recognized by the expert members of the parent discourse community, and thereby constitute the rationale for the genre [...]. In addition to purpose, exemplars of a genre exhibit various patterns of similarity in terms of structure, style, content and intended audience. If all high probability expectations are realized, the exemplar will be viewed as prototypical by the parent discourse community [...]. (Swales, 1990a, p. 58)

Swales here argues that texts play a significant role in many communicative events (1990a, p. 45). Although focussing on written English, he does not exclude from genre studies other sources of insights and perceptions such as participants' accounts, picture/document records of sites, and observation findings. This open-mindedness and advocacy of ethnographic studies can be found in Swales (1998) and Bhatia (2008).

Purpose, according to Swales, is the very parameter that separates a genre from a random group of sentences. For example, a news report is meant to be informative and tell readers an account of everyday happenings; job advertisements express a company's intention to make job vacancies known to audiences. Swales proposes to use 'sets of communicative purposes' instead of a single purpose when describing and defining a genre (1990a, p. 47), because he finds a genre's purpose is seldom single, as in the case of news reports, courtroom examinations, and article abstracts. He emphasizes this observation in Swales (2004, pp. 60–98) and suggests that purpose should be identified ethnographically. However, he does not consider the interrelations among different purposes of the same genre. Bhatia further problematizes this issue and examines multiple purposes of specific genres using a number of concepts including genre mixing, genre conflicting, and genre bending (Bhatia, 1997a, 2004).

The present research follows Swales' definition of purpose as the overarching parameter to understand, analyze and explain the macro move/step structure of civil judgments, their typical lexicogrammatical features and the rhetorical strategies used. The investigation of purposes is conducted through internet research, library research, and specialist interviews. However, the analysis of judges' rhetorical strategies and their practical considerations needs a conception of genre which is more suitable for professional genres.

Swales's definition of genre works well when studying academic genres (Chang and Swales, 1999; Hyland, 2004). Nevertheless, in order to analyze various professional genres in usage, a more flexible definition seems necessary. Recent research has examined the way genres are handled from a wider perspective (Bhatia, 1995, 1997; Bremner, 2008; Swales, 1998). Bhatia concentrates on professional genres and proposes:

> It (genre) is a recognizable communication event characterized by a set of communicative purpose(s) identified and mutually understood by the members of the professional or academic community in which it regularly occurs. Most often it is highly structured and conventionalized with constraints on allowable contributions in terms of their intent, positioning, form and functional value. These constraints, however, are often exploited by the expert members of the discourse community to achieve private intentions within the framework of socially recognized purpose(s). (Bhatia, 1993, p. 13)

As in Swales (1981, 1990a), Bhatia takes 'communicative purposes' as the main criterion to define and analyze genres. Beyond this, more attention is paid to the conventionality of genre and the versatility of exploiting generic conventions because professional practices are significantly different from academic ones. In academic communities, generic conventions play a dominant role and only established scholars enjoy limited freedom to make variations in their writing style. But the rule of conventionality in professional communities is less restrictive, and most experienced community members often manipulate the generic conventions to realize their 'private purposes' (Bhatia, 1995). It is therefore necessary to study judges' 'private purposes' when analyzing civil judgments.

2.4.2 The analytical dimensions

The ESP scholars adopt a number of analytical dimensions in their study of academic and professional genres, such as coherence and interdiscursivity. Coherence has been discussed in Swales (1990b). Swales' account of coherence is more socially oriented, and he discusses coherence as one characteristic attributed by readers to texts, while the Sydney School scholars describe coherence as one inherent function of texts Halliday, & Hasan (1976), Martin (1992), and Halliday & Matthiessen (2004). Using parameters of purposive, schematic and local expectations, Swales investigates what kind of coherence can be acquired from texts, and in what ways it can be acquired. The discussion of coherence in the present research adopts the framework established by Swales (1990b). Additionally, the thematic chains and cohesive devices discussed in Martin (1992) are also drawn on in order to add textual substance to the argument.

Interdiscursivity is frequently exploited to interpret professional genres, such as in Bhatia (2004, 2008) and Candlin and Maley (1997). The difference between intertextuality and interdiscursivity is discussed in Fairclough (1992, p. 85), but the instantiation of the two concepts in professional genres is defined in Bhatia (2008). The present research uses the concept of intertextuality to examine direct or indirect law citations in civil judgments, attending to the citing of texts and the location and functions of citations (Swales, 1986a). In addition, the concept of interdiscursivity refers to the interrelationships among a number of discursive values in civil judgments, including argumentation, reporting, persuasion, and sequence. Furthermore, interdiscursivity explains why legal specialists embed other discourse like administration and conciliation into legal discourse for situation-specific purposes. This embedding or mixing of discourse is different from the explicit quotation of texts in civil judgments which falls under the concept of intertextuality.

Specialist interviews are a successful method when analyzing professional and academic genres (Bhatia, 1993; Hyland, 2000). Specialist accounts in this research are acquired through both general interviews and text-based interviews (Hyland, 2000, p. 132). General interviews are usually open-ended. Specialists are presented with very general questions which are intended to encourage them to reflect on their career experiences and to tell interesting stories. Text-based interviews are more specific, and the guide questions used are all based on the analysis of genre exemplars. The intention is to ask specialists for comments and evaluations on the researcher's provisional findings; the specialists are, of course, encouraged to add their own understanding to specific issues. The method of acquiring specialists' accounts in this research is also reinforced by narrative inquiry (Connelly, & Clandinin, 1990) and the personal experience method (Clandinin, & Connelly, 1994).

2.5 Legal discourse studies

This section reviews some studies of legal discourse to explain the broad context of the research and the specific sources from which the researcher draws insights. The broad context includes Bhatia (1987), Kurzon (1997), Maley (1994), Gibbons (1994) and Wagner (2010), and specific sources for research insights include a number of international research project on legal discuss led by Bhatia and other scholars (Bhatia, Candlin, Engberg, & Trosborg, 2003a; Bhatia, Candlin, & Gotti, 2003b; Bhatia, Engberg, Gotti, & Heller, 2005; Bhatia, Candlin, & Engberg, 2008; Bhatia, Candlin, & Sharma, 2009). Bhatia (1987) and Wagner (2010) stress the importance of studying legal language in social contexts. The present study of civil judgments includes not only an analysis of legalized words and expressions used in civil judgments, but also an analysis of judges' rhetorical strategies and the contextual implications of these expressions and strategies.

According to Bhatia (1987), the primary concern of studies of the language of the law is to analyze legal language 'as the vehicle for social action' (1987, p. 227). Wagner points out that 'law and language are closely linked to social and cultural events within a specific period of time and space' (2010, p. 78). In relation to the legal words and grammars, i.e., register, and legal genre and discourse, Kurzon suggests that 'legal registers, in terms of special words and expressions, may be of secondary importance, any study of legal discourse should perhaps become mainly a study of legal genres' (1997, p. 119).

This research into civil judgments seeks to interpret rather than to critique. Studying legal language interpretively rather than critically is not new Maley (1994), Gibbons (1994) and Bhatia (1994). Maley suspects the effect of the 'plain language movement' which tries to simplify legal language to everyday language without a serious concern for legal conventions and practices. She further distinguishes legal language 'that is integrated deeply into institutional structures, practices and ideologies and which may or may not be open to reform' and legal language 'that is unhelpful, peripheral, and therefore dispensable' (1994, p. 49), arguing that the latter is open to reform while the former needs to be handled more cautiously. After studying and interpreting a number of textual features in English legislative statements, Bhatia stresses that 'legislative statements have good reasons to be what they are, and one should try to understand this genre on its own terms rather than by imposing standards of ordinary expressions from the outside' (1994, p. 153).

Within the above broad context, this research specifically draws on Bhatia et al. (2003a, 2003b, 2005, 2008, 2009) for methodological/analytical insights. One analytical theme in examining civil judgments is to uncover judges' writing variations in constructing this highly conventional and institutionalized genre. Bhatia et al. (2005) study the tension between vagueness/ambiguity and specificity that constitutes the generic integrity (Bhatia, 1993, p. 145) of normative (legislative, judicial and arbitration) texts. The studies reported in this volume discuss the issues of vagueness in normative texts through analyzing the lexico-grammar of modifications, conditionals and adverbs, and through analyzing the background 'communicative necessities' (2005, p. 17). The contributions in this volume are important for the present study because they identify the legitimacy of legislators' and judges' writing variations in their application and interpretation of the law.

Bhatia et al. (2003a, 2003b, 2008) attempt to discover how one legal text (arbitration law) is constructed in different countries when they have to follow a common model prepared by the UN. In addition to the findings about the social construction of the legal text, the research method used in these three volumes is appropriate for an in-depth genre analysis of civil judgements. The methodology includes three steps: (1) linguistic analysis of texts; (2) grounded account of the drafting and interpretive practitioners; and (3) explanation of issues identified in 1 and 2 by reference to socio-cultural, economic and political, linguistic and legal factors (2003a, p. vi). However, the three research steps are possible only when the researcher can access sufficient data. Because of the confidentiality of some litigation practices in Mainland China, it is sometimes difficult to access original textual or account data for the applied genre analysis of civil judgments. The issue of confidentiality is discussed in Bhatia et al. (2009), who suggest that it is possible to reconstruct the studied professional practice through an analysis of alternative textual and account data. The method of reconstruction is important for a complete and in-depth analysis of civil judgments and the background litigation practices.

2.6 Conclusion

This chapter attempted to contextualize this study by reviewing the three traditions of genre studies, their common concerns and distinctive focus, and also by reviewing a literature of legal discourse studies. It is not intended for this research to draw on one single school for theoretical constructs and analytical strategies, and the researcher makes an attempt to synthesize those elements which are useful for the analysis of civil judgments. An applied genre analysis of civil judgments requires an analysis of typical and meaningful lexico-grammatical features, but an all-inclusive Sydney School-type linguistic analysis is not intended. Swales and Bhatia's definitions of genre emphasize generic convention and versatility, which is important to interpret from a socio-cultural perspective judges' conventions and variations in writing civil judgment. The analytical dimensions of the North American School supply a variety of parameters which are useful for the handling of civil judgments and related legal texts on a textual level. The review of legal discourse studies sets up a broad context for the present research and identifies specific sources from which insights into analytical themes and methods can be drawn.

Chapter 3

Research Methodology

3.1 Introduction

This chapter aims to establish the analytical framework for the present research by drawing on the literature review of the previous chapter. The research procedure and the specific analytical dimensions are first introduced by highlighting and discussing some established methods of genre analysis. The concepts of metadiscourse, coherence, and interdiscursivity are then explained and illustrated to obtain the readily applicable dimensions for analyzing civil judgments as text and as genre. Although other parameters like sentences, paragraphs, predicative verbs, and quoted/quoting texts are also needed, it is the above three that are conceptually complicated and which are taken as analytical themes in the study of civil judgments.

3.2 Research Procedure

Genre studies traditionally focus on textual and immediate contextual analysis (Swales, 1981, 1990a). Although Swales takes the concept of 'discourse community' as one crucial concept in defining genre, the analysis of academic genres mostly focuses on move/step structures and lexico-grammar features (Swales, 1990a). This method serves the ESP pedagogic purpose, but the present research needs to consider a broader professional context and specialists' professional practices in order to understand the linguistic and generic features of civil judgments. The multi-perspective and multidimensional framework elaborated in Bhatia (1993, 2004) is therefore adopted.

The linguistic analysis in this research identifies the move patterns of civil judgments, the purpose of each move, and the lexical and grammatical patterns. The lexico-grammar analysis is not as all-inclusive as in Martin (1992) and Martin and White (2005) because linguistic analysis alone is insufficient for a 'thick description' oriented analysis of civil judgments. Only textual features which are meaningful in litigation practices are identified. The aim of linguistic analysis is not to analyze the text itself, but to find how discursive and socio-legal meanings are negotiated and textualized.

After the linguistic analysis, ethnographic investigations are employed for situation-specific contextual analysis. Information sources like original institutional documents, specialist accounts, and observations of real professional practices are essential to acquire a comprehensive and in-depth understanding of litigation practices of which civil judgment is a part. This research draws on Bhatia's distinction between immediate context and more general context (Bhatia, 2004, p. 125). This distinction, although less theoretically complicated, is more pragmatic than other similar constructions of the concept, like the situational and cultural context in Halliday (1978). In addition to Halliday's construct of field, tenor and mode, Bhatia uses the participants' relationship, attitude, social distance, goals and intertextual relationship to explain the immediate situational setting of a genre, and uses social and professional culture to explain the more general context. This research encompasses both the immediate context and a broader socio-political context of civil judgments to produce meaningful explanations of the textual findings.

In an endeavour to provide the thick analysis of academic and professional genres, Bhatia uses the following diagram to show the multi-perspective and multidimensional analytical model:

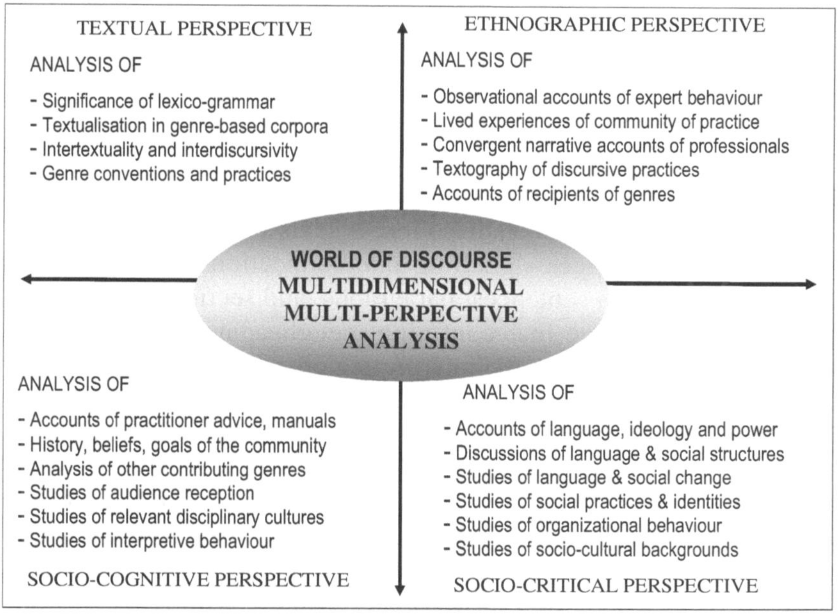

Table 3.1. A multi-perspective and multidimensional model of genre analysis, quoted from Bhatia (2004), p. 163.

This research draws on the above framework and analyzes civil judgments from a number of dimensions, including rhetorical patterns, lexico-grammatical features, accounts of lawyers and judges, the professional culture of Chinese judicial systems, and other contributing genres (indictments and defences). The data are acquired through library/internet searches, approaching particular institutions or specialists, and interviewing litigation practitioners. The important themes to be used in the research are now discussed.

3.3 Text-internal resources

3.3.1 Metadiscourse

Different theoretical perceptions relate to the concept of metadiscourse. Some argue metadiscourse is texts about texts, referring to grammatical devices signalling interconnections among textual components such as sentences, paragraphs, and sections (Mauranen, 1993). Others believe that confining metadiscourse to the textual function only undermines the interpreting power of this concept, and they further utilise the interpersonal function (Hyland, 1996, 2005). Two common concerns underlie these two perceptions. Firstly, metadiscourse adds no propositional meaning to texts and its removal does not influence the meaning conveyed by the texts. Secondly, metadiscourse makes texts more accessible to readers, communicates writers' commitment to their arguments/discussion to readers, and conveys writers' intention to negotiate meaning with readers. Both two concerns highlight writers' awareness of readers and writers' efforts to 'convey personality, credibility, considerateness of the readers' (Crismore et al., 1993, p. 40). Metadiscourse, in the present research, fulfils both the textual and interpersonal functions. Particular attention is paid to the metadiscursive devices realizing the judges' interpersonal intentions.

These basic theoretical considerations have engendered complicated categorizations of metadiscursive devices (Van de Kopple, 1985; Crismore et al., 1993; Hyland, 2005). A full account of the detailed metadiscursive categorization is not relevant here because this research only makes use of several devices applicable to civil judgments. Two frequently occurring metadiscursive devices (hedges and emphatics) are particularly explored in order to explain how and for what purposes Mainland Chinese legal professionals, i.e. judges and lawyers, claim their personal identities in this highly institutionalized genre.

According to Hyland:

> Hedges are devices such as *possible, might* and *perhaps*, which indicate the writer's decision to recognize alternative voices and viewpoints and so withhold complete commitment to a proposition. (Hyland, 2005, p. 52)

Writers withhold their complete commitment either because they consider the argument may not be identical to truth or because they intend to show their deference in order to gain readers' ratification of claims (Hyland, 1996, p. 256). The second reason does not hold value for the interpretation of civil judgments because judges are neutral adjudicators on behalf of the disputing parties and enjoy an unchallenged status unless charged with malpractice. Judges do not and need not show deference or humbleness in writing judgments; they instead need to exercise their power appropriately, writing formally and authoritatively. The appropriate use of hedging and emphatics are two possible ways for judges to achieve this.

Hedges used in civil judgments are analyzed, categorized, and interpreted in view of their specific textual/contextual situations. There are more efforts in studying these hedging devices on their own rather than efforts in grouping or describing them according to some pre-established theoretical constructions. Emphatics refers to grammatical devices which stress writers' personal attitudes or commitment to what they are arguing. This study does not use name certainty markers (Crismore et al., 1993, p. 52) or boosters (Hyland, 2005, p. 53) because the term 'emphatics' more directly describes the primary function of lexico-grammars such as 'any, naturally, obviously, explicitly', and 'extremely', as judges use them. Certainty markers highlight writers' intentions to show their complete commitment to the truth-value of the proposition, and boosters are used to close down alternatives and constrain conflicting views. While both explanations can illuminate an interpretation of judges' considerations in writing civil judgments, neither is entirely appropriate from a legal point of view.

Metadiscourse is important for civil judgments and Mainland Chinese judges because it supplies a legitimate device for judges to establish their personalities. This is especially meaningful considering Chinese judges' personal identities are usually subsumed by the collective identity of the People's Courts and the state as a whole. For example, it is common for judges to show their personal analysis and understanding through emphatics when they could otherwise produce a direct statement:

> The defendant's action has **directly** harmed the plaintiff's social reputation [...] so the defendant **naturally** should bear the liability [...].
> The defendant's argument is **obviously** unreasonable [...].

Besides contributing to the persuasiveness of judges' opinions, emphatics are here used to express the judges' personal evaluations towards factual or evidential issues. 'Directly' and 'naturally' clearly convey the judge's negative feelings towards the defendant's actions. 'Naturally' implies that the defendant has no excuse to refuse to compensate. The judge says the defendant's argument is 'obviously unreasonable' not only because the defendant's argument is completely groundless but also because there is a negative feeling towards the fact that the defendant pursued some unreasonable aims.

3.3.2 Coherence

The concept of coherence in this research draws on Swales (1990b), Martin (1992), Sanders & Noordman (2000), Sanders et al. (1992) and van Dunne (1996). There are two approaches to defining the concept of coherence. Firstly, coherence can be described as one attribute of texts which is not concerned with readers' interpretations. Sanders argues 'discourse shows coherence' (Sanders & Noordman, 2000, p. 38). Researchers of this theoretical orientation devote considerable effort to examining cohesive devices in texts (Halliday & Hasan, 1976). Secondly, coherence can be seen as a characteristic attributed to texts by readers' interpretations. A text is coherent because readers can acquire from it logical and interconnected cognitive representations (Enkvist, 1990, p. 11). In order to acquire a coherent understanding of texts, readers have to make connections between texts and situational/cultural contexts, drawing on their experience, knowledge, and interpretation. In analyzing coherence in texts, cohesive devices in the discourse are 'viewed as important though not necessary features of discourse' (Sanders et al., 1992, p. 2). A more crucial element is readers' expectations, which include purposive, schematic, and local expectations (Swales, 1990b, p. 189).

This research uses a slightly modified concept of normative coherence and narrative coherence (van Dunne, 1996) in order to examine the coherence of civil judgments. According to van Dunne, normative coherence means that legal texts are in agreement with the whole legal system because they can be justified by related law and legal norms. Narrative coherence entails that facts and legal decisions are all based on an appropriate use of evidence. This discussion is not sufficient for the analysis of civil judgments because it does not consider the consistency of text. This study therefore uses linguistic coherence to incorporate a necessary analysis of textual consistency, and uses discursive coherence to refer to normative coherence and narrative coherence, an understanding of which requires some mastery of legal knowledge.

The analysis of linguistic features in chapter 6 is qualitatively oriented. No attempts are made to use statistical analyses because this describes only the general rather than genre-specific textual features of civil judgments, which offers little insight in a 'thick-description' of civil judgments. The concepts of 'transitivity' and 'theme' (Halliday & Matthiessen, 2004, p. 64) are exploited to understand the extent to which specific texts meet readers' interpretations and expectations of coherence. The analysis of individual sentences is less meaningful than chains of sentences. Only by grouping sentences of one paragraph or section together can the researcher determine whether there is a convergent or divergent tendency among the choices of verbs and the contents of individual sentences. This convergent or divergent tendency governs the degree of coherence of texts (Martin, 1992, p. 488).

Theme is defined as 'the element which serves as the point of departure of the message; it is that which locates and orients the clause within its context' (Halliday & Matthiessen, 2004, p. 64). It is an important indicator signalling the topic of sentences and the immediate context surrounding the clause. Understanding the themes in the writing of judges' opinions is crucial to capture the essence of their arguments. For example, it is preferred that there are consistent choices of themes in judges' writing and the chosen themes are interconnected meaningfully. Otherwise, the arguments are less coherent and less accessible to specialist and non-specialist readers. In addition to the themes of individual sentences, this research also considers the chains of themes, aiming at analyzing the consistency and sudden changes occurring in these chains.

A number of realizations of themes, including ideational, interpersonal and textual are discussed in Halliday and Matthiessen (2004), and more than one pattern of thematic progression is elaborated in Bloor (1995). These two realizations are not relevant here because sentences used in civil judgments are not and cannot be as versatile as those used in novels or stories, as shown in Halliday and Matthiessen (2004, p. 100). Most sentences in civil judgments start with one of the litigation participants (plaintiff, defendant, witness, judge, etc.), or one particular factual element (disputed contract, short-delivered goods, patent rights, and so on). They are mostly single words or simple noun phrases, having no complicated internal grammatical structures.

The primary goal of examining the chain of themes is to reveal the consistency and changes in the choices of themes while also discussing the underlying institutional and professional restrictions. A thorough analysis of sentence themes is not intended. The textual features studied are sometimes linguistically simple but more effort is required to interpret and explain these features in the context of Chinese judicial culture.

3.4 Text-external resources

The importance of intertextuality and interdiscursivity for discourse analysis is acknowledged in a number of studies including Hyland (2004), Bazerman (2004), and Devitt (2004). These two concepts are important because 'intertext' refers to the fact that a text is never completely isolated; it always sits in an interwoven web of a number of other texts. The pioneering study of this can be seen in Swales (1986a). Scholars in applied linguistics are not satisfied with a pure linguistic analysis of intertexts and have expanded the study of intertextuality to the level of interdiscursivity, by drawing upon insights from the social constructionist movement, the research of New Rhetoric and composition studies, and also the work of critical discourse analysis.

The difference between these two concepts is explained by Fairclough:

> Intertextuality is basically the property texts have of being full of snatches of other texts, which may be explicitly demarcated or merged in, and which the text may assimilate, contradict, ironically echo, and so forth [...]. The concept of intertextuality sees texts historically as transforming the past – existing conventions and prior texts – into the present [...]. (Fairclough, 1992, p. 84–85)

Fairclough distinguishes between 'manifest intertextuality' and 'interdiscursivity' or 'constitutive intertextuality'. The former refers to prior texts explicitly appearing in another, while the latter mainly refers to the interwoven relationships among different discourse, as discussed in Devitt (1991).

In addition to the work of Swales (1986a) and White (2004), Bazerman (2004) analyses levels of intertextuality and techniques of presenting intertexts, Bremner (2008) studies intertextual practices in workplace communication and looks at how ESP practitioners can provide students with more textual support through intertextual analysis. Bazerman (2004) proposes six ways of presenting intertexts, including direct quotation, indirect quotation, and mentioning of a person/document/statements, etc. This classification is useful, but pure categorization is insufficient for an in-depth analysis of various academic and professional genres. A consideration of socio-cultural context is required to examine why writers construct specific texts the way they do.

Candlin and Maley (1997) use the concept of interdiscursivity to analyze the interplay of mediation and litigation discourse, which refers to the mixing of different discursive values in the present research. Through a grounded analysis of transcriptions of mediation talk, they successfully demonstrate that the generic integrity of mediatory discourse is unavoidably invaded by legal and therapeutic discourse, because the mediators have been given much legally-oriented professional training. Their theoretical contribution suggests that the concept of interdiscursivity can successfully explain the frequent interplays between various professional discourses. However, their work does not involve professionals' exploitation of generic resources systematically; neither do they make a clear distinction between intertextuality and interdiscursivity. The present research draws on the discussion of interdiscursivity in Bhatia (2004, 2008, and 2010).

Bhatia argues:

> Interdiscursivity is always across discursive events (may be genres, professional activities, or even more generally professional cultures). It is often based on shared generic or contextual characteristics across two or more discursive constructs and some understanding of these shared features is a necessary condition to an adequate understanding of the new construct. Interdiscursivity thus can be viewed as a function of appropriation of generic resources across three kinds of contextual and other text-external boundaries: professional genres, professional practices, and professional cultures. (Bhatia, 2010, p. 36)

The implication here is that intertextuality discusses the relationship among texts, while interdiscursivity, in the field of professional discourse studies, usually examines specialists' appropriation of text-external generic resources. Interdiscursivity can occur on and across a number of levels like discursive values, professional practices, professional cultures and even socio-cultures. Civil judgments encompass several tasks at one time: to declare judges' decisions on parties' disputes, to persuade parties to accept these decisions as fair, and to demonstrate judges' professional competence. These different tasks need to be realized by different discourses. An attempt is made to examine specific issues such as what discursive values civil judgments usually carry, what the relationship among these values is, why judges include discourses other than legal discourse, and what contextual factors have made the inclusion of multiple discursive values possible and legitimate. These issues are examined by analyzing rhetorical purposes of texts, lexico-grammatical features in texts, internal structures of texts, and specialists' accounts related to texts. The analysis seeks to demonstrate whether a civil judgment is an ideal mono-discursive genre or a multi-discursively constructed discursive artefact in litigation practices.

3.5 Data Collection and analysis

The present research draws on two data sources: civil judgments and specialists' accounts. The judgments are publicly accessible through the internet or published materials. A corpus of 100 civil judgments was randomly compiled. Care was taken to choose only those judgments which were delivered after the year 2000, because newly rendered judgments more effectively reflect the judicial realities of the PRC. No preference was given to the types of disputes, be they contractual, personal injury, or damage of property. The textual analysis starts from a detailed reading and analysis of 30 judgments in the corpus. The researcher read carefully through each of these 30 judgments, aiming at marking and discovering repeatedly occurring lexico-grammatical features and discursive patterns. Any unclear features and patterns thus found in these 30 judgments were examined against another 20 judgments. The remaining 50 judgments are used as data for verification of findings. Altogether, 41 example texts from 25 judgments are cited in this book to illustrate the researcher's analysis and argument (Appendix I). The textual analysis and specialists' accounts reveal that the writing of civil judgments in China is highly standardized and convergent, and that the quoted texts and cases are representative of the corpus and of the judges' discursive practices in civil judgments.

The specialists' accounts were acquired from seven lawyers and three judges. The lawyers come from law firms in Beijing, Zhejiang and Henan in the People's Republic of China. Most have been practising for over eight years. The three judges work in intermediate courts in Zhejiang and Henan. Two of them have a litigation career of five and 20 years respectively. The third has been drafting judgments for six years in a court in Hangzhou, the capital city of Zhejiang province.

The interviews were both general and text-based. The general interview solicited specialists' reflections and thoughts on their roles/participation in legal communities, their professional practices, and their lived experiences. Lawyers and judges are expected to produce 'a narrative of some sort regarding all or part of their own life-experience' (Wengraf, 2001, p. 5). The text-based interview sought to verify the findings of the above textual analysis, and specialists were welcome to add their own perceptions. Fifteen formal recorded interviews of 45–60 minutes were held.

The interpretation of the interview data used in this research is influenced by Seidman (1998). Seidman believes that the interview should consist of three sections: interview one – focused on life history; interview two – the details of experience; and interview three – reflection on the meaning (Seidman 1998). These three sections can provide a full understanding of the research subject, but Seidman's study is solely based on analyzing in-depth interview data. The present research is primarily discourse-based, and the interview is used to supplement the textual and discursive analysis. The purpose of the research is to interpret meaningfully civil judgments in view of their socio-legal contexts; there is no intention to strictly follow a particular research procedure. These three stages are adopted and undertaken in one interview.

Supplementing these two major data sets are several secondary data sources. As a highly inter-textual and inter-discursive genre, civil judgments include a number of other discourses, such as indictments, defences, and witnesses' testimonies. The further analysis of these discourses is indispensable for an in-depth and comprehensive applied genre analysis of civil judgments.

Chapter 4

The Rhetorical Moves of Civil Judgments

4.1 Introduction

This chapter reports the analysis of move patterns in civil judgments and discusses the issues of readability and accessibility (Barnes, 2006; Little, 1998; Wald, 1995) of this genre. Four steps of analysis were conducted in order to identify the move patterns in civil judgments. Firstly, the corpus was analyzed in order to discover the overall move pattern in this genre. Secondly, the communicative purposes and internal structures of specific moves were examined. Thirdly, the content of specific moves was analyzed in order to see what was textualized by judges in these moves. Finally, effort was made to examine the judges' rhetorical practices in writing civil judgments and their situation-specific considerations behind these practices.

The issues of readability and accessibility are discussed in this chapter because civil judgments seem to have multiple target audiences. Readability is an important concept which is continuously discussed in studies of plain English/language in the legal field (Barnes, 2006; Kimble, 1994; Turnbull, 1997; Williams, 2004). Researchers examine the readability of various legal texts mainly to solve ordinary non-specialists reader problems and to consider the difficulty involved in reading these texts. It has been suggested that legal language should be examined more critically and that better solutions should be found to strike an appropriate balance between providing the necessary legal precision and certainty and supplying sufficient access to the law for non-specialists (Barnes, 2006, p. 131; Turnbill, 1997, p. 22). These studies indicate that civil judgments in China simultaneously serve several different purposes: for litigation participants, the texts report the facts, the issues, and the court decisions; for courts of appeal, the texts report the actual litigation process which is meant to be supervised; for other judges, the texts provide precedents for deciding similar cases in future; for layperson readers, the texts inform them of legal knowledge in specific contexts. Although Su argues that civil judgment includes both specialists and non-specialists as the target readers (2001a, p, 16), Mainland Chinese judges, as demonstrated in the corpus, seldom make special rhetorical arrangements to make their writing easily accessible to non-specialist readers. What is found when reading this genre is a text of between two and ten pages without explicit discourse markers or other signposts that demarcate the textual boundaries among the component sections.

4.2 The move[1] pattern

Civil judgments have no explicit discourse markers like numbers or subtitles which can directly indicate the overall move pattern of this genre. They also include some basic legal concepts such as claim, defence, fact, and opinion, the understanding of which is necessary to analyze this highly institutionalized and conventionalized genre. However, a number of conventional signposts including 'the plaintiff claimed, the defendant argued', and 'this court holds' are explicitly used in this genre, and their identification can facilitate move analysis in this genre. In the present research, the analysis of each judgment is conducted by a careful reading of the text, with the dual

1 The researcher's understanding of the concepts 'move' and 'step' draws on Swales' analysis of academic discourse (Swales, 1981, 1990a) and Bhatia's analysis of professional discourse (Bhatia, 1993). They use 'move' and 'step' to refer to conventional component sections of a particular genre, the awareness of which will reduce readers' cognitive effort in handling the genre.

purpose of acquiring a general understanding of the text and of revealing the meaningful textual features. An analysis of all civil judgments in the corpus finds the following move pattern (an example of a genre analysis of an entire judgment can be found in Appendix V):

Civil Judgment

- Move 1: Heading
  - Step 1: Case Number
  - Step 2: List of Litigation Participants
- Move 2: Introduction
- Move 3: Parties' Arguments
  - Step 1: Plaintiffs' Claim
  - Step 2: Defendants' Defence
  - Step 3: Evidence (*optional*)
- Move 4: Judges' Arguments
  - Step 1: Facts
  - Step 2: Issues (*optional*)
  - Step 3: Evidence (*optional*)
- Move: 5 Judges' Opinions
  - Step 1: Interpretation of Law
  - Step 2: Application of Law
  - Step 4: Opinions
  - Step 5: Opposite Opinions (*rarely available*)
- Move 6: Court Decisions
  - Step 1: Decisions
  - Step 2: Notification of the Right to Appeal
  - Step 3: Signature Line

Table 4.1. The move pattern of civil judgment.

This table shows that the move pattern in civil judgments is standardized, i.e., all civil judgments include the same moves arranged in the same order. All moves *Heading, Introduction, Parties' Arguments, Judges' Arguments, Judges' Opinions,* and *Court decisions* are obligatory, and each is presented in a fixed position in the civil judgment. This largely fixed textual arrangement facilitates reading because specialist and non-specialist readers can easily locate particular sections of interest.

All moves are easily identifiable because of the explicit signposts initiating each move. For example, the move *Court Decisions* always starts with signposts like 'to sum up the above, a judgment is hereby entered', and 'the judgment is handed down as below'. The move Judges' Arguments usually starts with signposts like 'the following facts were ascertained on the basis of the evidence provided by the Plaintiff' or 'it has been ascertained by this court through examination'. The standardized move pattern makes civil judgments a highly conventionalized genre with few variations. In the above table, the steps *Evidence* and *Opposite Opinions* are not universal for all judgments, although they can be important sections demonstrating the judges' argumentation and negotiation in writing a civil judgment. The following analysis handles each move in turn and examines their purposes and internal structures.

4.3 Move 1 and 2: *Heading* and *Introduction*

Heading and *Introduction* are the two most standardized moves in civil judgments. The corpus examination reveals that the two moves provide a blank-filling task for Mainland Chinese judges. *Heading* lists, in a fixed order, some conventional information related to the civil judgment, including the court's name, the case number, the plaintiffs, the plaintiffs' agents, the defendants, and the defendants' agents. *Introduction* briefly introduces the parties' dispute and the trial process. The following example case is between a person (the plaintiff) and a hospital (the defendant), who both assigned agents to act on their behalf in court. The quoted text is the *Heading* and *Introduction* of the final judgment:

- Chaoyang District Court of Beijing
- Civil Judgment
- (2003) CMCZ No. 9980

- Plaintiff: Wang Rongfu, male, born on October 12, 1935, Han Zhu, retired from Beijing Zhaowei Electronics Group, (*address*)No.5, flat 2, 201, Gaojiayuan, Chaoyang District of Beijing.
- Agent: Wang Qiang (the son of Wang Rongfu), male, born on March 10, 1964, Han Zu, teacher of the Medicine Division in Peking University, (*address*) No. 14, flat 1, Unit 5, Building 25, the Medicine Division of Peking University, Haidian District of Beijing.
- Agent: Liu Ruishuang, male, born on September 25, 1968, Han Zu, teacher of the Medicine Division in Peking University, (*address*) 49, Huayuan Bei Lu, Haidian District of Beijing.
- Defendant: Jiuxianqiao Hospital, (*address*), 6, Street 1, Jiuxianqiao, Chaoyang District of Beijing.
- Legal Representative: Cheng Mingzhe, Director.
- Agent: Deng Liqiang, lawyer from Beijing Huawei Law Firm.
- Agent: Gao Qiying, female, born on September 14, 1953, secretary in Medical Affairs Office of Jiuxianqiao Hospital, (address), the Resident Hall of Jiuxianqiao hospital.
- With respect to the dispute over the medical contract between the plaintiff – Wang Rongfu and the defendant – Beijing Jiuxianqiao Hospital (hereinafter referred to as Jiuxianqiao Hospital), this court accepted the case, constituted a collegial bench, and held open hearings. Wang Qiang and Liu Ruishuang, the agents acting on behalf of the plaintiff (Wang Rongfu), and Deng Liqiang and Gao Qiying, the agent acting on behalf of the defendant (Jiuxianqiao Hospital), appeared in courtroom and attended the proceedings. Now the hearing of this court has been closed. (Example text 1, case 1)

Two obvious rhetorical observations of this text do not require a detailed understanding of the reported content. Firstly, the textual layout is easy to follow because all reported information is clearly itemized. Secondly, the text is not easy to read because it employs highly legalized lexico-grammar, including many legal terms, numbers, phrases, and an exclusive use of declarative sentences. On the basis of these two rhetorical observations, three research findings are presented below.

4.3.1 The introduction of litigation participants

An introduction to litigation participants, i.e. the judges, the parties, and the agents, is required in all civil judgments, but there is no universal way of introducing these different participants. In the above text, some participants are introduced with very detailed personal information, including gender, dates of birth, and exact addresses, while others may be introduced only with names and affiliated institutions. This variation in introducing litigation participants is demonstrated below:

(*the detailed introduction of the plaintiff and his agent*)

- Plaintiff: Wang Rongfu, male, born on October 12, 1935, Han Zu, retired from Beijing Zhaowei Electronics Group, (*address*) No.5, flat 2, 201, Gaojiayuan, Chaoyang District of Beijing.
- Agent: Wang Qiang (the son of Wang Rongfu), male, born on March 10, 1964, Han Zu, teacher of the Medicine Division in Peking University, (*address*) No. 14, flat 1, Unit 5, Building 25, the Medicine Division of Peking University, Haidian District of Beijing.

(*the brief introduction of the defendant and its agent*)

- Defendant: Jiuxianqiao Hospital, (*address*), 6, Street 1, Jiuxianqiao, Chaoyang District of Beijing.
- Legal Representative: Cheng Mingzhe, Director.
- Agent: Deng Liqiang, lawyer from Beijing Huawei Law Firm.

The plaintiff and his agent are introduced in such a detailed way that some information seems quite redundant for non-specialist readers, like *Han Zu (ethnicity),* and *No. 5, flat 2, 201, Gaojiayuan (address).* The introduction of the defendant and his agent is brief, which seems to satisfy non-specialist readers for whom issues beyond what the case is about, the parties to the dispute, and the judge's dispute rulings are irrelevant. The difference between the detailed and the brief plaintiff introductions can be explained by Chinese judges' institutional and professional considerations when they write the judgment.

Heading may have different meanings for different groups of readers. For litigation participants, it simply signifies a standardized section of a judgment which provides no new information. For non-specialist readers, it identifies the parties in the litigation. For specialist readers, it is an important section reporting essential information about the litigation participants, including ages, addresses, locations, affiliations, etc. This information is necessary to judges a particular party's capacity for civil conduct i.e. the capacity to act on his/her own in litigation, and necessary also to judge the court's jurisdiction i.e. the right to hear the case.

The law requires a detailed introduction for some litigation participants. For example, 'the General Principles of the Civil Law of the PRC' (1986) defines the concept of 'capacity for civil conduct' with the following two articles:

> *Article 11*
> A citizen aged 18 or above shall be an adult. He shall have full capacity for civil conduct, may independently engage in civil activities and shall be called a person with full capacity for civil conduct [...].
>
> *Article 12*
> A minor aged 10 or above shall be a person with limited capacity for civil conduct [...].

These two articles take age (*18 years or above*) as the only criterion to decide whether an individual has the full capacity for civil conduct. Therefore, the individual parties' ages must be introduced in the civil judgment. In the above text, the plaintiff (*Wang Rongfu*) is 'male, born on October 12, 1935'. At the time of trial, he was therefore over 68 and an individual with the full 'capacity of civil conduct'. He had the right of self-representation or to assign some agents (*Wang Qiang, Liu Ruishuang*) to act for him in the court trial.

Similarly, the parties' addresses determine whether the court has the jurisdiction to hear the case, as illustrated in 'the Civil Procedural Law of PRC' (1991):

> *Article 22*
> A civil lawsuit brought against a citizen shall be under the jurisdiction of the People's Court of the place where the defendant has his domicile [...].

Article 23

The civil lawsuits described below shall be under the jurisdiction of the People's Court of the place where the plaintiff has his domicile [...].

Article 22 stipulates that, in most cases, the court in the defendant's domicile (dwelling place) has jurisdiction over the dispute, while Article 23 lists several conditions under which the court in the plaintiff's domicile has jurisdiction. The court of appeal and other interested specialist readers need to know the exact addresses of both parties in order to judge whether the court has jurisdiction in the present trial. The judges must therefore report the two parties' addresses in the above text: 'No.5, flat 2, 201, Gaojiayuan, Chaoyang District of Beijing' and '6, Street 1, Jiuxianqiao, Chaoyang District of Beijing'.

Not all litigation participants are introduced in detail in *Heading*. Legal persons, i.e. corporations or organizations, are conventionally introduced with brief and standardized information like company's names, legal representatives, and addresses. This simpler introduction is reasonable because the essential information related to even a small company can be countless; it is not possible to list all such information in the limited textual space of a civil judgment, and most of this information is irrelevant when adjudicating particular disputes.

When specific information about a legal person is needed, judges may obtain it from related authorities. Legal persons are usually registered with government institutions. In China, they have to be registered with the local Administration for Industry and Commerce and other specialized institutions like the Health Bureau, the Police Department, and the Environmental Protection Bureau. Judges can easily access these government institutions for the required information. To sum up, judges introduce litigation participants not according to judicial preferences but according to the case-specific situation and the requirements of the law. The content of the introduction to the parties carries legal significance, which is either explicitly required by law or important to decide a legal issue. The omission of any necessary content may lead to reading difficulty for specialist readers.

4.3.2 *The absence of lawyer*

When parties get involved in a lawsuit, it is expected that they will first go to lawyers and make preparations for complex litigation. This may not be true in Mainland Chinese judicial cultures. The plaintiff in the above text does not hire a lawyer to act on his behalf in court. The plaintiff here seems to trust his son, i.e. the agent more than he trusts a lawyer. This tendency for parties to choose relatives and friends to act on their behalf occurs commonly in the corpus. Although all the plaintiffs and defendants in the corpus choose to assign one or several agents to act on their behalf in court, many actually turn to non-specialists for help. The following three texts illustrate how the choice of agents varies:

(*with lawyers as agents*)

- Plaintiff: Zhang Tielin, male, U.K. (nationality), born on June 15, 1957, director of Beijing Moon Movie and Television Company Ltd., lives in 1201, Unit 3–4, No. 412, Huizhong North Lane, Chaoyang district, Beijing.
- Agent: Xie Gang, lawyer of Beijing Guofang Law Firm.
- Agent: Zhang Zhixia, lawyer of Beijing Guofang Law Firm. (Example text 2, case 2)

(*with lay persons as agents*)

- Plaintiff: Wang Rongfu, male, born on October 12, 1935, Han Zu, retired from Beijing Zhaowei Electronics Group, (*address*) No. 5, flat 2, 201, Gaojiayuan, Chaoyang District of Beijing.
- Agent: Wang Qiang (the son of Wang Rongfu), male, born on March 10, 1964, Han Zu, teacher of the Medicine Division of Peking University, (*address*) No. 14, flat 1, Unit 5, Building 25, the Medicine Division of Peking University, Haidian District of Beijing.
(Example text 1, case 1)

(*with both lawyers and lay persons as agents*)

- Defendant: Jiuxianqiao Hospital, (*address*), 6, Street 1, Jiuxianqiao, Chaoyang District of Beijing.
- Legal Representative: Cheng Mingzhe, Director.
- Agent: Deng Liqiang, lawyer of Beijing Huawei Law Firm.
- Agent: Gao Qiying, female, born on September 14, 1953, secretary in the Medical Affairs Office of Jiuxianqiao Hospital, (address), the Resident Hall of Jiuxianqiao hospital. (Example text 1, case 1)

These three texts reveal a common phenomenon in Mainland Chinese civil litigation, i.e. the parties do not hire a lawyer to help them deal with intimidating litigation. Some parties seem to rely more on non-specialists rather than on lawyers. The litigation participant (*Wang Rongfu*) in the second text above appointed his son as his agent in court. His son was a 'medical teacher' in Peking University and his medical expertise was perhaps a significant advantage in the surgical dispute between the plaintiff and the defendant. In litigation, however, legal knowledge is usually more important than the subject knowledge related to the dispute, and a lawyer is clearly more adept at handling litigation than a doctor.

Similarly, in the third text, the defendant (*Jiuxianqiao Hospital*) assigned one of its staff members as its agent. This was done either because it lacked sufficient confidence in the lawyer engaged (*Deng Liqiang*) or because it preferred to use its own staff to facilitate communication with the lawyer. The tendency for the parties to use related persons (relatives, staff members, friends, etc.) as agents is common in the corpus: companies usually assign staff members, and individuals usually choose their friends or relatives. This tendency may occasionally go to extremes where a case seems to transform into a family dispute instead of a court trial. In the following dispute between two neighbours, the plaintiff (*Li Enqi*) sued the defendant (*Qiao Jingjuan*) and claimed that the frequent noise made by the defendant disturbed his life. The litigation participants were introduced as below:

- Plaintiff: Li Enqi, male, born on March 12, 1936, HAN Zu, worker in Design Office of Thermo Power Plant, lives in X, High Building, South Zhongshan Gate Lane, Hedong District, Tianjin.
- Agent: Li Dan (daughter of the plaintiff) [...]
- Agent: Luo Peng (relative of the plaintiff) [...]
- Defendant: Qiao Jingjuan, female, born on August 10, 1934 [...]
- Agent: Zhong Sheng (son of the defendant) [...] (Example text 3, case 3)

This text shows that both the plaintiff and the defendant asked their sons and relatives to be their agents. The impression is thus given that this is a negotiation or mediation between the two families. The parties' preference for relatives and friends as litigation agents indicates the influence of traditional Chinese culture over modern litigation practices. Chinese people still believe that courts are only one part of the government; they believe judges are their parenting officers (父母官) who will put everything right for them, and relationships (关系) are still an important factor they consider when they have to turn to other people for help. Discussing the social status of lawyers and people's distrust of lawyers in Mainland China, *The Beijing Youth Daily* reported:

> It is unbelievable for someone not to hire a lawyer in court trials in foreign countries, but it is quite common at home. About 80 % percent of civil cases have no lawyers as agents, some of them have no agents and some have lay persons as agents. Although lawyers, as a profession, have been developing fast in recent years, they remain a mysterious group for ordinary people. Ordinary people have so much doubt about lawyers' charges and service quality. When getting into a case, quite a lot of people believe lawyers do not help a lot, or they do not know how to hire the appropriate lawyer [...]. (*Beijing Youth Daily*, February 12, 2004) (Excerpt 1)

It can be concluded that the absence of lawyers in civil judgments is not simply a textual variation of writing judgments; it reveals that Chinese people quite often have no incentive to hire lawyers or do not know how to hire lawyers when they get involved in litigation. The legal profession in Mainland China still has considerable room for improvement. An acknowledged fact is that Mainland Chinese lawyers do not acquire as important a social status as they deserve. The common anxiety among Mainland Chinese lawyers is not how eloquent they can be in courtroom examinations or what professional legal opinions they should produce in relation to difficult factual or legal issues, but how they can acquire as many cases and clients as possible, as pointed out in Sun (2009, p. 22). Most lawyers invest considerable time and effort to persuade companies and individuals to accept them as agents or legal counsellors.

4.3.3 *Simplified information in the move* Introduction

The move *Introduction* is usually a small paragraph which leads the whole judgment by introducing the parties' dispute and briefly summarizing the whole trial process. The introduction of the parties' disputes is standardized, and the brief summary of the trial process is general and imprecise. This move does not give specialist and non-specialist readers a sufficient opportunity to access the reported litigation. The standardized way of introducing disputes is illustrated by the example below:

> The plaintiff X **sued** the defendant Y **for** violating his copyright.

Sentences of such a kind are written in such a standardized way that judges need do nothing but fill in the parties' names and a general indication of their disputes. The information carried by such sentences discloses little information about the litigation, because the parties have been introduced in the move *Heading* and the dispute (violating his copyright) is only a general indication of what actually happened.

In the whole civil judgment, the move *Introduction* is the easiest way for non-specialist readers to know what actually happened in the court trial. Judges are required to consider both the readability and accessibility of their writing. Readability means the writing should be readable for specialist and non-specialist readers, and accessibility requires that the writing discloses sufficient information related to the background litigation. The analysis suggests that while the move *Introduction* usually summarizes the trial process in a readable way, it is seldom accessible. The text below is from the above case where the plaintiff claimed the frequent noise made by the defendant disturbed his life:

> This court accepted the case on September 26th, 2001. On November 30th, the judge, Huang Qingnan, heard the case openly as required by the law. Yan Tieying, the plaintiff's agent, and Zhao Shuzhou and Sun Jingliang, the defendant's agents, participated in the courtroom examinations. This case has now been closed.

This text demonstrates how the judges in this case summarized the trial process. At the linguistic level, the lexico-grammar and sentences are well structured. Although it uses specialized words and expressions like 'hear the case, agents, participated in the proceedings', and 'closed (the case)', the text is readable even for non-specialist readers. The problem here is that insufficient information has been reported relating to the actual litigation. For example, the text does not mention the process of judge selection. The judge is presented as given: 'the judge, Huang Qingnan, heard the case'. One may argue that the process of nominating judges for a particular trial is recorded in archived files stored by the court, and it is unnecessary to list this information in every litigation document. This sounds reasonable because the lawyers participating in the trial lack access to the archived information. However, it does not consider the interests of other readers, including legal specialists, non-specialists, and even courts of appeal.

Strict legal regulations govern the nomination of judges or collegial panels for specific cases, so at least some basic information should be disclosed. *The Civil Procedural Law of PRC (1991)* stipulates:

> *Article 40*
> The trial court shall hear civil cases through a collegial panel or a sole judge. The collegial panel must have an odd number of members [...].
>
> *Article 142*
> When hearing simple civil cases in which the facts are evident, the rights and obligations are definite, and the disputes are minor, the trial court may apply the simplified procedure stipulated in this Chapter [...] and have the cases heard by a sole judge [...].

Article 40 stipulates that a trial court can have a case heard either by a collegial panel or by a sole judge. Article 142 stipulates the situations in which a trial court may assign a sole judge or a collegial panel to hear a case. In addition to these two regulations are other related issues like the parties' right to challenge the appropriateness of a particular judge and the judges' obligation to withdraw from cases where they have a vested interest. The application of these related laws and the process of forming the collegial panel are not disclosed to specialist and non-specialist readers. Commenting on this insufficient disclosure of information in the move *Introduction*, one specialist informant reported:

> Judges always want to tell a full but imprecise trial story [...]. The whole trial process are too comprehensive to be managed within one or two small paragraphs, so what they do is mention everything very briefly and vaguely. If necessary, they should report important moments in the trial in a precise way, rather than trying to cover everything so generally. (Excerpt 2, lawyer A)

4.4 Move 3 and 4: *Parties' Arguments* and *Judges' Arguments*

The move *Parties' Arguments* reports the respective claims and arguments of the plaintiffs and defendants, which includes the steps *Plaintiffs' Claim* and *Defendants' Defences*. The move *Judges' Arguments* reports the judges' identification of the facts and issues. This section studies the purposes of these two moves, their production, and some of their typical rhetorical patterns, with particular attention paid to the interdiscursivity between narration and argumentation, and the issues of readability and accessibility.

4.4.1 Narration or Argumentation

Ideally, both *Parties' Arguments* and *Judges' Arguments* need to be argumentative because the former reports the parties' attempt to convince judges to accept their description of the facts, and the latter reports the judges' attempts to identify facts through analysis and reasoning. However, the investigation demonstrates that both moves are filled with non-argumentative narratives.

Parties' Arguments reports how the plaintiffs and defendants describe the dispute in their own favour. This move can basically be seen as a battlefield upon which the opposing parties rhetorically fight each other. Their writing is meant to be as persuasive as possible because the sole purpose is to convince the judges to accept their respective arguments. However, in 60% of civil judgments in the corpus, this move does not introduce evidence supporting the parties' arguments; rather, it presents the parties' arguments as given rather than as persuasively constructed. In order to examine how this move is produced, the researcher compared this move with the original documents submitted by the parties to the court (plaintiffs' indictments and defendants' statements of defence). The purpose here is to compare how parties write their original arguments with how these original arguments are interpreted and recontextualized by the judges in the move *Parties' Arguments*.

Parities' Arguments does not contain the original arguments made by the plaintiffs and defendants, although this is obviously indicated by the move title. It is instead the judges' understanding and reporting of the parties' original indictments and statements of defence. This move, as indicated by the title *Parties' Arguments*, may be assumed to protect the parties' rights to be heard by providing a faithful representation of their arguments. In practice, however, it is common for judges to tailor the parties' arguments according to the judges' understanding of the dispute. Such a process of recontextualization is illustrated by the example step *Plaintiffs' Claim* below. In this case, the plaintiff (*Qin Tao,* a writer) sued the defendant (*Sohu,* one of the biggest commercial websites in China) and claimed the defendant had published his article without authorization:

> The plaintiff, Qin Tao, claimed: Sohu (Ltd.), without my permission, copied one of my articles in my personal blog in 2006, and I sued Sohu (Ltd.) for its violation of my copyright. During the trial, Sohu (Ltd.) and I signed a reconciliation agreement under which Sohu (Ltd.) should pay me 50,000 RMB for compensation. Until now, Sohu (Ltd.) has not fulfilled its duty of payment, so I sued and required the court to order Sohu (Ltd.) to pay me 50,000 RMB as agreed in our reconciliation agreement. (Example text 4, case 4)

This text illustrates how this example step provides some brief information about the plaintiff's arguments. The lack of argumentation in this text is perhaps surprising. Except for the two obvious attributing expressions ('claimed' and 'sued and required'), no serious argumentative effort is indicated. For example, there is no evidence or detailed explanation to support this plaintiff's specific claims nor an introduction to this plaintiff's suffering, and the language used is mostly language of 'doing' (Halliday, 1989), like 'Sohu copied', 'I sued, Sohu and I signed', and 'pay me', which conveys narration rather than argument.

Moreover, the lack of argumentation is also evidenced by the imprecise words and expressions used in the above text. A number of issues are reported ambiguously. For example, a lack of precision means the particular article referred to by 'one of my articles' is unknown. Similarly, the reader is not told how 'copied' was achieved, what the major contents of the 'reconciliation agreement' are, and what consists of the claimed '50,000 RMB'. It is not reasonable to assume that the plaintiff's strong incentive to persuade the judges would produce such ambiguous expressions to present his argument. In order to see whether simplifications of information appear in this judge's recontextualization and whether the plaintiff is given the right to be heard, the plaintiff's original indictment is presented below for the purpose of comparison:

> Claims: 1, To order the defendant to stop the violation immediately [...]
> 2, To order the defendant to pay the plaintiff the due amount of X for compensation
> 3, To order the defendant to reimburse the plaintiff [...]
> 3, To order the court fees to be borne by the defendant.
>
> Facts and reasons: [...] The plaintiff has made it clear 'prior negotiation and authorization are required for citation or quotation of the copyrighted materials'. On August 9 of 2005, the plaintiff posted in her blog the article 'Six thoughts about Baidu going crazy, Matsa coming, and Alibaba being sold'. The defendant reposted this article on its own website on August 9 2005 but it did not negotiate with the plaintiff or acquire prior authorization, did not mark the article source, and did not pay the author [...]. The plaintiff argues that she, as the lawful copyrighter, should enjoy the legal protection of her writings [...] the defendant should respect the author's copyright, but it reposted the plaintiff's article illegally several times and thus acquired huge profits. So the defendant should be held responsible for its violation of the plaintiff's copyright. The plaintiff hereby files this case with the Court for your adjudication [...]. (Example text 5, case 5)

The plaintiff's original document explicitly includes values of argumentation like 'claims, facts and reasons', and 'opinions (the plaintiff argues)'. The text shows that the plaintiff's claims include monetary and non-monetary ones. This original fully fledged argumentation is replaced by a simple sentence in the move *Parties' Arguments* ('I sued Sohu (Ltd.) for its violation of my copyright'). The 'facts and reasons' in the plaintiff's original document tell a full story relating to the development of the dispute between the plaintiff and the defendant. The narrative elements used include time (*August 9, 2005*), place ('plaintiff's blog' and 'defendant's website'), the subject matter ('the defendant reposted the plaintiff's copyrighted materials'), and the modifications of action ('several times, without prior negotiation and authorization', 'without paying the plaintiff'). The corresponding wording in the judges' recontextualization is 'Sohu (Ltd.), without my permission, copied articles in my personal blog in 2006'. The plaintiff's original document also provides multiple arguments to support the plaintiff's claims, such as 'the defendant should respect the author's copyright, reposted the plaintiff's article illegally several times', and 'acquired huge profits'. However, the judges' recontextualization omits this information.

A similar type of recontextualization occurs also in the defendants' original statements of defence, which are significantly simplified when the judges write the step *Defendants' Defences*. It can be concluded that the judges' concern in writing the move *Parties' Arguments* is not to respect the parties' right to be heard. Rather, the judges recontextualize the parties' original arguments in such a way that summarizes the parties' arguments, ignores all modifications and reports only the propositional meaning. The result is that the parties' original argumentation is turned into a brief narrative, and the parties' persuasive effort is not presented/heard. These brief narratives may sit more harmoniously with other sections of a civil judgment but sacrifice the protection of the parties' procedural satisfaction (Zhao & Sharma, 2003).

In summary, although judges need to take into account only the facts and not personal opinions of the parties when writing judgments, the omission of so much information seems problematic. The inclusion of some of the omitted information would construct the judgment in a more argumentative way, which is important to respect the parties' rights to be heard in trials. Noticing the lack of argumentation in civil judgments and other legal genres, the Supreme People's Court of the PRC recently initiated a Five-year Reform Outline[2] in order to improve the quality of argumentation in Chinese litigation genres. The Court particularly identified two areas needing improvement, namely, 'the judges' legal analysis and the judges' examination of evidence' and 'the judges' argumentation with an attempt to record the process of litigation and open the judges' reasoning in judgments' (see footnote 2).

4.4.2 The correspondence between Parties' Argument and Judges' Arguments

This section addresses the unexpected correspondence between the moves *Parties' Argument* and *Judges' Arguments*. The adversarial nature of litigation creates frequent tensions between the arguments of the three litigation participants: the plaintiffs, the defendants, and the judges. Their arguments in relation to facts and laws are not always in agreement. However, the analysis of the corpus reveals an almost universal correspondence between the factual description in the step *Plaintiffs' Claim* (step 1 of the move *Parties' Arguments*) and the factual descriptions in the move *Judges' Arguments*. *Plaintiffs' Claim* reports the plaintiffs' understanding of the dispute and their claims, while *Judges' Argument* reports the facts identified by

2 The reform in writing litigation documents should be accelerated, and the quality of litigation documents should be improved. The reform focus is on improving the judges' legal analysis and the judges' examination of evidence and on improving the judges' argumentation in litigation documents. Litigations documents should record the process of litigation and open the judges' reasoning in judgments, thus making each litigation document a symbol display of the judicial justice for the public and a lively sample to be used in law popularization. – *Five-year Reform Outline of People's Courts (1999)*, by Supreme Court of PRC (Excerpt 3).

the judges. It is unreasonable to conclude that judges in all the judgments agree with the plaintiffs, as indicated by specialist informant interviews. It is more common that judges agree with the plaintiffs on some aspects of the disputes and agree with the defendants on others. The correspondence between these two moves seems to indicate the other considerations of judges.

The following analysis tries to examine how such a correspondence occurs. In the following case, the plaintiff (seller) sold the contracted metal silicon to the defendant (shipper and buyer). For some reason, the sold goods were returned to the plaintiff. On examination, some of the returned goods were found to be damaged, so the plaintiff sued the defendant to get compensation for the damaged goods. The table below illustrates how the same events were handled in the step *Plaintiffs' Claim* and the move *Judges' Arguments* (the texts are quoted verbatim):

Plaintiffs' Claim (step 1 of the move *Judges' Arguments*)	*Judges' Arguments*	
	Based on aforesaid confirmed evidence, the court finds the following facts: On Jan. 12, 1999, the plaintiff and KNT signed silicon purchase contract [...]. After made the contract, the plaintiff bought the silicon [...].	*Contract and contract implementation*
	Later, the plaintiff carried the 115 ton-bags to Tianjin new port by land. The cargos were put into 6 containers [...].	*Transportation of goods from factory to port*
The plaintiff claimed: In Jan. 16, 1999, the plaintiff freighted metal silicon in containers (6X20') from Tianjin Xingang to Pusan port, South Korea.	The plaintiff delivered the 6 aforesaid containers to the defendant, Oasis. On Jan. 26, 1999, Oasis signed a clear bill of lading No. KYcr006, titled TWH Warehouse, as the agent of TWH, to the plaintiff.	*Shipping to the buyer*
Vessel 'Victory Star V904E' took in charge of the cargo. The defendant as the carrier singed and issued the clear bill of lading No. KYCR006. The bill recorded clearly the numbers, seal numbers and the name of metal silicon in each of container.	The B/L showed: the shipper was plaintiff; the consignee should be assignee of the instruction from the National Agriculture Bank; shipping port was Tianjin Xingang; port of destination was Pusan, Korea; carrier was vessel "Victory Star V904E"; cargos were 115 bags of metal silicon (gross weight: 115345 kg), in six 20' containers.	*Bill of Lading, i.e., certificate of shipping*
	The numbers of the containers and seals were clearly marked; hand-over form was CY-CY with cash against delivery. The cargos were shipped on time.	*Shipping to the buyer*

Table 4.2. Correspondence between *Parties' Arguments* and *Judges' Argument.*

The table demonstrates how the facts identified by the judges in *Judges' Arguments* closely correspond with the brief factual description provided by *Plaintiffs' Claim.* The difference is that *Judges' Arguments* contains more detail and more elaborative information related to the dispute. *Plaintiffs' Claim* reports three events:

- In Jan. 16, 1999, the plaintiff freighted metal silicon in containers (6X20') from Tianjin Xingang to Pusan port, South Korea.
- Vessel 'Victory Star V904E' took in charge of the cargo.
- The defendant as the carrier signed and issued the clear bill of lading No. KYCR006. The bill recorded clearly the numbers, seal numbers and the name of metal silicon in each of container.

The three events are all picked up and elaborated further by the move *Judges' Arguments.* The first event, 'In Jan. 16, 1999, the plaintiff freighted metal silicon in containers (6X20') from Tianjin Xingang to Pusan port, South Korea', is divided into specific topics related to the contract and contract implementation, including the shipping port (Tianjin Xingang) and the destination port (Pusan port), packaging particulars ('put into 6 containers by [...] sealed by [...]'), the source of the metal silicon ('the plaintiff bought [...] from [...]'), the methods of transportation to the shipping port (*by land*), and the deadline for shipping (*Jan. 26, 1999*). The effort to elaborate is even more obvious when the single time (*Jan. 16, 1999*) is replaced by several more precise ones including *Jan. 12, 1999* (the signing of contract), *Jan. 26, 1999* (the deadline of shipping), and *Jan. 22, 1999* (the issue of the inspection certificate).

Similarly, the second event, 'Vessel "Victory Star V904E" took charge of the cargo', is reported in more detail, such as the legal status of the vessel (*carrier*), the detail of cargo (*115 bags of metal silicon*), the shipping method (*in six 20' containers*), etc. The third event, 'the bill recorded clearly the numbers, seal numbers and the name of metal silicon in each of container', is particularized into a number of details related to the bill of lading, including the title (*No. KYcr006*), the signer (*Oasis*), the signing time (*Jan. 26, 1999*), the content (*shipper, consignee, shipping port, port of destination, carrier*), and the seal (*clearly*).

The above comparison and analysis is not meant to be exhaustive, and there are further similarities between *Parties' Arguments* and *Judges' Arguments* in the same judgment. The conclusion here is that a close correspondence exists between the two moves, which is closer than might be expected given the general understanding of the adversarial nature of litigation. This close correspondence suggests that the parties' arguments are recontextualized by judges to introduce briefly the facts identified by judges, rather than to guarantee the parties' rights to be heard, as indicated by the move title (*Parties' Arguments*). Because the law does not explicitly regulate that judges should introduce their identified facts in *Parties' Arguments*, it is only the judges' professional convention that does this. The judges' adherence to this convention indicates their familiarity with the inside knowledge of the profession[3].

4.4.3 Use of evidence

4.4.3.1 Insufficient connection between evidence and *Parties' Arguments*

Evidence is an integral element in litigation and civil judgment because the acceptance of specific arguments and factual descriptions is legally required to be based on the examination of evidence. This section attempts to study how the litigation participants, i.e. the plaintiffs, the defendants, and the judges, use evidence to support their argumentation in this genre. As mentioned in the previous analysis, the *Five-year Reform Outline of People's Courts (1999)* identified two focus areas of judges' writing which need significant improvement ('the judges' legal analysis and the judges' examination of evidence'

3 In fact, one judge as specialist informant claimed that he directly quotes the parties' original arguments in writing the move *Parties' Argument*. However, this practice was challenged in a subsequent interviewing with other judges and lawyers as specialist informants, all of whom criticized the lack of professional competence in such a practice.

and 'the judges' argumentation'), in order to enhance the quality of civil judgments and other litigation documents and to record 'the process of litigation' and opening 'the judges' reasoning in judgments'.

In the corpus, only three judgments do omit discussion of the evidence. The remaining 97 all discuss various evidential issues, such as the evidence presented by the parties, the court examination of evidence, and the evidence accepted by the court. Although the judges' discussion of evidential issues demonstrates that they attempt, at least somewhere in the civil judgment, to incorporate argumentative or negotiable values in their writing, such attempts seem insufficient, and most evidential issues are not handled in an argumentative way either.

Evidence is more often listed separately rather than being incorporated into the judges' on-going argumentation. Some typical instances of listing evidence in civil judgments are presented below:

- The plaintiff submitted 23 documents to the court to prove his claims, facts and arguments, including B/L, commodities inspection report, certificate of the original products, purchase contract, invoices, freight returning notice, bill returning certificate and so on. (See details list)
- Defendant, X, submitted to the court an agency agreement made between Oasis and TWH, three faxes of the disputed cargo between X and the Y.
- Plaintiff X provided this court with 28 pieces of evidence.
- Defendant Y provided this court with three sets of evidence.

The above texts demonstrate how the parties' evidence is reported in civil judgments. Evidence is usually put at the end of the steps *Plaintiff's Claim'* and *Defendants' Defence,* functioning as a whole to provide collective support for all the arguments reported in the two steps. No effort is made to sort out the connection between specific evidence and specific arguments, which is left for specialist and non-specialist readers to determine.

The first two texts above provide enough specific evidence such as 'B/L', 'commodities inspection report', 'certificate of the original products', 'purchase contract', 'invoices', 'agency agreement', and 'three faxes', but the text meanings are not precise. The list of evidence is not exhaustive and it is indicated that more exists ('and so on'). Readers are not told the selection criteria by which some evidence is reported while other evidence is ignored. The arguments to be supported by the listed evidence are also referred to generally ('his claims, facts and arguments'); readers may doubt whether the judges have an intention to disclose their analysis relating to the connection between the parties' arguments and the specific evidence provided. For example, the first text is quoted from the case related to an international trade of metal silicon between the plaintiff (seller) and the defendant (buyer). Since the plaintiff sued and claimed that the delivered goods were returned because of the defendant's faults, it is evident that the *purchase contract* and *invoices* are relevant in proving the occurrence of costs. But other details, like 'B/L', 'commodities inspection report', and 'certificate of the original products', need more explanation in order to explain their immediate relevance, or at least need to be proved relevant to specific arguments.

Even less precision occurs in the last two texts above, 'the plaintiff provided the court with 28 pieces of evidence' and 'the defendant provided the court with three sets of evidence'. No necessary explanations are given. Although lawyers or other specialists may realize that the detailed information may be accessed in the courts' archive files, such expressions are insufficiently precise for civil judgments. These expressions all indicate is that the parties do provide the court with some evidence which is not relevant unless the evidence presented can be accepted. If the examination and acceptance of specific evidence is not discussed, the imprecise introductions of evidence in the above texts make little sense.

The separation between evidence and specific arguments makes it difficult for specialist and non-specialist readers to capture the connection between them. The judges' introduction to the evidence here is better seen as a simple report of the parties' presentation of evidence, with no attention paid to the parties' intentions. It can be concluded that the judges' introduction to the evidence in *Parties' Arguments* serves no purpose of argumentation; it is a rhetorical convention which exists for its own sake and does not carry much practical significance (Zhang, 1999, p. 26). Judges are not willing to remove it because the law does not explicitly allow them to do this. A similar way of introducing evidence is also identified in the move *Judges' Arguments,* as illustrated in the next section.

4.4.3.2 Insufficient connection between evidence and *Judges' Arguments*

The identified facts reported in the move *Judges' Arguments* are not sufficiently supported by evidence either. Judges' writing in this move is less argumentative because they report the evidence as one group, while they report the identified facts as another. The evidence and facts are not sufficiently connected. As shown in this research, judges mostly report the collection and examination of evidence in order to support the facts identified in the trial. Some judges report the collection and examination of evidence before the identified facts, and others report this after the facts. The evidence and facts are separated in both cases; it is difficult to determine why much evidence is reported in condensed paragraphs and what the relationship is to the facts identified.

This way of reporting the facts is not persuasive and it can barely convince the losing party of the legitimacy of these facts. The judges' report of the evidence reads more like a report of work results than a convincing support for the facts. The facts thus presented are not reasonably supported by evidence and are presumed as given rather than negotiated.

However, examination of the evidence on its own reveals that some judges attempt to disclose through the introduction of evidence more information relating to the litigation practices, although the evidence as a group is not sufficiently connected with the facts. About 40% of civil judgments in the corpus supply a certain amount of analysis of the parties' evidence, which is a recent trend in writing civil judgments and may be seen as an echo of the Supreme People's Court's reform goal 'improving the judges' legal analysis and the judges' examination of evidence' (*Five-year Reform Outline of People's Courts,*

1999). In the following case, the defendant (the borrower) took out nine loans from the plaintiff (the bank) and could not repay the money in due course. The text below is the judges' discussion of both parties' evidence:

> After examining and cross-examining the evidence provided by both parties, this court accepted the following evidence (with reasons given): 1, five notices of collecting over-due debts with the debtor line signed by 'Li Yupu', provided by the plaintiff. Because [...] the defendant has no evidence proving the signature is not authentic [...] 2, [...].
> This court refused to accept the following evidence (with reasons given): 1, the statement of Zhao Taikuan's testimony [...] because Zhao Taikuan's absence from the courtroom hearing was not approved by this court [...] 2, 13 lists of Li Yupu's loans provided by the plaintiff [...] 3, [...].
> According to the accepted evidence, this court found the following facts: [...]. (Example text 6, case 6)

This text shows how both parties' evidence was examined and cross-examined and then categorized into two groups: accepted evidence and rejected evidence. Specific reasons were also produced, explaining why specific evidence was accepted or refused. For example, 'five notices of collecting over-due debts' was accepted because the defendant signed for receipt of the notices; 'the statement of Zhao Taikuan's testimony' was not accepted because the witness did not appear in the court as required by law. This kind of evidential analysis enables specialist and non-specialist readers to access the judges' reasoning processes in litigation. The litigation practices are thus made more open because the more litigation practices are explicitly textualized, the more transparent this genre will be.

Making judges' reasoning more transparent restricts the possibility of judicial malpractice in litigation, as specialist readers including lawyers, peer judges and law professors are able to see the legitimacy of accepting or refusing specific evidence. In the above text, the imprecision in some sentences negatively influences the generic authority of the judges' writing. For example, the phrase 'five notices of collecting over-due debts' is too general for a clear report of the evidence. A number of doubts in relation to these 'five notices' need to be clarified, such as whether they were issued at one time or in a sequence, how long the intervals were between individual notices, and when exactly these notices were issued. These questions are not introduced in the above evidential examination, and they become more imprecise when the judges discuss them again in a subsequent text from the same judgment:

> [...] June 20, 2003, the plaintiff made a list of the above 13 loans borrowed by Li Yupu, and sent the defendant, Li Yupu, five notices of collecting over-due debts. Li Yupu signed his name in the 'debtor' of these five notices [...].

This further discussion makes the original imprecise expression even more ambiguous. On *June 20, 2003*, *five pressing notices* were sent to the defendant. The literal meaning of this sentence is that five notices were issued on the same day, which seems unlikely because it is rare for a bank to send five notices about one matter to one debtor within a single day. It is more reasonable that from that day (*June 20, 2003*) on, five notices were issued, but the exact date when the last notice was issued is still not told. The exact interval between the exact issue date and the trial date is an important element in deciding to what extent the defendant had a malicious intention to refuse to repay the money. Such imprecise expressions indicate that judges' examination of evidence has considerable room for more transparency.

To conclude, a sufficient connection between evidence and identified facts is necessary when judges intend to deliver convincing judgments related to the parties' disputes in specific cases. The facts identified by judges are intended to resolve the parties' disputed understandings of the facts. Since the parties usually present their own understandings of the facts with evidence, they expect judges to base the legally identified facts on solid evidence as well. When the evidence and the identified facts are sufficiently connected, the parties can see the reasons for the judges' acceptance of some facts and their rejection of others. This convinces specialist and non-specialist readers of the legitimacy not only of the facts identified by the judges but also of the background litigation practices.

4.4.3.3 Sufficient connection between evidence and *Judges' Arguments*

Although most civil judgments contain an insufficient linkage between the facts and the evidence, there are civil judgments (13 in the corpus) which include an integrated combination of facts and evidence. The judges in these 13 judgments seem to make an effort to follow the judicial reform goals established by the Supreme People's Court of the PRC. These judges organize the facts in itemized groups and discuss them in detail, which discloses more information relating to the judges' reasoning processes to specialist and non-specialist readers and improves the accessibility and transparency[4] of this genre.

In the case below, the plaintiff (Xinli Corporation) sued the defendant (an entertainment company) because the defendant made an illegal use of the plaintiff's music for profit. The following text reports the facts identified by the judges:

> [...] in 2001, Xinli Corporation produced and issued VCD disk 'LEON MUSIC MOVIES COLLECTION' [...]. [T]he Asian office of IFPI (the International Federation of the Phonographic Industry) produced testimony document proving the MTV video 'LEON MUSIC MOVIES COLLECTION' was produced by Xinli Corporation [...].
>
> December 12, 2003, Beijing office of IFPI entrusted Liu Ying (its agent) [...] to record the defendant's playing of the songs and burn it into two disks [...]. Suzhou Notary Office notarized this process of evidence collection [...]. (Example text 7, case 7)

This text reports the judges' finding of two specific facts: 'Xinli Corporation produced and issued a VCD disk' and 'to record the defendant's playing of the songs and burn it into two disks'. Each fact is followed by supporting evidence: 'the Asian office of IFPI produced testimony document' and 'Suzhou Notary Office notarized this process of evidence collection'. This close connection between facts and

4 Transparency in the present research studies to what extent the judge's writing in civil judgment has disclosed sufficient information related to the background litigation.

evidence leaves little scope for the judges to reason randomly, because their reasoning has to go beyond reasonable doubt by supporting specific facts with sufficient evidence.

The second quoted case is between Yao Zhongjian (the plaintiff) and Science Press (the defendant). The two parties signed a publishing contract which allowed the defendant to publish one of the plaintiff's books. After the first print, the defendant reprinted the book for sale and did not pay the plaintiff for this reprinting. The facts were identified by the judges:

> [...] October 13, 1998, Yao Zhongjian signed a publishing contract with Science Press. The main content of this contract include: Yao Zhongjian granted Science Press the exclusive license to print 'HANDBOOK' in paper form in the People's Republic of China within the duration of this contract [...]. The above fact was proved by evidence No. 1 provided by Yao Zhongjian and evidence No. 1 provided by Science Press. (Example text 8, case 8)

The fact identified in this text is that 'Yao Zhongjian signed a publishing contract with Science Press', which is supported by 'evidence No. 1 provided by Yao Zhongjian and evidence No. 1 provided by Science Press'. The reported evidence is attributed to an identifiable source: 'evidence No. 1 provided by Yao Zhongjian' and 'evidence No. 1 provided by Science Press'. This attribution of sources makes the judges' writing precise because it avoids the possibility of multiple interpretations by disclosing detailed information of the judges' reasoning process.

One characteristic of these clearly established connections between evidence and facts is that they are mostly written by the judges from one court: *Haidian People's Court* in Beijing. Contextual investigation reveals that the judges in *Haidian People's Court* seem to enjoy a special situation where they have an incentive to produce more argumentative writing in civil judgments, while most other judges are slow in adding argumentation to the traditionally narrative style of civil judgments. The political and judicial cultures in Mainland China are essentially quite conservative and the pace of judicial reforms is extraordinarily slow. It is felt that one reason for this conservativeness and slowness is that any radical social or political changes in a country of billions of people could invite chaos. A mature and frequently used strategy for introducing reforms in Mainland China is to first implement them cautiously and selectively at trial locations. Once successful, the reforms are introduced more widely. Although there are no official documents saying *Haidian People's Court* is one such experimental site for Chinese judicial reform, certain documents support the conclusion that this court actually enjoys a special status compared to other trial courts.

To determine the status of *Haidian People's Court* in the Chinese judicial system, one of the specialist informants brought the following two legal news reports to the notice of the present researcher. They come from the most influential newspaper controlled by the Central Government of China (*People's Daily*) and the most influential legal newspaper managed by the Supreme People's Court of the PRC (*People's Court Daily*):

> Luo Gan (the supreme official in charge of Chinese judicial affairs) congratulated that *Haidian People's Court* was awarded the title – 'the excellent court of the PRC'. He said *Haidian People's Court* was a good example [...]. [T]he judges in this court improved both their political awareness and their professional competence. Combining legal knowledge and scientific/technological knowledge, they skilfully heard and concluded a number of cases. They also earned people's praises. (*People's Daily*, December, 12, 1998) (Excerpt 4)

> As an excellent representative of over 3000 basic courts in the PRC, *Haidian People's Court* aimed at judicial justice, cultivated excellent judges, got first-class achievements, won the Party and People's trust, and built a good image of People's Court and People's judges in the public. (*People's Court Daily*, January 1, 2008) (Excerpt 5)

People's Daily and *People's Court Daily* are the voice of the central government of the PRC and the Supreme People's Court of the PRC. The above two articles reflect the policies decided by the central government and the Supreme People's Court. The first article specifically attributes the news to one of the top leaders at that time, Luo Gan. The reporting of this name (Luo Gan) is itself solid evidence suggesting the reported comment came from the central government of the PRC because Luo Gan is one of the seven standing members of the Political Bureau. These seven standing members represent the group which exercises supreme governing power over all the socio-political aspects of Mainland China. Luo Gan's acknowledgement of *Haidian People's Court* as *the Excellent Court of PRC* demonstrates the special status this court enjoys in the Chinese judicial system.

Similarly, the second article above represents the Supreme People's Court's acknowledgement of the special status of *Haidian People's Court*. The conclusion to be drawn here is that civil judgments issued by *Haidian People's Court* differ in their argumentation from civil judgments of other courts. Mainland Chinese judges seem to produce argumentative civil judgments in a certain context, i.e. with the acknowledgement and support of the authoritative people and government.

Although the judges in *Haidian People's Court* enjoy the privilege of making improvements in civil judgments, this incentive may be highly risky for judges in other courts as they do not enjoy the privilege of leading the country's judicial reform. Many litigation practices in Mainland China follow unwritten conventions, as what is happening in the judicial reform. There are no official documents explaining how the Chinese judicial reform will be conducted and which courts will be chosen as trial sites; however, the authorization of *Haidian People's Court* to lead the Chinese judicial reform is given by an authoritative person (*Luo Gan*), as indicated in the above text. Judges from other courts, without such authorization, are usually cautious about breaking traditions, even though doing so could improve the quality of argumentation in civil judgments, because they worry about potential challenges to their authority. This also explains why Mainland Chinese judges refuse to break the convention of recontextualizing the parties' original arguments in less argumentative ways, as indicated in the previous analysis.

4.5 Move 5: *Judges' Opinions*

A clear report of the issues in *Judges' Opinions* is important for a number of reasons. Firstly, specific issues summarize the judges' professional analysis of the facts and indicates that the judge's legal analysis will be focused on the essential points of the parties' dispute. Secondly, the judges can itemize their writing in the move through the specific issues, which will improve the readability of this move and give readers a better chance to understand this legalized move. This section attempts to examine judges' reporting of issues in the move *Judges' Opinions*. In this move, judges need to demonstrate their mastery of legal knowledge, their ability to do legal reasoning, and their ability to write persuasively. The specific tasks judges need to accomplish include the reporting of issues and the interpretation and application of law.

As demonstrated in the corpus, issues are usually handled in three different ways. Firstly, 80% of civil judgments in the corpus do not introduce issues. The move *Judges' Opinions* reads like a single-paragraph essay reporting the judges' views on specific laws and their application of laws. Non-specialist readers have little opportunity to understand the judges' specialized opinions because this writing is less reader-friendly. Secondly, 18% of civil judgments present issues at the beginning of this move. Thirdly, 2% of civil judgments combine the issues and the judges' opinions together, itemizing the opinions related to specific issues. The following analysis uses example texts to discuss and illustrate these three ways, paying particular attention to their respective advantages, disadvantages, and the judges' considerations in using them.

4.5.1 The omission of issues

Most civil judgments in the corpus (80 %) do not even include the word *issue*. After summarizing the parties' arguments (*Parties' Arguments*) and reporting the judges' identified facts (*Judges' Arguments*), the judges immediately turn to their legal opinions (*Judges' Opinions*) which are signalled by the standardized signpost phrase *the court holds* or other similar expressions. The case below concerns a sex scandal between a well-known Chinese actor (*Zhang Tielin*, the plaintiff) and an unknown actress (*Zhou Meiying*, the defendant). One newspaper (*Chengdu Business Times*) is involved as the second defendant. The actress told the newspaper that the actor attempted to give her money for sex, which the newspaper later reported as entertainment news. However, the actor sued and claimed that he had not offered money for the reported sex and that the two defendants seriously harmed his reputation. The following text is the move *Judges' Opinions* in the final judgment:

> This court holds: According to the stipulations of the General Principles of the Civil Law of PRC, citizens enjoy a legal protection of their reputation and it is not permitted to damage other people's reputation by insults or calumnies. Because the law of the place where an infringing action is committed shall be applied in handling the lawsuit related to the damages caused, the General Principles of the Civil Law of PRC should be applied in the present case where Zhang Tielin's (with a foreign citizenship) reputation was damaged. Zhang Tielin claimed Zhou Meiying's statements in Chengdu Business Times (June 29, 2003 and July 4, 2003) damaged his reputation while Zhou Meiying argued that she never said things like 'offered money for sex or proposed a strange request'. According to the reports from the media on and after that day [...] Zhou Meiying's statements in those newspaper articles were real [...]. Zhou Meiying's statements damaged Zhang Tielin's reputation, and she should be held responsible [...]. [H]er arguments cannot be accepted by this court. Chengdu Business Times reported the sex scandal [...] on the basis of Zhou Meiying's statements [...]. [T]he reports are basically real, and does not exaggerate or distort facts. So Chengdu Business Times shall not be held responsible. (Example text 9, case 2)

The overall meaning of this text is that *Zhou Meiying* (the defendant) intentionally gave false statements to *Chengdu Business Times* (the second defendant) in order to earn publicity, and these false statements damaged Zhan Tielin's (the plaintiff's) reputation. Without an explicit report of the issues, the single paragraph *Judges' Opinions* poses great reading difficulty for specialist and non-specialist readers.

In order to achieve a more reasonable understanding of the reading difficulty of the above text, the researcher presented it to several non-specialist readers (five PhD students in communication studies and two PhD students in applied social sciences) for their feedback (see Swales, 2004, p. 71 for the assessment of text readability). These non-specialist readers initially refused to try because they were intimidated by the specialized content and by the less than reader-friendly writing. When further requested, five of them read it. One of them reported his understanding with the following statement:

> This is something about the pop star's sex scandal, Zhang Tielin is famous and this actress is trying to use him to promote her own publicity. This actress is responsible for her misbehaviours and the newspaper is innocent.

This statement and a number of similar ones demonstrate non-specialist readers' common-sensical understanding of the above *Judges' Opinion*. Different informants' common-sensical understandings share a commonality: They all overlook the judges' discussion of the law. In subsequent verifications, the informants reported that they could not distinguish between the discussion of law and the discussion of facts because there were no signposts indicating this. Such reading difficulty could have been avoided if the judges had arranged their writing into clearly itemized or numbered sections.

The *Judges' Opinions* cited above and other similar ones are difficult to read because the judges condense several issues into one single paragraph which does not discuss the judges' opinions in a reader-friendly way. It is possible the judges do not realize their writing could create difficulty for specialist and non-specialist readers; it is also possible that the judges' understanding and analysis of the case at trial have not produced clear issues that can be itemized. Both of the two possibilities negatively influence the readability and authority of civil judgments as a legal genre.

4.5.2 The presence of issues

20% of the civil judgments in the corpus have the move *Judges' Opinions* organized in a clear and reader-friendly manner, because specific issues are listed at the very beginning of this move or are used as subtitles to itemize the entire move. Compared to other traditional civil judgments of low readability and transparency, these 20 % of judgments disclose more information related to the judges' factual analysis and legal interpretation, such as the judges' choice, interpretation and application of law. the judges in these judgments show a stronger intention to report the results of their analysis of facts and the application of law, which can be seen as another effort made by Chinese judges to implement the judicial reform initiated by the Supreme People's Court.

The introduction to specific issues at the beginning of this move makes the judges' reasoning process more accessible to specialist and non-specialist readers. This move is mainly about *opinions*, so the first thing readers need to know is on what issues the judges are presenting their legal *opinions*. In litigation, it is normal that contentious issues exist among the parties; otherwise, they would not go to court in the first place. This research finds that judges may have a clear understanding of the parties' issues and may be confident in their legal opinions on specific issues, but they should report them in a way that can be seen as fair.

In the case below, the plaintiff (Sony Corporation) claimed that the defendant (West Entertaining Company) illegally used an MTV program owned by the plaintiff. In the move Judges' Opinions of the final judgment, the judges discussed three contentious issues between the two parties, as indicated by the following text:

> This court identifies the following issues:
> 1, the nature of the MTV program in question and its copyright ownership;
> 2, whether West Entertaining Company has the right to use the MTV program;
> 3, whether West Entertaining Company has violated the plaintiff's copyright and what responsibility West Entertaining Company should bear.
> …

> Based on the found facts and evidence, this court gives opinions in relation to the following issues:
> 1, the nature of the MTV program in question and its copyright ownership
> This court holds [...] the MTV program in question is one kind of production created by method of film-making stipulated by the Copyright Law of PRC, and should be protected by the Copyright Law of PRC [...]. [This court] accepts that Sony Company (the plaintiff) has the copyright of the three MTV programs in question.
> 2, whether West Entertaining Company has the right to use the MTV program in question
> This court [...] does not accept West Entertaining Company's argument that it has acquired the authorization from the Music Copyright Society of China.
> 3, whether West Entertaining Company has violated the plaintiff's copyright and what responsibility West Entertaining Company should bear
> This court holds [...] West Entertaining Company [...] violates Sony Company's copyright [...] and should stop the violating action and compensate Sony Company for its loss [...]. (Example text 10, case 7)

In this text, the judges explicitly state specific issues before giving their legal opinions in relation to them. The three reported issues, plus explicit discourse markers like *based on the found facts and evidence* and *this court holds*, create a clear internal structure to this text. In order to understand these judges' opinions, non-specialist readers do not necessarily read the detailed elaboration of every issue, because the beginning and ending of each itemized section clearly states what the issue is and what the judges' opinions are.

In the corpus, the introduction of specific issues is sometimes not included in the move *Judges' Opinions*. Rather, it may be included in the move *Parties' Arguments*, which is believed by some judges to be a better place to highlight the parties' contentious issues. However, this writing variation is neither a legal requirement nor a professional convention, which shows some judges' personal preferences in handling issues in civil judgment.

The introduction to issues in the move *Judges' Opinions* may become a professional convention, although it is also not legally required. It is more reader-friendly when readers do not need to refer back to previous pages for issues when they read the judges' opinions. Readers can easily see specific issues being discussed and the judges' legal opinions on them. When issues are clearly itemized within the whole move, the connection between specific issues and the judges' opinions on them can be even more easily identified, because they are textually more closed. Such itemization is sometimes not explicit and the move is not divided into numbered subsections led by specific issues; rather, the issues are reported in separate paragraphs, which does not hinder reading.

Judges use paragraphing for a number of practical reasons. They do not want to deviate greatly from the traditional way of omitting issues in civil judgments. Secondly, they may believe that it is unnecessary to list issues independently, as integrating them with the opinions can function better. They may also have personal preferences for this particular rhetorical structure because the Supreme People's Court's *Five-year Reform Outline* suggests that judges should improve the quality of civil judgments. These possibilities may hold the same value, and a conclusion here is that because some judges are actively taking measures they believe appropriate to improve the quality of civil judgments, some new professional conventions in writing civil judgments are gradually emerging.

4.6 Move 6: *Court Decisions*

The move *Court Decisions* is the most important though shortest move in civil judgments. *Court Decisions* is the judges' final legally enforceable decision on the parties' dispute. It is through this move that the law exercises power with regard to the parties' rights and obligations. As non-specialist readers, the parties most often pay their sole attention to this move. Although placed at the end of the civil judgment, *Court Decisions* is the move the parties will always read first. This section analyzes this move from three points of view: its textualization features, its internal rhetorical structure and the problem of imprecision.

The importance of this move requires judges' writing to be highly readable, which has encouraged the judges to standardize it to a considerable extent. The text below is the final judgment in the international trade of metal silicon dispute. The plaintiff sued the defendant to get compensation for damaged returned goods. This was supported by the judges, as indicated below:

> [...] in accordance with the stipulations of Article 42 (1) 1–3, Article 55, Article 71 and Article 72 of the Maritime Law of the PRC, the judgment is hereby given as follows:
> **I** Defendant Y shall compensate plaintiff X for the loss of cargo in amount of [...];
> **II** Other litigation requests of plaintiff X shall be dismissed.
> Of the court fees [...] plaintiff X shall pay [...] and the remaining [...] shall be borne by defendant Y.
> The payment of the above sums shall be completed within ten days of this judgment coming into effect.
> Should there be any objection to this judgment, a statement of appeal with copies in the number of the opponent parties may be submitted to this court within 15 days upon the service of this judgment, for appealing before the court of appeal Guangdong Higher People's Court. (Guangzhou Maritime Court of PRC, Civil Judgment (2001) GHFCZ No. 212)

The text first itemizes the judges' material decisions, i.e. decisions relating to the facts and cites the relevant documents; the text above only uses paragraphs. The material decisions are numbered because more than one decision is given and because numbering makes the text more readable for non-specialists. Furthermore, as material decisions are decisions that decide the material rights and obligations of the parties, numbering them makes them more distinctive from decisions related to procedural matters. Interviews with judges revealed that the numbering of material decisions is common practice, the absence of which may imply a lack of such knowledge.

These interpretations can be applied to the following text as well. The text below is from a personal injury case where the plaintiffs X and Y got hurt in Z's (the defendant) supermarket. X and Y's claim for compensation was finally supported by the judges:

> In conclusion, according to Article 134 (7) of the General Principles Civil Law of PRC and Article 6 (2) of [...] the court gives the following judgment:
> Within seven days of this judgment coming into effect, Z (Ltd.) shall pay 60,000 RMB (including 5,000 RMB having been paid) to Y and Z as compensation.
> Of the court fees, X shall pay [...] Y shall pay [...] Z (Ltd.) shall pay [...]. [A]ll payment shall be completed within seven days of this judgment coming into effect.
> Should there be any objection to this judgment, a statement of appeal with copies in the number of the opponent parties may be submitted to this court within 15 days upon the service of this judgment, for appealing before the Beijing First Intermediate People's Court. (Example text 11, case 9)

It is clearly unnecessary to number material decisions if there is only one. This text includes only one material decision: 'within seven days of this judgment coming into effect, Z (Ltd.) shall pay 60,000 RMB (including 5,000 RMB having been paid) to X and Y as compensation'. The other decisions are all about procedural matters, such as 'court fees' and 'statement of appeal'.

Based on the understanding of the above two texts, the standardized internal structure of *Court Decisions* is presented as below:

[...] judgments are given as follows:	*Signpost*
This court rejects the plaintiff's claims.	*Step 1 (decisions over material matters)*
The court fees 10,000 RMB are born by the plaintiff.	*Step 2 (decisions over procedural matters)*
If any party is dissatisfied with this judgment, he/she may submit this case to the court of appeal [...].	*Step 3 (notice of the right to appeal)*

Table 4.3. Steps in the move *Court Decisions*.

The table shows that *Court Decisions* consists of one signpost sentence and three steps: decisions over material matters, decisions over procedural matters, and notice of the right to appeal. There are no optional elements, and all four components occur in a fixed order. The textualization of each step is also standardized. For example, the judges use a number of typical signposts like 'in conclusion, the court makes the following judgment according to, in accordance with [...] the judgment is hereby given as follows', and 'according to [...] this court gives the following judgments'.

Although the standardization in this move improves the clarity of the judges' writing, it may sometimes harm the transparency of this genre. One example is the judges' invoking of law. The imprecision in invoking the law makes this move less convincing. Judges usually invoke specific laws to support their final decisions in this move. There are some conventional strategies for invoking the law, such as 'in accordance with the stipulations of Article 42 (1) 1–3, Article 55, Article 71 and Article 72 of the Maritime Code of the PRC, according to the Civil Procedure Law of the PRC article 64 section 1', and 'according to the Copyright Law of PRC article 46 (1), article 47 (1)'. These expressions are signs of intertextuality which lead to direct quotations and interpretations of the law. However, these standardized expressions are all that judges supply in relation to the legal basis for their decisions. Neither full quotations nor necessary interpretations of the law are given. Neither specialist nor non-specialist readers will comprehend what these standardized expressions exactly refer to; the extra burden of discovering the relevant laws is imposed on the reader. This way of invoking the law discloses insufficient information related to the litigation practice.

The analysis of the move *Court Decisions* and other previous moves demonstrates that the writing of civil judgments requires a mastery of legal and rhetorical rules and conventions. These rules and conventions suggest that the legal genre of litigation that is civil judgments in Mainland China represents more the collective voice of the court and judges as a profession than the voices of individual judges. One feature of the Chinese judicial culture is that judge's individual voices are always intentionally underplayed, while the collective and institutional voice is always valued and acknowledged in civil judgements and other legal genres.

4.7 Conclusion

The preceding analysis demonstrates that civil judgments are a highly structured and standardized legal genre, with all the judgments in the corpus demonstrating a universal move pattern. Judges arrange these moves in the same sequential order. Some moves (*Heading, Introduction,* and *Court Decisions*) are more standardized than others (*Parties' Arguments, Judges' Arguments,* and *Judges' Opinions*). The information reported in these moves and the way it is reported are, nevertheless, mostly standardized. Judges need to follow the standardized rules and conventions and fill in the case-specific information, which compromises their professional expertise and competence.

However, in less standardized moves (*Parties' Arguments, Judges' Arguments,* and *Judges' Opinions*), greater freedom is afforded judges to exploit their professional expertise and competence. Judges need to use a number of information sources like indictments, statements of defence, and courtroom records in order to identify facts, analyze issues, and form legal opinions. Judges' effort and work in these moves often produces narrative rather than argumentative writing. For example, when judges introduce legal facts in the step *Plaintiffs' Claim* and the move *Judges Arguments*, they prefer to report only the results of their factual identification, paying no attention to the process of the identification. Thus, specialist and non-specialist readers have no chance to know the legitimacy of the reported facts. This kind of narrative writing, according to Gu (2000) and Zhang (1999), is more readable but less accessible because the reported information is taken as given rather than as negotiated.

Although judges conventionally write civil judgments in a narrative not an argumentative style, certain situations have encouraged judges to make their writing more accessible and more argumentative. This research finds that the Supreme People's Court of the PRC and the top leaders of China are dissatisfied that developments in Chinese litigation practices lag behind the advancement of China's fast-developing economy and consequently recently (1997) initiated a nationwide judicial reform to improve professionalism in litigation practices and judges' writing of legal documents. Some courts like *Haidian People's Court* in Beijing, have been chosen as implementation sites and have been given the right to lead the reform. Judges from these courts have both an incentive and a pressure to write civil judgements in more accessible and argumentative ways.

Chapter 5

The Lexico-Grammar of Civil Judgments

5.1 Introduction

This chapter analyzes some of the typical lexico-grammatical features used in civil judgements, with special attention paid to temporal and monetary expressions and to metadiscourse. Firstly, the moves *Parties' Arguments* and *Judges' Arguments* are closely examined to reveal the typical lexico-grammatical construction of facts, particularly judges' use of numerical expressions in facts. Numerical expressions are so frequently used that an average of 80% of sentences in civil judgments include at least one temporary or monetary expression. Drawing on the concept of 'accounts'[5] (Orbuch, 1997), the close correspondence between the move *Parties' Arguments* and the move *Judges' Arguments* examined in the previous chapter is further studied. Secondly, two frequently used metadiscursive devices (emphatics and hedging) are analyzed to discover judges' methods of establishing their personalities in the moves *Parties' Arguments* and *Judges' Opinions*.

5 This concept helps the researcher to sort out the contentious relationships among the litigation participants' views, namely, the plaintiffs, the defendants, and the judges. Each of the three litigation participants try to create an account of the facts and law for their own benefits, but tension usually exists between their respective accounts. While the plaintiffs' and defendants' accounts enjoy an equal status, judges' accounts are definitive.

5.2 Monetary expressions

The corpus demonstrates that civil judgments include numerous numerical expressions in the moves *Parties' Arguments* and *Judges' Arguments*, and their use does not vary according to the types of cases. They are equally exploited in cases of finance, personal injury, and neighbourhood disputes. Numerical expressions are used by judges to discuss mainly two types of issues: time and money. The following analysis examines some issues relating to the monetary numerical expressions, such as the context of their appearance, the pattern of their textualization, and judges' considerations when using them.

5.2.1 Financial cases

Monetary numerical expressions appear in both financial and non-financial cases. In financial cases, the parties use them in their description of facts and their claims, and judges use them in the report of identified facts and the analysis of the parties' claims. In non-financial cases, the parties use them in their claims and judges use them in the analysis of these claims. In this section, the use of monetary numerical expressions in financial cases is analyzed. The analysis asks: how judges make their writing clear and exact, why some judgments are imprecise and inaccessible, and how judges handle the same monetary issues in the moves *Parties' Arguments* and *Judges' Arguments*.

In civil judgments of financial cases, monetary numerical expressions frequently appear in the moves *Parties' Arguments* and *Judges' Arguments*. The numerical expressions in *Parties' Arguments* display the objectivity of the parties' arguments by particularizing them appropriately. By listing individual amounts of money, the step *Plaintiff's Claim* (see Table 4.1) can provide detailed information relating to specific damages the plaintiffs have suffered, which can convincingly support the total amount of money subsequently claimed as compensation. However, to make the judges' recontextualization of the plaintiffs' original arguments 'plausible and convincing' (Xu, 2003, p. 32), one basic requirement in relation to these monetary numerical expressions is that the summation of specific numbers reported should match the final total claimed as compensation.

This match can be reached either by repetition or by calculation. When the facts are simple and no complicated plots are reported in the step *Plaintiffs' Claim*, this match is usually acquired through repetition. In the case below, the defendant broke an expensive insured antique bottle. The plaintiff (X, an insurance company) sued and claimed that the defendant should reimburse it (X) for what it had paid the bottle owner in this incident. The claim amount is 1.2 million RMB, which is repeated four times, as illustrated below:

> The plaintiff X (an insurance company) claimed: [...] The insured amount was **1.2 million RMB** [...]. [A]fter the site investigation [... we] approved that the loss was **1.2 million RMB**. [...] because the defendant's careless action had caused the damage of the insured goods, and we had to pay **1.2 million RMB** [...]. [W]e filed the suit and required the defendant to compensate us for the sum of **1.2 million RMB** (Example text 12, case 10, emphasis added by the present author).

In this text, the exact repetition of numerical expressions (*1.2 million RMB*) is discursively meaningful because it implies the judges' reluctance to use simple anaphoric devices, like 'this', 'that', 'it', etc. After the first introduction of '1.2 million RMB', it might be expected that '1.2 million RMB' will be replaced with other alternatives in the subsequent discussion, like we approved that loss, we have to pay this money and we filed the suit requiring the defendant to compensate us with that money.

The use of these anaphoric expressions with 'this' or 'that' presuppose that readers and writers have a mutual agreement on some aspects of communication, including the collaborative intention of communication, the agreed understanding of communication strategies, and the common knowledge of context. These mutual and usually implicit agreements enable writers and readers to successfully produce, communicate, and consume the other party's discourse. In the adversarial context of litigation, the parties cannot afford to have this agreement because of the contentious tensions between their views. This research finds that it is normal practice for judges to express their intended meaning as clearly as possible in writing through exact repetition or other strategies. The likelihood of misinterpretation is thus restricted when the meaning is delivered rather than inferred. Judges' retaining of these repetitions in civil judgments indicates the judges' clear awareness of the parties' tensions.

Repetition occurs not only when the use of numerical expressions is simple but also when it is more complicated. The plaintiff in the following case directed a TV drama for the defendant (an entertainment company). After the completion of this drama, the plaintiff did not get the agreed salary from the defendant. The plaintiff therefore filed a lawsuit with the court and claimed that the agreed salary should be paid in due course:

> The plaintiff claimed: The defendant hired me as the director of a TV series with twenty episodes – *I and My Father* and signed the agreement with me on August 1, 2002. According to the agreement, the defendant should pay me **300 thousand RMB** (**15 thousand for each**) [...] according to a supplementary agreement, the defendant should also pay me **164 thousand RMB** for writing the script [...]. So I filed the suit with this court requiring the court to order the defendant to pay **464 thousand RMB** (including the director's salary of **300 thousand RMB** and the writer's salary of **164 thousand RMB**) (Example text 13, case 11, emphasis added by the present author).

In this text, the plaintiff claimed that he should be paid '300 thousand RMB' as director and '164 thousand RMB' as the script writer, which is textualized as '464 thousand RMB (both the director's salary of 300 thousand RMB and the writer's salary of 164 thousand RMB)'. In addition to the exact repetition of the specific numbers of '300 thousand RMB' and '164 thousand RMB', the judges also explicitly provide the total number '464 thousand RMB'. Because the summation of the two individual numbers is not complicated and its absence does not leave much room for misunderstanding, the judges' intention of including the total sum is more likely to show the authority and exactness of their writing than to add new information to this text. In addition, the exact repetition of individual numbers and the explicit stating of the total number improve reader-friendliness. One does not need to go back to previous sentences, paragraphs or even pages in the civil judgment to understand what is being discussed.

Since numerical expressions are frequently used in civil judgments and most are case-specific, non-specialist readers may overlook them because their primary reading purpose is to find the judges' opinions and decisions related to specific disputes. However, lawyers and judges do examine the correctness of these numerical expressions, which was confirmed by the majority of specialist informants interviewed. Specialists check the correctness and the legitimacy of individual and composite numbers to evaluate the quality of civil judgments and, more importantly, the legitimacy of the background litigation practices.

The research demonstrates that lawyers read these numerical expressions because they have a professional interest in carefully reading legal genres and because they acknowledge that a large proportion of civil judgments in Mainland China are not well-written (Cohen; 1997; Gechilk, 2005). This is also verified by a few judgments in the corpus. In these particular judgments, the information carried by numerical expressions is unclear, as illustrated by the case below. The plaintiff (a pedestrian) was hit by a moving car driven by the defendant. The plaintiff received proper treatment after being immediately sent to hospital and recovered after six months. The defendant paid only a small portion of the medical fees incurred, so the plaintiff sued and claimed:

> [...] After the accident, the plaintiff was sent to the central hospital of Zhejiang Lishui [...] the total medical fees were **299972.34 RMB**; the defendant paid **198700 RMB** but refused to pay **the rest** [...]. To sum up, the plaintiff required the court to order the defendant to pay **48266.44 RMB** [...] (Emphasis added by the present author).

The text shows that the plaintiff bore the total medical fees (*299974.34 RMB*) of which the defendant paid a portion (*198700 RMB*). The plaintiff went to court because the defendant refused to pay the rest; the amount seems to be 101272.34 RMB (the deduction of *198700* from *299972.34*). However, the amount claimed in the above text is *48266.44 RMB*. The mismatch between 101272.34 and *48266.44* is problematic. As an authoritative genre, civil judgments should be constructed carefully, and when this type of mistake occurs it should be removed before sending the judgment to the parties. The three numbers in this text are information the judges provided in relation to the plaintiff's description of facts and claims. No other information is supplied to explain this mismatch. The mismatch may have originally appeared in the plaintiff's indictment but should have been identified and corrected in the judges' written judgment. This type of mistake harms the integrity and authority of civil judgments and also the credibility of the judges' litigation practice.

Turning from the judges' use of monetary numerical expressions in the step *Plaintiffs' Claim*, the following analysis attempts to study the relationship between this step and the move *Judges' Arguments*, particularly in relation to their respective handling of the same monetary issues. The research discovered that a difference exists when judges recontextualize the plaintiffs' original arguments in the step *Plaintiffs' claim* and when they again discuss these same arguments in the move *Judges' Arguments*. This difference indicates how judges achieve this purpose in litigation.

Section 4.4.2 indicates that a close correspondence exists between the move *Parties' Arguments,* particularly its step *Plaintiffs' Claim,* and the move *Judges' Arguments*. Judges recontextualize the plaintiffs' original arguments in indictments not to faithfully report these arguments but to report their identified facts on the basis of these arguments and to make the move *Parties' Arguments* sit more harmoniously with other moves in the civil judgment. The judges' intention is explicitly evidenced by the use of numerical expressions in the two moves. In the case below, the defendant took out nine loans from the plaintiff (a bank) and could not repay the loan within the loan period. The judges in this case introduce facts both in *Parties' Arguments* and in *Judges' Arguments*, as indicated below:

> (*Parties' Arguments*)
> Plaintiff X claimed: Defendant Y took out nine loans from our bank from May 1994 to October 1999, the total sum was **270,260 RMB**, and took out 4 loans in other people's name with a total sum of **42,000 RMB**. The total sum of the **13** loans was **RMB 312,260**. After we requested for paying back several times [...].
>
> (*Judges' Arguments*)
> According to the accepted evidence, this court found the following facts: on September 10, 1989, Y borrowed **63,000 RMB** from X in the name of [...] on June 26, 1994, Y **borrowed 5,000 RMB** from X in the name of [...] on April 28, 1995, Y borrowed **100,000 RMB** from X [...] on October 29, 1999, Y borrowed **2,000 RMB** from X [...] (Example text 14, case 6, emphasis added by the present author).

Comparing the above two texts, it is found that *Plaintiffs' Claim* only lists the aggregate sums: 270,206 RMB ('Y took out 9 loans [...] the total sum was 270,260 RMB'), 42,000 RMB ('took out 4 loans in other people's name with a total sum of 4,200 RMB') and 312,260 RMB ('the total sum of the 13 loans is 312,260 RMB'). However, *Judges' Arguments* displays detailed information relating to the individual loans, including the date of borrowing and the interest thus incurred. Non-specialist readers may argue that there is nothing improper in this textual arrangement, because whether the total or individual numbers come first does not prevent readers from getting the whole story; for specialists, however, the location of the two figures has important implications.

A full report of individual figures and related information suggests an intention to challenge hard evidence and an effort to conduct investigations. This intention and effort are completely missing in a report where only the total number is provided. In practice, the reporting of summative figures only is, as suggested by specialist informants, seldom used by the plaintiffs and their specialist agents who are well aware that the omission of individual numbers will deprive them of the opportunity to present more convincing arguments. Providing only a summative figure suggests that the plaintiffs have no hard evidence to support their claims, which is not necessarily true in the plaintiffs' original arguments.

At his indictment, it is reasonable that the plaintiff in the above case produced most of the total and individual numbers and necessary related information, and that these all contributed to the facts for the judges' examination and acceptance. The total figures were reported in *Parties' Arguments* in order to demonstrate the plaintiff's main argument, while the individual figures and related information were reported in *Judges' Arguments* as part of the facts. This rhetorical choice is legitimate because judges' writing of civil judgments is based on their professional understanding and analysis of a number of trial documents including, among others, indictments, statements of defence, and courtroom records. Although the plaintiffs are allowed to produce their own facts favourably, judges have the power to decide what aspects of their descriptions can be accepted as legal facts, which might be similar or at variance from the plaintiffs' descriptions.

5.2.2 Non-financial cases

Although the facts in non-financial cases are not related to financial disputes, it is common for the plaintiffs to claim monetary compensation for their loss or suffering. Similarly, the judges use monetary numerical expressions to report the parties' monetary claims and their analysis of these claims. The analysis of judges' use of monetary numerical expressions in non-financial cases reveals the judges' handling of some controversial issues in Mainland China, like compensation for mental distress.

There is no consensus in Mainland China on whether and in what way the compensation for mental distress should be accepted in a civil trial. Some legal experts believe that its acceptance is required by the rule of law and that it is beneficial for the development of China's modern legal system. But government officers, who are usually more powerful than judges, argue that its acceptance encourages an overuse of lawsuits which will negatively influence the fast-developing Chinese economy. The contentious views on this issue are also reflected in civil judgments.

Some civil judgments in the corpus involve disputes such as divorce, neighbourhood rights, and personal reputations. In these non-financial cases, the plaintiffs mostly claim non-financial remedies to restore their rights plus a claim of financial compensation. For example, when a defendant damages a plaintiff's reputation, the most immediate and reasonable remedy available for the plaintiff and the court is to order the defendant to apologize in a proper manner, aiming at minimizing the negative influence of the defendants' tortious (law-breaking) action. Moreover, as Mainland China has been expanding the protection of citizen's personal rights in the past three decades, the plaintiff whose reputation is damaged is also entitled to claim financial compensation. The *General Principles of the Civil Law of the PRC* stipulate that a person can ask for compensation for mental distress when his/her rights are violated (Article 120).

The following case involves a dispute within a family. A man died of a serious disease. His wife and daughter (the plaintiffs) sued his sister (the defendant) because they believed that the defendant transferred the deceased to a new hospital without their permission. When they requested the defendant tell them the name of the new hospital, the defendant refused. Before the man's death, the defendant tried every method to stop the plaintiffs from seeing the man, even after he had died and been cremated. The plaintiffs sued and argued that they were deprived of the right to accompany the husband (and father) before his death. The text below is the plaintiffs' claims:

> [...] The defendant had seriously violated the plaintiffs' rights. After many fruitless negotiations with the defendants, the plaintiffs filed this suit requiring the court to order that: 1, the defendant should **deliver the death certificate immediately to the plaintiffs**; 2, the defendant **should apologize to the plaintiffs in public**; 3, the defendant should **pay the plaintiffs 500 thousand RMB as compensation for mental distress**; 4 the defendant should **bear the court fees** (Example text 15, case 12, emphasis added by the present author).

In this text, the plaintiffs claimed two non-monetary remedies ('deliver the death certificate' and 'apologize') and two monetary ones ('compensation for mental distress' and 'the court fees').

Among the four claims, the first one is most likely to be accepted by the judges and the fourth one is mostly likely to be rejected. 'Deliver the death certificate immediately to the plaintiffs' is a remedy which will unsurprisingly be supported by the court. Whether the defendant stopped the plaintiffs from seeing the man for a good reason, the plaintiffs are his wife and daughter and have a lawful right to his death certificate. Ji points out that 'apologize in public' is not common in the judicial context of Mainland China (2005), as Chinese people usually have a negative association with lawsuits and judges tend not to embarrass the parties in public, particularly in family cases.

As for the third claim, 'compensation for mental distress', there is evidence suggesting this is 'even less pragmatic in litigation practices' (Xiong, 2003, p. 157). Although it is theoretically possible for the plaintiffs to be awarded compensation for mental distress and it is also a fact that the plaintiffs in other civil trials commonly claim compensation for mental distress, it is not reasonable to expect the compensation claimed to be supported by the court. The normal result is either an award of no money or a sum of negligible worth compared to the size of the compensation claim. It is possible for the plaintiffs to claim one million RMB as compensation for mental distress and end up with an award of 10,000 RMB. This huge contrast between the money claimed and the money awarded is common. To seek a plausible explanation for this contrast, it is necessary to see the *General Principles of the Civil Law of PRC*:

> *Article 120*
> If a citizen's right in his/her name, portrait, reputation or honor is infringed upon, he shall have the right to demand that the infringement be stopped, his reputation be rehabilitated, the negative effects be eliminated and an apology be made; he may also demand **financial compensation for loss and suffering** (Emphasis added by the present author). *General Principles of the Civil Law of PRC*, 1991

Although this Article 120 does not mention the expression *compensation for mental distress*, it conveys the legislators' intention to introduce it to Chinese litigation. The *financial compensation for losses* in this article is usually interpreted by legal specialists as financial compensation for mental pains the plaintiffs suffer as a result of the defendants' infringing action. However, no legal authorities have produced any specific stipulations for the award of this compensation. The legal basis for handling compensation for mental distress in litigation is limited and vague.

It is possible that the lack of specific law indicates that the legislators and the government only intend to discuss compensation for mental distress on paper; they are not in favour its application and compensation for mental distress in the present context of China. The Supreme People's Court of the PRC produced the following official statement:

> *Article 10*
> If a citizen's or legal person's reputation are infringed upon, the wrongdoer should compensate for any financial loss that results from the infringement; **if the citizen claims compensation for mental distress, the court may decide this on basis of the nature of faults, the detail of infringements, the results of mental distress, and other relevant elements**. *Stipulations in relation to the lawsuit about reputation,* by the Supreme People's Court of PRC. (Excerpt 6, emphasis added by the present author)

In this article, the Supreme People's Court stipulates that one can ask for compensation for both *financial loss* and *mental distress* for his/her suffering. Nevertheless, there are subtle differences between the two concepts. 'The wrongdoer should compensate' signifies that the court has an obligation to see 'compensate for any financial loss' to be awarded. However, 'the court may decide this (compensation for mental distress)' only 'if the citizen claims compensation for mental distress' means that judges are not legally required to consider compensation for mental distress when the parties do not request this.

This vague and limited legal basis implies that legislators and the Supreme Peoples' Court have a conservative attitude towards the application of compensation for mental distress. Plaintiffs need to be cautious when they make this claim because court fees are in proportion to the money claimed as compensation for mental distress. A claim for higher compensation leads to the higher court fees. If plaintiffs are not awarded their claims, they have to bear a proportion of the court fees according to the extent to which they lose.

This is illustrated by the following case. The plaintiff claimed the defendant had damaged his reputation, which was accepted by the court. However, of the one million RMB claimed by the plaintiff as compensation for his mental distress, the court only awarded 10,000 RMB. The text below is the court decision:

> To conclude, according to [...] the judgment is given as follows:
> 1. The defendant should publish a statement of apology in [...]
> 2. The defendant should pay the plaintiff 10, 000 RMB as compensation for mental distress [...]
> 3. [...]
>
> As for the court **fees 15,010 RMB, the plaintiff shall bear 14,860 RMB** and the **defendant shall bear 150 RMB** (to be paid within 7 days of this judgment coming into effect) (Author's emphasis added.).

This text shows that the judges supported the material claim made by the plaintiff but ordered him to pay most of the court fee (*14,860* out of *15,010*). As the losing party, the defendant was ordered to pay only *150 RMB*. It seems that the winning party (plaintiff) actually lost money, even though he was awarded *10,000 RMB* as compensation for mental distress.

The law stipulates that the losing party should bear the court fees. If a party has some of his claims supported and others rejected by the court, he should bear the proportion of the court fees according to the extent to which he loses. The judges in the case above accepted the plaintiff's material claim of his reputation being damaged but refused his high claim for compensation for mental distress. The judges decided that the defendant should stop his action immediately and publish a statement of apology in a national newspaper. The plaintiff's claim 'one million RMB as compensation for mental distress' was not accepted and the money awarded was '10,000 RMB'. As a result, the plaintiff was ordered to bear 99% of the court fees, i.e. the claimed 'one million RMB' is divided by the awarded '10,000 RMB', which is the law.

Some evidence shows that the compensation awarded for mental distress in Mainland China seldom exceeds 50,000 RMB. The difficulty in getting compensation for mental distress is publicly acknowledged, as stated in the following news report:

> Now it is common for the plaintiffs to claim compensation for mental distress [...]. So some judges remind [...] not to claim unreasonably high compensation for mental distress [...]. [T]his will lead to higher court and lawyer fees, also these high compensation will not be accepted [...]. According to the stipulations of Shanghai High People's Court, the **maximum amount of awarded compensation for mental distress is 50,000 RMB**. If the plaintiffs make extremely high claims, he, very possibly, will win the case but lose money. *Shanghai Commerce* (*2004, 10, 14*) (Excerpt 7, emphasis added by the present author)

The plaintiffs and the judges might have a different understanding of this phenomenon of 'win the case but lose money' as stated in this news report. The plaintiff in the case above may believe the high compensation for mental distress (one million) is an appropriate sum to ameliorate the damage to his reputation and to stress the defendant's malicious intent. The judges may consider this high compensation claim as the plaintiff's strategy to earn publicity, so they usually consider non-monetary remedies first, such as stopping the infringing action, requiring a statement of public apology, and the elimination of negative effects.

To conclude, the study of monetary numerical expressions in non-financial cases reveals the contrasted considerations of compensation for mental distress between plaintiffs and judges. While plaintiffs may have case-specific considerations in claiming high compensation for mental distress, as demonstrated in the *step Plaintiffs' Claim*, judges' consideration and handling of this compensation in civil judgments usually reflects the requirements of law and judicial cultures, as demonstrated in the move *Court Decisions*. Although judges sometimes omit individual compensation claims by plaintiffs when they recontextualize the plaintiffs' arguments in the step *Plaintiffs' Claim*, this investigation shows that in this step they never omit the plaintiffs' compensation claim ed for mental distress. Judges intend to use the contrast between compensation claim for mental distress and the final amount awarded by the court to reflect the state's policy on compensation for mental distress and to indicate their following of this policy.

In the current Chinese judicial context, non-monetary remedies are mostly thought sufficient for non-financial disputes. Even when there may be a possibility of awarding higher compensation for mental distress, judges have no right to decide this; the law at least does not explicitly given them such a right. A pure consideration of facts does not justify judges' decisions; more importantly, they need to take into account the policy of the Supreme People's Court and the government, as discussed above.

5.3 Temporal Expressions

Temporal numerical expressions are heavily used by judges in the move *Parties' Arguments*. This research finds that judges use most of these temporal expressions in the first step of this move, *Plaintiffs' Claim,* while they conventionally use none in the second step, *Defendants' Defence*. Approximately half (54 %) of judgments in the corpus do not include a single temporal expression in the *Defendants' Defence* step.

5.3.1 The step Plaintiffs' Claim

Judges' writing in this step is intended to report the plaintiffs' views of facts and their claims. In order to summarize the plaintiffs' views of facts, judges conventionally use many temporal numerical expressions. In the case below, the plaintiff ate some food in a restaurant managed by the defendant. Because the food was not properly cooked, the plaintiff became seriously ill. The plaintiff filed this lawsuit in order to get compensation for the pain and discomfort he had suffered. In the following text, the judges describe the food the plaintiff ate in the restaurant and the different hospitals to which he had gone for treatment to recount a clear and exact story of this incident:

> The plaintiff claimed: **July 6, 2006**, the plaintiff went to the restaurant managed by the defendant [...]. **July, 19, 2006**, the plaintiff found half of his body began to lose sense and power [...]. **July, 24,** the plaintiff went to the Third Affiliated Hospital of Beijing University [...]. **July 28**, doctors of the Third Affiliated Hospital of Beijing University invited doctors from [...] to have a medical conference [...]. **July 29**, the plaintiff was transferred to [...]. **August 17, 2006**, the plaintiff went to Beijing Friendship Hospital [...]. [F]rom **August 17** to **August 30, 2006**, the plaintiff stayed in this hospital [...]. (Example text 16, case 13, emphasis added by the present author).

In this text, the judges use temporal expressions heavily: 'July 6, 2006 – July, 19, 2006 – July, 24 – July 28 – July 29 – August 17, 2006 – August 17 – August 30, 2006'. Because what is discussed is an incident occurring over two months, in everyday communication it would not be necessary to use eight temporal expressions to report its development. One or two dates would be sufficient to tell the incident to non-specialist readers. The heavy use of exact temporal expressions indicates that it was necessary to list the problematic incidents experienced by the plaintiff, and is testimony to the plaintiff's persuasive effort. The judges stressed that the plaintiff changed hospitals several times before doctors finally diagnosed his illness. The implied seriousness of the illness and the difficulty of diagnosis are important facts for the judges to consider. These temporal expressions and the reported actions demonstrate the judges' understanding of the plaintiff's efforts to attribute blame to the defendant.

One advantage of using these exact temporal expressions is that the readability of texts is significantly increased. The chronological sequence of description, as one kind of the language of 'doing' (Halliday, 1989, p. 7), makes an obvious contrast with the language of 'thinking' in other parts of civil judgments. In reading the lengthy *Plaintiffs' Claim* step above, it is unnecessary to read every word to understand the intended meaning. The eight temporal expressions used can be seen as discourse markers implicitly segmenting the text. In order to achieve a general understanding, one can easily approach specific temporal expressions, read the immediately following sentences, and then put them together to get a summary. To make things easier, seven of the eight sentences have the same subject (the plaintiff) and the same syntactic structure (the plaintiff + verb). Such textual arrangements significantly reduce the effort needed to understand the text, which is further studied in chapter 6 by drawing on the concept of coherence.

5.3.2 The step Defendants' Defence

In this step, judges report the defendants' arguments against the plaintiffs' arguments and claims. Compared to the heavy use of temporal expressions in *Plaintiffs' Claim*, around half (54%) of civil judgments in the corpus include no single temporal expression in the *Defendants' Defence* step. The following *Defendants' Defence* step is taken from the same food case:

> The defendant argued: We accept the fact that the plaintiff ate in our restaurant and fell ill and we sincerely apologize. After the incident, we published an apology in the media, so we do not agree with the plaintiff's claim that we should publicly apologize in influential newspapers or magazines in Beijing. As for the medical fees [...] we agreed to compensate the plaintiff within the reasonable limit. The compensation for mental distress claimed by plaintiff is too high and we request the court to decide this according to the situation. (Example text 17, case 13)

This text includes no instances of temporal expressions. According to this text, the judges seem to conclude that the defendant argued only against the plaintiff's claim and offered no disagreement relating to the plaintiff's description of the facts. This judges' conclusion is possible for specific cases, but is questionable when they give this same conclusion in all civil judgments in the corpus.

In order to see how the defendants write their original arguments, the researcher analyzed the defendants' statements of defence and compared them with the *Defendants' Defence* step in civil judgments. A similar comparison is made in chapter 4, where the purpose is to examine the difference between the plaintiffs' arguments and the judges' recontextualization of these arguments. Following the same method, the following comparison is conducted. The quoted case handles the dispute between a transportation company (the defendant) and one staff member (the plaintiff). The plaintiff got hurt while doing his job and sued the defendant in order to get compensation for his injury. However, the defendant argued the plaintiff had not followed the company's regulations and so should not be compensated for his injury. The text quoted below is from the defendant's *statement of defence*:

> [...] I arranged for the plaintiff to transport goods to Gansu on **September 3, 2004** [...] in order to avoid the toll booth and earn money for himself, the plaintiff took a new road which had not been completed **about 4 or 5 am, September 5, 2004** [...] **about 6 am, September 5, 2004**, the truck driven by B [...] (Emphasis added by the present author).

This example text shows how the defendant understands the incident occurred. A chronological arrangement of temporal expressions is again employed: 'September 3, 2004 – about 4 or 5 am, September 5, 2004 – about 6 am, September 5, 2004'. In this sequence, the defendant not only identifies the particular date but also reports the detailed chronological development of the incident. It is further verified by specialist informants that defendants usually insist on fully presenting their own description of facts even when they have no significant disagreement with the plaintiffs' description of facts. Of course, the judges will decide whether their description of facts is relevant for the litigation, as demonstrated by the following statement:

> The judges do not literally report the parties' arguments in *Plaintiffs' Claim* and *Defendants' Defence*. Among a number potential issues and problems related to

> the dispute between the parties, only those that are relevant will be analyzed and discussed. The judges have the right to analyze the parties' arguments and identify the facts, which is required by law. However, to briefly report the identified facts in *Plaintiffs' Claim* instead of the two parties' own description of facts is a professional convention, which is not required by law. Because the identified facts usually involve time and money elements, the judges have to keep them in *Plaintiffs' Claim*. (Excerpt 8, lawyer B)

In civil judgments, the 'statement of defences' is only one of many documents judges may consider when they attempt to identify legal facts. Like the judges' recontextualization of the plaintiffs' arguments in civil judgments, the judges are allowed to analyze the defendants' arguments and retain only those elements which are legally relevant to civil judgments. Judges do not mention the defendants' description of facts either because they believe the defendants have not proposed factual descriptions which are significantly different from the plaintiffs' or because they synthesize both plaintiffs' and defendants' descriptions and report the results in the *Plaintiffs' Claim* step. As a result, the *Defendants' Defence* and *Plaintiffs' Claim* steps are more closely connected as component sections of civil judgments and not as two independent texts intended to faithfully report the respective arguments of the plaintiffs and defendants. It can be concluded that judges' use of temporal expressions in the two steps demonstrates how judges analyze the parties' descriptions of facts and thus identify the legal facts. The close connection between these two steps indicates the judges' understanding in regard to the tension between the two parties' views, i.e. the plaintiffs and the defendants.

5.4 Metadiscourse in civil judgment

The following sections of chapter 5 discuss the use of metadiscourse in civil judgments. Metadiscourse, in this research, refers to Chinese words that express judges' evaluations of the texts or their interpersonal negotiations of meaning with potential readers. Judges' use of metadiscourse in civil judgments is explicitly identifiable because the metadiscursive expressions used carry the judges' interpersonal communication and always stand out from other standardized language used in civil judgments, for example, '可能性极小' (extremely unlikely), '一般' (normally), and '通常' (generally). The analysis of the corpus reveals two frequently used metadiscursive devices: emphatics and hedging. As a highly standardized and institutionalized genre, civil judgments are traditionally held as not creative or interpersonal. What judges need to do is to familiarize themselves with the standardized words, expressions and rhetorical structures, which is a common belief among laypersons in Mainland China. This belief conceals one important fact beneath the highly standardized and institutionalized surface of this genre, namely, judges need to evaluate the parties' arguments and make their own decisions (Rowe, 1999, p. 10). The judges' job in writing civil judgments is never a simple task of blank-filling; instead, the competing arguments made by the plaintiffs, the defendants, and the judges are all reflected in texts. This gives legitimacy to the occurrence of metadiscourse in civil judgments.

Plaintiffs and defendants in litigation enjoy the opportunity to present their usually competing arguments to judges, with the purpose of convincing the judges to support their respective views. To achieve this, the parties', i.e. the plaintiffs and defendants, arguments are usually rhetorically constructed to serve their own ends, although there are standardized rules and conventions to follow. Similarly, judges enjoy the right to weigh up the parties' competing arguments, interpret the related law, and finally award legal decisions, which demands much rhetorical effort in addition to following the standardized rules and conventions. Writing rhetorically is therefore common for both judges and the parties who usually bear different interests in litigation. Arguments in civil judgments are seldom constructed neutrally, be it *Plaintiffs' Claim, Defendant' Defence* or *Judges' Opinions*. Although the analysis in chapter 4 shows some sections of civil judgments read more like narratives than arguments, these narratives are appropriately loaded with a number of rhetorical devices, including emphatics and hedging.

The following analysis of emphatics and hedging in the *Plaintiffs' Claim* and *Defendants' Defence* steps is based on a research finding verified by specialist informants which reports that judges do not usually add their own metadiscourse to their recontextualization of the parties' original arguments in these two steps. Rather, judges are usually expected to remove metadiscourse which carries overly strong personal attitudes from the parties' original arguments when they recontextualize them in the civil judgment. If some of the parties' metadiscourse is retained in these two steps, the judges must have a reason to do this or it would suggest a lack of professional competence in writing civil judgments.

5.4.1 Emphatics in the step Plaintiffs' Claim

In *Plaintiffs' Claim*, judges retain the emphatics used by plaintiffs to emphasize the seriousness of defendants' tortious (law-breaking) actions and the suffering the plaintiffs have experienced. The plaintiff in the case below claimed that the defendant's speech had damaged his reputation. In the *Plaintiffs' Claim* step, the judges retain a number of emphatics in their writing:

> The plaintiff claimed: The defendant's talking [...] is **completely malicious** (纯属恶意诽谤) slander and **cannot be** factual **at all** (根本不是事实) [...]. [T]he defendant has **seriously damaged** (严重侵犯了) my reputation [...].

These expressions emphasized in bold face do not contribute much propositional meaning to the texts, the omission of which would not influence specialist and non-specialist readers' understanding. However, these expressions strengthen the persuasive power of the text. This text evaluates the defendant's infringing action and argues that the defendant spread wrong statements in order to harm the plaintiff's reputation. Instead of expressing the plaintiff's argument with an emotionless description of facts, the text modifies each sentence with emphatics: 'completely malicious' slandering, 'not' be factual 'at all', and 'seriously' infringed. The cumulative power of adding 'completely' and 'malicious' together indicates the plaintiff's strong negative attitude towards the defendants' action. 'Cannot be factual at all' implies that the defendant's wrong statements are easy to capture, which of course need to proved by evidence. The last one, 'seriously infringed', stresses the legitimate basis for the plaintiff's filing of the lawsuit and the reason why the plaintiff was claiming compensation for his suffering.

The judges retain these emphatics in this civil judgment to explicitly demonstrate the plaintiff's intention to blame the defendant and his intention to persuade the judges to accept his claims. There is always a tension between the plaintiffs' and the defendants' views in litigation, and it is the judges' job to understand and resolve this tension in civil judgments, something outsiders might not realize.

Plaintiffs may use different strategies to demonstrate the tension between their views and the defendants' views. Sometimes, they choose to stress sympathetically the suffering they have experienced because of the defendants' actions, but not to stress negatively the defendants' actions. The plaintiff in the text below accused the defendant of having prevented her from seeing her (the plaintiff's) husband.

> The plaintiff claimed: The defendant brought **life-long pains** (终身的痛苦) to the plaintiffs. After learning my husband's death, I suffered **so much** (悲痛欲绝)**,** spent **countless very painful sleepless** (长期的彻夜不眠) nights **and completely lost my mind** (精神恍惚) **[...]**. [T]he defendant's action **very seriously** (严重侵犯) infringed my rights [...] (Example text 18, case 12, emphasis added by the present author).

This text demonstrates the plaintiff's use of emphatics not to negatively stress the defendant's action, but to describe herself as a helpless and weeping widow. Her intention here is to convey the depth of her suffering to the judges: 'life-long pains', 'suffer so much', 'countless very painful sleepless nights', and 'completely lost my mind'. These emphatic expressions tell a tragic story in order to attract sympathy for this suffering, which is summarized in the final sentence: 'defendant's actions very badly infringed the plaintiffs' lawful rights'. The judges' retaining of this long and emotional description of suffering demonstrates that they understand the tension between the plaintiff and the defendant is not negotiable.

There are two considerations deciding the plaintiffs' choice between stressing the defendants' actions negatively and describing their suffering sympathetically. Firstly, when the plaintiffs recognize the defendant's tortious (law-breaking) actions, they may choose to describe the defendant's actions in detail because this is more direct. Otherwise, it is better for them to describe their own suffering sympathetically, which is indirect but carries equal persuasion. Secondly, when the plaintiffs intend to persuade the judges to punish the defendants' tortious (law-breaking) actions, they may attempt a very detailed description of the defendant's actions to prove the defendants' malicious intent. However, if the plaintiffs' intention is to get remedial compensation, they may spend more effort on proving the suffering they have experienced, because only demonstrable suffering will be compensated in Mainland Chinese litigation. It can be concluded that judges have a good understanding of both considerations and the tension between the parties; they would otherwise remove these emphatics in their recontextualization of the parties' original arguments in civil judgments.

5.4.2 Emphatics in the step Defendant's Defence

The *Defendants' Defence* step realizes the judges' recontextualization of the defendants' arguments. Because of the usual tension between plaintiffs and defendants, the defendants also use emphatics to argue against the plaintiffs' claim, but in a different way. Unlike the plaintiffs, the defendants seldom use emphatics heavily and cumulatively. Rather, defendants use emphatics more selectively in the *Defendant's Defence* step, which is less noticeable and requires considerable effort to identify. The judges' retaining of these emphatics indicates their effort to retain some of the defendants' intentions carried by these emphatics in civil judgments. This will disclose more information relating to the interaction between the defendants and the plaintiffs and will improve argumentation in civil judgments.

The investigation suggests that a majority of defendants have less incentive than plaintiffs to demonstrate the tension between their views in litigation. The defendants' intention is usually to mitigate, or avoid the plaintiffs' claim technically rather than to give emotional feedback or comment on the plaintiffs' arguments or claims, which is explained by the following lawyer's statement:

> The defendants in a majority of civil cases have actually harmed the plaintiffs' rights, to a greater or lesser degree. I personally do not expect the defendants, as wrong-doers of various kinds, to talk as aggressively as the plaintiffs will do. By demonstrating too strong a desire to escape the responsibility, the defendants will harm their purpose of mitigating or avoiding the blame from the plaintiffs, because they do not show the expected understanding towards what the plaintiffs suffer. (Excerpt 9, lawyer C)

The following text is quoted to explain the defendants' use of emphatics, which differs from the above case in which the plaintiff claimed that the defendant had damaged his reputation:

> The defendant argued: I **never** (从未) said 'offered money for sex' […] I **only** (只是) told Y fact, I gave them information in private talks and I didn't open it to public […].

This text demonstrates how the defendant justified her own actions in order to avoid being blamed by the plaintiff. The defendant here uses two simple emphatics, 'never' and 'only' to modify her argument against the plaintiff's claim. 'Never' is used to emphasize the defendant's denial of the plaintiff's accusation and to indicate a strong sense of innocence. 'Only' is used to mitigate her action of disclosing the plaintiff's private information to the media. It seems that the defendant attempts to persuade the judges that what she said is true and has nothing to do with malicious intention to harm the plaintiff's reputation.

The two emphatics include a meaning difference because the omission of 'never' does not change the propositional meaning of the defendant's argument, while the missing of 'only' does. The primary purpose of using 'never' is to express the defendant's personal intention of persuasion and a personal resentment at being accused. However, 'only' not only carries the personal intention, it also delimits the meaning of the defendant's arguments. For example, 'I told facts to Y' and 'I only told facts to Y' are not two different expressions of the same meaning. Without being modified by 'only', the defendant can also tell other things in addition to facts to the media, which is an interpretation that can ruin the defendant's effort to avoid blame.

In the following case, the defendant was accused of unlawfully publishing the plaintiff's works for profit.

> The defendant argued: We expressed a **very sincere** (深深的歉意) apology to the plaintiff for publishing his works [...]. We have given **all** (全部) payment the plaintiff should earn to the acting editor-in-chief **at one time** (一并支付) [...]. [W]e, **in fact** (实际上), have completed the duty of paying [...] (Example text 19, case 14, emphasis added by the present author).

This text reveals the defendants' typical intention of using emphatics, which is verified by the earlier specialist statement (Excerpt 9). This text seems to acknowledge the accusation made by the plaintiff, but an intention to avoid blame can be identified. Firstly, the defendant includes within his arguments an apology ('we expressed a very sincere apology'). 'Very sincere' means the defendant realized the plaintiff's suffering and was willing to apologize for that. The defendant's strategy here is to accept responsibility in order to construct himself as a responsible publisher. The construction of personal responsibility is an important element convincing judges that the defendant had no malicious intentions and that he should thus not bear responsibility beyond what is necessary, namely, the compensation should only cover damages that have actually occurred and should not include those that have no immediate effect. 'All at one time' and 'in fact' stress the immediacy and completeness of the payment. The fact of payment, if accepted by the judges, can be hard evidence proving the defendant had no intention of taking advantage of the plaintiff.

To sum up, although the defendant in this text does not use emphatics as frequently as the above plaintiffs do, he does carefully select and arrange emphatics in his arguments. Each of the emphatics used is intended to argue against one specific argument proposed by the plaintiff or intended to justify one specific aspect of his own actions. The nature of litigation is such that defendants may have less incentive than plaintiffs to show explicitly the tension between their views because the defendant's purpose in litigation is to mitigate or avoid blame, not to give emotional comments on these accusations.

5.4.3 *Emphatics in the move* Judges' Opinions

After the analysis of emphatics in the judges' recontextualization of the parties' arguments in the two steps of *Parties' Arguments*, this section examines how judges use emphatics when they write their arguments in the *Judges' Opinions* move. As neutral adjudicators in litigation, the judges' primary tasks are to find the facts, to interpret the law and to apply the law to facts. The previous analysis demonstrates that both require judges to follow some standardized rules and conventions and to exploit their professional competence and expertise. In practice, judges enjoy and sometimes even create space to stamp their personality and express their personal understanding in civil judgments. This section examines judges' writing in the *Judges' Opinions* move in relation to their tasks: the interpretation of law, the application of law to facts, and the writing of legal opinions.

5.4.3.1 The interpretation of law

The first task judges need to do in *Judges' Opinions* is to interpret the law. The study of emphatics in this move reveals that judges may have other considerations when they interpret the law beyond immediately applying the interpreted law to the identified facts. For example, their writing will be read by other judges. Judges in courts of the same level refer to their judgments to decide similar cases. Judges in higher courts examine their judgments for supervision, and judges in lower courts take their judgments as established precedent[6]. Poorly constructed legal interpretations in civil judgments can be easily recognized by these specialist readers, which jeopardizes the writing judges' professional credibility and future career prospects. Such considerations give judges a strong incentive to demonstrate their professional competence and expertise through emphatics and hedging in this move.

The following text shows some of the typical ways judges textualize their incentive to demonstrate personality, professional expertise and competence in this move. This text is from a case in which the parties had a dispute over the defendant's use of the plaintiff's patent. The judges in this text express their views on the legal protection of patents in Mainland China:

> This court holds: [...] those patent rights enjoyed are legitimate and lawful and are protected by patent law [...]. **[A]ny**[7] (任何) units or individuals, without authorization of patent holder, should not use this patent in the following six ways [...].

The judges' interpretation of patent law in this text uses the all-inclusive emphatics *any*, not to refer to specific persons or units but to refer to all potential patent law breakers. If the judges consider the lawsuit under consideration, it seems unreasonable for them to use the all-inclusive *any* because they could have used the specific expression 'the defendant' instead. The judges here demonstrate an intention to discuss patent law at a general level. Another textual feature indicating this intention is that the judges list six different situations under

6 One could argue that the principle of precedent is not applicable in civil law countries including Mainland China, but this is only a theoretical assumption. In practice, judges in Mainland China do refer to judgments produced by other judges, particularly those from higher courts.

7 This sentence is a literal translation of the original text, because the English sentence (*No units or individuals, without authorization of patent holder, should...*) makes the original Chinese emphatics (任何, any) invisible.

which a patent holder's rights can be infringed even though not all of them are relevant in this trial. This text shows the judges' personal understanding that the interpreted legal regulation should be applied strictly in this and other similar cases. Their interpretation of law is intended not only to provide a legal basis for deciding the lawsuit before them but also to express the judges' professional competence at a general level, particularly for specialist readers.

The judges' intention to show their competence and expertise is more obvious in the text below. This is a case where the parties' contract was annulled by the court because it involved the illegal use of state-owned land:

> This court holds: [...] land is obligatorily administered by the state and the transfer of land ownership or rights of land-using **should and has to** (必须) be approved by the land administration organ of the state [...]. [W]ithout the approval of the land administration organ of the state, the plaintiffs have no right to transfer**, as they wish** (擅自) [...] (Example text 20, case 16, emphasis added by the present author).

The first emphatics used in this text is complex ('should and has to'), and there are no similar expression in the original legal regulation. The judges seem to think the separate use of 'should' or 'has to' is not sufficient to warn potential lawbreakers of the strict supervision of land transaction and of the state's determination to stabilize the land market. This complex emphatic indicates the judges' confidence in their interpretation of the land law. The second emphatic, 'as they wish', does not contribute much propositional meaning to the writing because the chance of misunderstanding the sentence 'without the approval of the land administration organ of the state, the plaintiffs have no right to transfer' is slim. What is conveyed by 'as they wish' are two aspects of interpersonal meaning. Firstly, this phrase shows that the judges have a strong negative attitude toward illegal land transactions. Secondly, the emphatic is used to signify that the parties in this case have a clear intention to break the law. It is further implied that lawbreakers in such cases do not take the land law seriously and have a malicious intent. A text with such emphatics clearly signals that the judges confidently show their negative attitudes toward the party who breaks the law intentionally.

The research finds that judges' confidence in their interpretation of law is not only based on their familiarity with the law but also on their familiarity with government policy. The judges and court in Mainland China usually follow government policies and use these policies in litigation. Zhang (2003) reports a similar finding in regard with the judges' litigation practice. The judges' interpretation of land law in the text above represents the government policy relating to land transactions in China, namely, all land transactions should be strictly administered by the government.

5.4.3.2 The application of law

The second task the judges need to complete in this move is to apply the interpreted law to identified facts. Judges will evaluate the parties' arguments against evidence and law. Since the facts and parties' arguments in specific cases vary extensively, this task demands more case-specific writing variations than standardized rules and conventions. The judges' intention to give personal comments and evaluations is explicitly evidenced by their use of emphatics. In the case below, one of the plaintiff's relatives got hurt in a hotel managed by the defendant, so he sued the defendant for compensation. The defendant's witness proved that the plaintiff's relative was solely responsible for his own incident, a claim supported by the judges. The following text is from the *Judges' Opinions* move of the final civil judgment:

> This court holds: The testimony of the defendants' witness […] is **very clear, quite trustworthy and of high acceptability** (清清楚楚，真实可信) […]. [T]he testimony […] is **objective and true** (客观真实) […] if X (the plaintiff's relative) had not been drunk, it is **extremely unlikely** (可能性极小) to have such incident […] (Example text 21, case 17, emphasis added by the present author).

The judges in this text evaluate the testimony of the defendant's witness and analyze the incident occurrence. It can be seen that emphatics are used very intensiely. The judges' intentions here are to show their personal comments and evaluations. The judges withhold the impersonal tone prevalent elsewhere in civil judgments and replace it with heavy appraisal-loaded expressions including 'very clear', 'quite trustworthy and of high acceptability' and 'objective and true'.

The judges' intention to demonstrate personal comments in the above text becomes more obvious when comparing it with their comments on the plaintiff's burden of proof, i.e. the duty to supply evidence, in the following text:

> because the plaintiffs refused to [...] there was no forensic medical or medical examination reports [...] so the plaintiffs **should bear the results** (应当承担) of not being able to provide evidence [...]. [A]lso, the plaintiffs' claim [...] was **not supported by sufficient evidence** (证据不足) [...] (Example text 22, case 17, emphasis added by the present author).

The judges in this text use no emphatics. The language used is formal and impersonal, which establishes a contrast with their comments on the testimony from the defendant's witness. This contrast demonstrates the judges' sympathetic attitudes towards the plaintiff and his injured relative as victims, even though they started the lawsuit on an inappropriate legal basis and thus lost the trial.

The investigation of the corpus reveals that judges equally use emphatics when they are discussing the innocent and tortious parties in *Judges' Opinions*. However, they seldom use emphatics when discussing a party who has experienced suffering but sued on a wrong basis. The judges' withholding of emphatics here indicates that the plaintiffs as victims should not be judged personally/ethically simply because their lawsuit is wrongly based, which can be corrected by initiating a fresh lawsuit. It can be concluded that judges' use of emphatics shows their personal/ethical attitudes towards the parties, in addition to their legal analysis of the disputes, and their withholding of emphatics in *Judges' Opinions* also indicates their ethical attitudes, i.e. a sympathetic understanding, towards the parties as victims. The use of emphatics in discussing the parties who sue on a wrong legal basis is believed by judges to be unnecessary and not legally professional.

5.4.3.3 The writing of legal opinions

The third task the judges need to do in this move is to give legal opinions in relation to the parties' dispute, in effect concluding the *Judges' Opinions* move. Because the judges' interpretation and application of law, i.e. the previous two tasks, usually involves much specialized content, this third task is usually the section non-specialist readers will read first when they read this move. As in the first task above, the judges include multiple emphatics to give personal comments and evaluations on various legal and ethical issues.

In the following case, the plaintiff lost his property when he travelled on a bus managed by the defendant. The plaintiff claimed that the defendant should have taken care of his property when travelling on the bus, while the defendant argued that he had no responsibility to take care of the plaintiff's personal property. The quoted text below shows the judges opinions on this particular issue:

> This court holds: The plaintiff did **not specifically declare** (并未特别告知) what was in his luggage [...]. [P]assengers (the plaintiff) **of course have more** (明显大于) duties in taking care of their personal property than the carrier (the defendant) does, [...] the plaintiff, **fully aware of the very fact** (明知) he was carrying something special [...] **carelessly handed it** (草率的交给) to the defendant [...]. [A]fter finding the property had lost, the defendant, **to fulfil his ethical duties**[8] [...] **actively collaborated and assisted** (出于道义上的原因，积极配合、协助) the plaintiff in his search of the lost property [...] (Example text 23, case 18, emphasis added by the present author).

The judges in this text comment on the plaintiff's and the defendant's actions in the dispute, based on their interpretation of contract law. Emphatics are closely used here. To comment on the plaintiff's action, the judges negative attitudes are expressed by 'not specifically declare', 'of course have more duties', 'fully aware of the very fact', and 'carelessly handed it over'. 'Not specifically declare' means that the plaintiff did not tell the defendant that the property he carried needed special care when he got on the defendant's bus, so he (the

8 This is a literal translation of the original sentence, in order to retain the Chinese emphatics in translation.

plaintiff) should be responsible for his own property when travelling on the bus. 'Of course carry more obligations' means that the plaintiff's claim is unreasonable because he cannot require the defendant to take care of his (the plaintiff's) personal property, particularly when he (the plaintiff) had failed to tell the defendant the value of the property. 'Fully aware of the very fact' and 'carelessly handed it over' stress that the plaintiff did not take care of his property properly.

All the emphatics above are used to indicate the plaintiff is at fault, while the judges use only one emphatic to comment on facts related to the defendant: 'to fulfil his ethical duties, (the defendant) actively collaborated and assisted' the plaintiff in his search for the lost property. The emphatics here indicates the judges' appreciation of the defendant's good intent because the defendant actually had no responsibility for the plaintiff's lost property, but he still 'actively' helped the plaintiff look for it. It is also implied that the plaintiff should not have initiated the lawsuit in the first place; instead, he should appreciate the defendant's help in this incident.

In addition to using emphatics to express their personal comments and evaluations on the parties' disputes, the judges also use emphatics to express their attitudes towards specific social issues which occur in litigation. In the following case, the plaintiff had dinner in a restaurant managed by the defendant and was served a dish of snails. The snails were infected with parasites and not thoroughly cooked, which resulted in a serious parasite-related illness for the plaintiff. He stayed in hospital for several months, suffering great pains and having to pay very high medical fees. The following text is from the *Judges' Opinions* move in the judges' judgment:

> This court holds: The defendant, as the owner of this restaurant, should bear **very high degree of obligation** (高度的注意义务) to guarantee the safety and hygiene of the food they provide [...]. [T]he defendant **had obvious and explicit subjective faults**[9] (主观上具有明显过错), so he should bear **full**

9 This is a literal translation of Chinese (主观上有明显过错, obviously unlawful intention). The Chinese word 主观上 (subjective) and 明显 (obvious) are usually put together to stress the wrong-doer's unlawful or malicious intentions.

> **responsibility for compensating** (负有完全赔偿责任) the plaintiffs for the caused personal and property injuries [...] (Example text 24, case 19, emphasis added by the present author).

Although the judges' writing in this text seems to indicate this case is not significantly different from other civil cases, three contextual factors make it a case where not only the parties' personal rights but also social interests are endangered. Firstly, snail has long been a traditional food in Mainland China. It is widely known that snail carries many parasites but is safe to eat if thoroughly cooked. State health organizations have for 50 years been warning people to thoroughly cook snail. The defendant's improper method of cooking indicates that he had no intention of attending to this government advice and no intention of taking care of his customers' health. Secondly, more than 40 customers in this incident were similarly infected, although some did not file lawsuits to claim compensation. Moreover, some people disclosed this incident to the media. The widespread reporting of the incident and the lawsuit drew a lot of public attention to the issue of food safety in Mainland China, which is socially and politically sensitive because the incident occurred in the capital of the PRC (Beijing). Lastly, this incident occurred immediately after the SARS epidemic, when the PRC government was exercising a strict policy on food safety. The government was afraid that the publicity around this incident might undermine people's confidence in food safety and public health.

It may be objected that these three factors relate little to judgment or court proceedings. Rather, the discussion takes the state, government, or politics as authority, which seems less relevant in the analysis of litigation and civil judgments. This is true for civil trials in common law countries where the judges and courts enjoy an absolute independence and freedom. However, the situation differs in Mainland China, where judges are linked to the government of various levels. The imprecision 'very high degree of obligation to guarantee' (高度的注意义务) is a very typical and highly indicative phrase used in Chinese political discourse rather than in Chinese legal discourse and is widely known by Chinese civil servants and judges. The judges' use of this sentence in writing their opinions explicitly suggests the government background of these judges. From a legal viewpoint, the imprecise emphatic 'very high', although expressing a strong personal attitude, cannot attribute the defendant's specific responsibility because it appeals to emotions rather than evidence-based analyses.

The other emphatics like 'obvious and explicit subjective faults' (主观上具有明显过错) and 'full responsibility' (负有完全责任) also reveal the judges' intention to follow the government strict policy on food safety as mentioned above. The judges decided that the defendant should bear fully responsibility for the disputed incident, and used emphatics as clear evidence suggesting they intend to decide this in a very confident and emotive way, which occurs more often in political than legal discourse. 'Full' means the defendant's responsibility for compensation is all-inclusive: the defendant should reimburse the plaintiff for participating in the lawsuit, should compensate for the plaintiff's suffering, and should compensate the plaintiff for potential future damages. The judges also have an implicit intention to make this civil judgment a precedent for future possible lawsuits by others involved in this incident.

To conclude, judges use emphatics in all three tasks in the *Judges' Opinions* move i.e. the interpretation of law, the application of law, and the writing of legal opinions, and they tend to use more emphatics in these three tasks. Judges' writing in these three tasks becomes lengthier, which may be attributed to the increased use of emphatics. However, a more reasonable explanation is that the demands of these tasks are less specialized and justify less standardized writing. The first task concerns the related law, the second applies the law to the dispute, and the third provides the judges' legal opinions on the parties' disputes. It is in the third task where judges enjoy greater freedom to use emphatics and to express their personal comments and evaluations, which will officially decide the parties' disputes.

5.4.4 *The absence of hedging in the steps* Plaintiffs' Claim *and* Defendants' Defence

The corpus demonstrates that judges do not include instances of hedging in the *Plaintiffs' Claim* and *Defendants' Defence* steps, which suggests that the plaintiffs and defendants do not use hedging in their arguments. Hedging was explained in Chapter 3 as a rhetorical device expressing writers' uncertainty or un-commitment towards what they are writing. The parties in litigation, submit their arguments to judges to persuade the judges to support their respective views in relation to the dispute. Seemingly little room is therefore left for uncertainty in or un-commitment to their arguments. The use of hedging in their arguments will suggest a lack of confidence or a lack of evidence, and will damage the credibility and persuasive power of their arguments.

5.4.5 *Hedging in the move* Judges' Opinions

The preceding analysis demonstrates that judges complete three tasks in the *Judges' Opinions* move: the interpretation of law, the application of law, and the writing of legal opinions. Hedging is used in the interpretation and application of law, but not in the writing of legal opinions. Because judges write their legal opinions to decide the respective rights and obligations of the parties in specific disputes, the opinions should be expressed by clear and exact language and avoid ambiguity. Legal opinions therefore disallow hedging. The following analysis examines how judges use hedging in their interpretation and application of law, and for what purposes.

5.4.5.1 The interpretation of law that is not readily applicable

It is assumed that to hear a trial in China is an easier job because the law is mostly available for specific cases, because Mainland China uses civil law and has a detailed written legal system including contract law, family law, patent law, tort law, transportation law, property law, etc. However, legislators obviously cannot legislate on all aspects of social life. Some disputes in the corpus are not addressed by extant litigation.

The plaintiff and defendant in the next case are step-brothers and their respective fathers died a long time ago. They went to court because they could not agree on how to bury their mother. The plaintiff buried the mother next to the tomb of his natural father (also the defendant's step-father). Days later, the defendant exhumed the coffin and buried it in his father's tomb (the mother's first husband). This case was new in litigation; the judges could refer to no similar precedent. The judges consequently took related social norms as the legal basis, as demonstrated in the following text:

> This court holds: When the deceased has a will, the disposition of the body, **normally** (一般情况下**)**, should follow the instructions of the will [...]. [T]his conforms to **general** (一般的) social ethical standards [...]. [**N**]**ormally** this will be supported by law [...]. [W]hen there is no will [...] the disposition of the body should be decided by all direct relatives [...]. [**N**]**ormally** (一般情况下) this will also be supported by law [...]. [A]fter the spouse's death, if the living wife (husband) married again, should she (he), after death, be buried with the ex-spouse or present spouse [...] there no explicit law regulations [...]. [**N**]**ormally** (一般) it should be decided according to the **general** (一般认识标准) social ethical standard [...] (Example text 27, case 21, emphasis added by the present author).

The judges construct a lengthy legal argument in this text to adjudicate on the parties' disposition of their mother's body. Three different legal bases are introduced: the will, the decisions of all direct relatives, and the social ethical standard. Since no will or relatives' decisions were available in this case, the judges decided it according to the social ethical standard. Because the judges' argument here is to rule on an unprecedented dispute, they are expected to feel proud of their handling of it and their comprehensive argument taking the 'social ethical standard' as its legal basis. However, this judges' argument contains three 'normally' and two 'generally' hedges, which suggests that the judges do not intend their decision on appropriate legal bases to be definitive. The use of these five hedges suggests that they express caution in their argument rather than pride[10].

Judges' caution and reluctance to make strong claims are reasonable in the legal context of China. Mainland China's civil law does not explicitly endow judges with the right to create law. Judges must practise care when dealing with unprecedented disputes; otherwise they might be accused of misusing or over-interpreting the law. The best thing they can do in such a situation is to ask for the Supreme People's Court's opinion and then quote this opinion in their judgment. However, it is possible that the Supreme People's Court will withhold an official opinion on a specific dispute because it is not a dispute of social interest, and it is also possible that the Supreme People's Court will return the dispute to the trial judges because of bureaucracy. The judges in this case have to handle the new dispute according to their own analysis and understanding, without reference to the Supreme People's Court's opinions.

The judges use 'normally' and 'generally' to preclude possible challenges proposed by other legal specialists. In order to decide the disposition of a human body, the law explicitly recognizes the will of the deceased, but the other two criteria (the decisions of all direct relatives and the social ethical standard) are not stipulated by law. Using these criteria as legal bases therefore demands reasonable justification. The discussion and comparison of alternative legal bases is a new procedure for the judges who demonstrate in the text a rhetorical distance from their expressed opinions to protect themselves: the judges use 'generally' and 'normally' to indicate exceptions can occur to what they argue.

10 The judges' handling of this case was acknowledged by the Supreme People's Court of the PRC and the judgment of this case was published as official case (案例), i.e. precedent, on the website of the Supreme People's Court of the PRC.

5.4.5.2 The interpretation of law that is readily applicable

In some cases in the corpus, judges do not produce elaborative analyses or arguments when they interpret the law. They very often make the interpretation of law a mechanical and concise process requiring little rhetorical effort. Their normal practice is to directly quote the law, to explain it at a general level without referring to the case, and to apply the law without legal reasoning. This concise process discloses little information about the judges' rationale behind choice of law and the connection between the law and the case. In such situations, the judges' law interpretations are devoid of hedging.

However, some judges in the corpus reject mechanical and concise interpretations of the law in favour of more personal analyses and understanding. In the case below, the plaintiff (a writer) signed a publishing contract with the defendant (a big publishing house in China) to publish his book. Because the book rapidly sold out, the defendant reprinted it without obtaining the plaintiff's further approval and did not pay the plaintiff for the reprinted book. The plaintiff filed a lawsuit for compensation from the defendant, but the defendant argued that the standard terms[11] in their contract entitled him to reprint the book according to the market demand. The judges did not support the defendant's argument, as indicated in the following text:

> This court holds: When interpreting standard terms in contracts, the rights and interests of the party who does not make the contract should be considered first and the standard terms should be interpreted in ways that are, **as much as possible** (可能平均合理), reasonable, at the same time, fair to the contractors [...] standard terms are made by one not two parties, so specific clauses are**, possibly** (可能会), written by the contract maker for its own benefits; particularly, the contract maker**, possibly** (可能会), will use or insert vague expressions to harm the other parties' interests [...] (Example text 28, case, 8, emphasis added by the present author).

11 These terms are not negotiated by the two parties. They are prepared by one party only and then presented to the other party for approving and signing.

The law being interpreted in this text is as follows:

> Article 41: If a dispute over the understanding of the standard terms occurs, it shall be interpreted according to **normal understanding**. Where there are two or several kinds of interpretation, the interpretation unfavorable to the party supplying the standard terms shall be preferred. Where the standard terms are inconsistent with non-standard terms, the latter shall be adopted. (Emphasis added by the present author). *The Contract Law of PRC, 1999*

Article 41 of the Contract Law of the PRC regulates the interpretation of standard terms in a contract. The imprecise expression 'normal understanding' indicates a legitimate ground for the judges' personal analysis and discussion of how the standard terms should be interpreted. Other parts of Article 41 are precisely and unambiguously drafted and should not create difficulty for judges' interpretation and application of it. Two ways standard terms should be interpreted are clearly given: 'where there are two or several kinds of interpretation, the interpretation unfavourable to the party supplying the standard terms shall be preferred' and 'where the standard terms are inconsistent with non-standard terms, the latter shall be adopted'.

However, the judges in the example text above go beyond a simple interpretation of Article 41. Rather, they supply a detailed analysis for the legitimacy of the two ways of interpreting the standard terms: 'particular clauses are', 'possibly', 'written by the contract maker for its own benefits'; 'particularly, the contract maker, possibly, will use or insert vague expressions to harm the other parties' interests'. This interpretation of legislators' intent may be common to judges in common law countries as suggested by studies like Solan (2005) and Tiersma (2001), but the analysis of the corpus reveals that it is quite extraordinary in Chinese litigation practice. Even in this text, the judges do it in a cautious way, namely using the hedging 'as much as possible' to claim there are exceptions to their analysis and to preclude potential challenges against their own interpretation of standard terms.

A detailed legal analysis of the above text might suggest that it is written not only for the present trial; the judges may have other intentions as well. This judgment was produced by the *Haidian People's*

Court in Beijing by the head judge of the collegiate bench, *Song Yushui*. The analysis of section 4.4.3.3 in Chapter 4 identified that 'Haidian People's Court is the distinguished court of the PRC and trusted by the government and People and presents a positive image of the People's Court and People's judges in public'. The special status of *Haidian People's Court* is acknowledged by the Supreme People's Court who has appointed it to be an example court for the whole PRC judicial system to follow. *Haidian People's Court* not only decides specific disputes, but is expected to provide an exemplar in litigation practices for other Chinese courts.

Moreover, the judges in the text above are able to write their judgment more argumentatively, as advocated by the Supreme People's Court. The head judge of the collegiate bench is *Song Yushui*, who is also the chief judge of intellectual trials in *Haidian People's Court*. She has been recognized as an exemplar judge by the Supreme People's Court and even writes a column in Mainland China's most comprehensive and authoritative law website <www.chinacourt.org/zhuanti1/songyushui/>, accessed at 2010/10/1, which is co-hosted by the Supreme Court and the Central Government of the PRC. One aspect of *Song*'s professional competence that has been constantly stressed is her excellent combination of professional and academic competence. In addition to being a qualified judge, she has published a number of academic journal papers which have contributed much to the discussion of controversial issues such as vagueness of contract terms, methods of mediation, comparison of legal cultures, and cultural influences on litigation practices. Her articles are widely read by Chinese legal specialists and her judgments are frequently referred to by other judges when deciding similar cases. *Song* occupies a special position from which she is allowed and, more importantly, required to interpret law in a more argumentative way. Her interpretations can therefore read more like academic essays than simple mechanical applications of law. This is because she has to illustrate for legal specialists, i.e., lawyers and judges, how and why laws should be interpreted.

5.4.5.3 The application of law

This section supplies more examples of judges' use of hedging devices in the *Judges' Opinions* move. Judges interpret law in order to apply the law to analyzing facts and evidence. The facts identified in litigation do not necessarily identify what actually happened in the past. They are collaboratively constructed during the court trial by the plaintiffs, defendants and judges. The judges will base their analysis of the parties' descriptions of facts on the interpreted law and on their own professional competence, which is indicated by the use of hedging in their writing. The case below has been discussed in the previous analysis. The plaintiff (an actor) sued the two defendants (an actress and a newspaper) because his reputation had been damaged by defendant A's (the actress's) erroneous statement published in defendant B's (the newspaper's) report. The judges ruled Defendant B was innocent because it had faithfully report A's statement, as indicated below:

> This court holds: The reports of *Chengdu Business Times* (defendant B) on the disputed sexual scandal […] are, **basically, true** (基本真实) […] its reports on X's (defendant A) statements […] are, **basically, true** (基本真实) […] (Example text 25, case 2, emphasis added by the present author).

The judges in this text analyze the truthfulness of Defendant B's report. It is held that Defendant B's report includes no distortion and exaggeration in its report of A's statement. This is an important fact because, if accepted, it will absolve Defendant B or responsibility, but the judges do not report this affirmatively. The two uses of 'basically true' indicate the judges' intention to give mitigated, rather than affirmative conclusions.

Strongly affirmative expressions like 'true' and 'completely true' are not preferred for practical reasons: the propositional meaning carried is too absolute and it can be falsified easily by Defendant A. For example, she can point out any potential linguistic inconsistencies between what she said and what was reported in the newspaper. The judges ruled Defendant B innocent of the charge not because the publication reported the exact words uttered by Defendant A, but because it faithfully reported what was meant by Defendant A. The hedged expression 'basically true' sufficiently expresses the judges' understanding and countermands possible future challenges by defendant A.

The judges' application of law sometimes requires an analysis of the parties' burden of proof and evidence. Judges need to decide whether the parties have appropriately fulfilled their burden of proof and produced sufficient evidence supporting their arguments. It is true that evidence should be objective, whose acceptance is a clear-cut yes or no question, but the burden of proof and the proving power of specific evidence needs to be analyzed and compared. Hedging normally appears in the judges' analysis and comparison of the parties' evidence and their burden of proof.

In the following case, the plaintiff (a design company) claimed that its patent was illegally used by the defendant (a construction company) in a project; the defendant argued that the technology being used in its (the defendant's) project was not the plaintiff's patented technology. Both the plaintiff and the defendant provided the court with evidence. The plaintiff provided the court with its patent documents supporting its claims, while the defendant provided only narrative evidence. In reality, the defendant could have provided more convincing evidence e.g. authentic documents of its own project. These project documents were potentially even more convincing than the plaintiff's patent document because they were an official record of the disputed on-going project. The defendant's refusal to supply these project reports unnecessarily complicated the court trial and rendered inaccessible the alternative narrative evidence.

The following text is the judges' analysis of the parties' burden of proof:

> This court holds: The plaintiff has, **preliminarily, proved** (初步证明了) the defendant […] used the disputed patent. The defendant has the duty and is, **comparatively more easily, able** (且更容易举证) to provide authentic evidence, so it (the defendant) should bear the results of not providing these evidence […] (Example text 26, case 20, emphasis added by the present author).

Hedging occurs twice in this text extract. The judges use it to directly analyze and compare the two parties' burden of proof and their fulfilment of the burden of proof. The defendant in this case did not make direct evidence available (authentic project documents), and the defendant's unknown motive for refusing to supply them legitimately allowed the judges to use the available indirect evidence (the plaintiff's patent documents) to decide 'the plaintiff has preliminarily proved' and to decide 'the defendant has the duty and is, comparatively more easily, able to provide authentic evidence'. The judges use 'preliminarily' to indicate their decision that the evidence produced by the plaintiff is sufficient to support his argument, and use 'comparatively more easily' to decide that the defendant should bear a greater burden of proof.

'Preliminarily' and 'comparatively' therefore not only mitigate the judges' personal commitment towards their argument, but also modify the argument's propositional meaning, which is a same case in the judges' analysis of facts above. The judges use hedging not only when it provides a safe opportunity to demonstrate their professional expertise and competence (they need not make unintended and easily challenged strong claims), but also when specific situations require this. Hedging is optional in the former situation but required in latter.

5.5 Conclusion

As an important legal genre, civil judgments officially close the litigation and decide the respective rights and obligations of the parties who submit their dispute to the court. The authoritative nature of this genre requires the language used to be clear, precise and unambiguous, and to supply the parties with an enforceable judgment. These three language requirements are magnified when judges have to use various numerical expressions to discuss temporal and monetary issues in the moves *Parties' Arguments* and *Judges' Arguments*, because even minor problems in these numerical expressions can create great reading difficult for specialist and non-specialist readers. Such reading difficulty is investigated and analyzed by Sun and Gao (2007, p. 35).

In order to decide the respective rights and obligations of the parties, judges must demonstrate their understanding and analysis of the parties' dispute, particularly, the countervailing tension between their views. They must also choose and interpret the law appropriately to build the legal basis for litigation. This tension explains why the parties undergo expensive and lengthy litigation proceedings. A clear understanding of the tension between the parties' views is therefore important for judges to capture the essence of the dispute, as demonstrated by the close connection between the *Plaintiffs' Claim* and the *Defendants' Defence* steps. The law in Mainland China stipulates that judges must attempt to mediate parties' disputes before they officially go to trial (Article 9 and 155, *the Civil Procedural Law of the People's Republic of China, 1991*). Only when the tension between the parties is so tight that it cannot be mediated will judges litigate and decide.

Although Mainland China has a comprehensive and systematic system of law, judges' building of legal bases for litigation is seldom simple, as indicated by the use of emphatics and hedging in the move *Judges' Opinions*. Judges may encounter difficulties when the law is general and imprecise and when no applicable laws govern new disputes. Judges need to decide specific ways to particularize general and imprecise law or find alternative authorities on which to build the legal basis for litigation, which requires considerable legal and rhetorical effort.

Chapter 6

Coherence in Civil Judgments

6.1 Introduction

This chapter looks at coherence in the step *Plaintiffs' Claim*, the step *Defendants' Defence*, and the move *Judges' Opinions* in civil judgments. By coherence, the researcher means the features of texts that enable readers to acquire a plausible and an intelligible comprehension and understanding of texts (Swales, 1990b; van Dunne, 1996). Coherence analysis of civil judgments is important in this research because civil judgments handle the parties' personal and property rights. A basic requirement for civil judgments is to supply a coherent reading for specialist and non-specialist readers; a basic requirement for judges is 'to avoid errors or misleading points in their writing' (Wang, 2009, p. 71). The following section attempts to study the judges' writing in civil judgments from the perspective of coherence, with particular attention paid to discovering how judges organize specific moves/steps in civil judgments, what specific mechanisms judges use to link individual sentences into a coherent text, how judges' writing can be read coherently, what knowledge is needed to reach this coherent understanding, and who has such knowledge.

6.2 Coherence in the step *Plaintiffs' Claim*

Judges recontextualize the plaintiffs' arguments in the *Plaintiffs' Claim* step by reporting the plaintiffs':

- description of facts,
- description of suffering, and
- claims of compensation.

The plaintiffs' claim for compensation is typically recontextualized into one single sentence in this step, so a complicated coherence analysis is unnecessary. The following analytical focus addresses the coherence of judges' recontextualization of the plaintiff's description of facts and suffering. Judges' coherent writing in *Plaintiffs' Claims* is important because it implicitly includes a brief report of legal facts, as demonstrated in the analysis of Chapter 4. A better understanding of this step is helpful for the understanding of other moves/steps in civil judgments. In the corpus, some judges use narrative stories in this step, aiming at telling how the parties' dispute has developed and in what way the plaintiffs' rights are infringed by the defendants, while others simply list the plaintiffs' main arguments. For the purpose of this research, the researcher names the narrative stories as plot-driven texts and the list of arguments as point-driven texts. Plot-driven texts report stories about the parties' dispute by supplying as much detail as possible. Point-driven texts do not tell narrative stories but report the plaintiffs' main arguments with regard to the facts and claims. The research finds that both plot-driven texts and point-driven texts appear in the judges' recontextualization of the plaintiffs' factual description, while point-driven texts only appear in their recontextualization of the plaintiffs' description of suffering.

6.2.1 Plot-driven texts in the judges' recontextualization of the plaintiffs' factual description

The judges use both plot-driven texts and point-driven texts to recontextualize the plaintiffs' description of facts, but for different case types. Plot-driven texts are used when the parties in cases constitute individuals and the cases involve less specialized areas, like neighbourhood disputes, customer rights, and family issues. Point-driven texts are used when the parties in cases constitute companies or organizations and the cases involve more specialized areas, like contract, copyright, patent, maritime, and insurance law. The analysis below examines plot-driven texts. Point-driven texts are examined in the subsequent section.

Judges use plot-driven texts to reconstruct chronologically the occurrence and development of the parties' dispute. The texts used have an identifiable beginning, development, and ending, and include a number of detailed time and place modifications. The reader can follow the reported story and reach a coherent understanding of the plaintiff's description of the facts. The case below was discussed in the previous analysis. The plaintiff (a passenger) lost property he was carrying when he travelled on a bus managed by the defendant. He held the defendant responsible for his loss, as demonstrated in the following text:

> The plaintiff claimed: August 29, 2006, the plaintiff, **carrying** his father's ashes, **got on** the bus (G07788) managed by the defendant from Lanzhou to Zhangye. Upon the defendant's request, the plaintiff **put** the casket holding his father's ashes into the bus' lower luggage hold. On the morning of August 30, after the defendants' bus arrived in Zhangye, the plaintiff **got off** the bus only **to find** the casket was gone. Following the defendant's advice, the plaintiff **circulated** notices and **went back and forth** from Lanzhou to Zhangye to find the casket. His effort was vain and he **had to pay** expensive transportation and boarding fees. (Example text 29, case 18 emphasis added by the present author)

The story recounted in this text includes sufficient detail to enable readers to see a sequential development of the disputed incident. Coherence in the text is achieved by the consistent linguistic arrangement: all sentences are active and declarative and most contain 'the plaintiff' as an actor. The verbs in individual sentences indicate a number of crucial moments in the development of the incident: 'carrying (his father's ashes) – got on – put (the casket) – got off – find (the casket was gone) – following (the defendants' advices) – circulated – went back and forth – (his effort) was (vain) – had to pay (fees)'. These verbs act as a chain holding together the four stages of the incident: 1, he ('the plaintiff ') carried his father's ashes and got on the defendants' bus; 2, he got off the bus and found the casket holding his father's ashes had gone; 3, he followed the defendants' advice ('circulated notices, went back and forth') to look for the lost casket; 4, his effort was in vain and cost him much money.

The judges use this text to identify the plaintiff's attempt to attribute blame. The plaintiff's father's ashes were lost because the defendant had not fulfilled his duty of as a carrier, and the plaintiff's subsequent search effort was in vain because of the defendant's improper advice. Although the text is the plaintiff's description of facts, it reports only the plaintiff's experiences and suffering and introduces nothing specific about the defendant's action. This could imply that the plaintiff lacked solid evidence to attribute responsibility to the defendant; he would otherwise have used such evidence to support his claims. The plaintiff's imprecise and general attribution of his suffering to the defendant ('upon the defendant's request' and 'following the defendant's advice') reinforces this assumption of insufficient evidence.

Commenting on judges' non-specialized writing of everyday disputes, one specialist informant made the following statement:

> It is common for me and my colleagues to handle a variety of everyday disputes in litigation, such as neighbours' quarrels, minor road accidents, minor personal injuries, and so on. In our report and discussion of these disputes, the purpose of writing is more than simply reporting a story of these incidents. Every sentence carries our professional understanding and analysis of a particular factual or legal issue. There might be slight rhetorical differences among our choices, but it is true that we all believe that the discussion of disputes, specialized or everyday, should be strategically arranged for case-specific purposes. (Excerpt 10, lawyer D)

The judges' recontextualization in this text achieves high coherence because all sentences contain the same subject ('the plaintiff') and because the choice of verbs is consistent and they are arranged chronologically. The judges limit distraction, i.e. no inclusion of other subjects, for specialist and non-specialist readers and discuss no legalized concepts and issues. Readers can thus easily acquire the intended coherent understanding. However, it cannot be concluded that the judges' recontextualization here requires no rhetorical or legal effort, which is evidenced by the neat and careful arrangement of subjects and verbs. Gao categorized and explained such legal writing strategies (2009, p. 198). This text is written in a plot-driven manner because the judges particularly desire a highly readable civil judgment for the benefit of non-specialist readers, and furthermore because the parties' dispute is not about specialized matters and is quite familiar for non-specialists. The rhetoric in this text is in fact as legalized as other sections of the same civil judgment, though in a slightly different way. The judges use each sentence to report one aspect of their understanding and analysis of the plaintiffs' factual description.

6.2.2 Point-driven texts in the judges' recontextualization of the plaintiffs' factual description

As demonstrated by the analysis in Chapter 5 (section 5.4), the plaintiffs can discuss in their description of facts:

- the plaintiffs themselves, or
- the defendants, or
- both the plaintiffs and the defendants.

Of course, there are different reasons for a particular choice. When the plaintiffs discuss both the defendants' and their own actions, the plaintiffs may fully understand how the dispute arose and developed, and they can further support it with evidence. When the plaintiffs discuss themselves only, they may lack a clear understanding of the defendants' actions or they may lack evidence to prove it. When the plaintiffs discuss the defendants only, it is possible that they have solid evidence to substantiate their claims against the defendant, which may be sufficient to persuade the judges. Although theoretically possible, plaintiffs seldom include their own faults and only discuss the defendant's in their description of the facts. It is self-evident that plaintiffs will not go to litigation if they themselves have faults. The previous section considered the plaintiffs' discussion of themselves, so this section will consider the discussion of both parties, i.e. both the plaintiffs and defendants, and their discussion of the defendants only.

6.2.2.1 The discussion of both the plaintiffs and the defendants

The step *Plaintiffs' Claim* uses point-driven texts to report the plaintiffs' factual description when the case involves specialized areas such as 'maritime', 'contract', 'patent', 'insurance', and 'copyright' law. Judges' normal practice in these cases is to identify and report the plaintiffs' important arguments, which produces a text consisting of a list of arguments, rather than the narrative story previously considered. In the case below, the plaintiff and the defendant signed a contract to establish a joint-investment corporation. After signing the contract, the defendant refused to fulfil his contractual duty, which made the plaintiff suffer a great loss. The plaintiff's description of facts is given below:

> The plaintiff X claimed: **X,** on September 25, 2001, **signed** a co-operation contract with **Y and Z**. **Y and Z** offer their land as a part of the investment, **X takes care of** (负责) other investment and they will collaboratively **manage** the land (32.4 *mu*) of *West Tiantong Yuan*. **X** has **done** a large amount of preparation work for the contract and **entrusted** a very experienced and qualified technical-service provider with much of the preparatory technical work. **Y and Z refused** to fulfil their contract duties, **refused** to provide the ownership certificate, and **signed** a new contract with another company at much lower price on April 12, 2002 which brought a loss to X. (Example text 30, case 16, emphasis added by the present author)

Non-specialist readers may find this text less easy to understand because it discusses the specialized content of contract law and because the connections between sentences are not easily identifiable. The judges' use of verbs does not seem to contribute to a coherent reading: 'signed – use land – takes care of – have done – [...] – refused'. Non-specialist readers have no easy way to detect the logical connection among these verbs, although individual sentences containing these verbs are largely intelligible.

The judges here cohere their writing with other rhetorical devices, namely, the choice of sentence topics. In order to understand the text coherently, the reader should examine how individual sentence topics are chosen and how they can be connected, which is conducted through the examination of themes. Theme, according to Halliday and Matthiessen, is 'the point of departure', which indicates the topic of the sentence; the other part of a sentence is rheme (2004, p. 64). In this research, the words and phrases beginning Chinese sentences are taken as themes and what follows are taken as rhemes. The examination of themes helps to identify the writer's main arguments in specific texts and their considerations in organizing these texts. In the text above, the judges carefully choose and arrange the topics of individual sentences in order to provide a coherent structure in their writing. This coherent structure can be captured by the following re-organization of this text:

(sentence 1) **X** signed co-operation contract with **Y and Z**.
(sentence 2) **Y and Z** offer [...],
(sentence 3) **X** takes care of [...]
(sentence 4) **they** (**X, Y and Z**) will collaboratively [...]
(sentence 5) **X** has done a large amount of preparation work [...]
(sentence 6) **Y and Z** refused to fulfil [...]

In this re-organization, the themes and rhemes of individual sentences establish two vertical chains: *X-X-X* and *Y and Z – (X) Y and Z – Y and Z*. This textual re-organization reveals that judges do make rhetorical effort to construct their writing. The plaintiff (*X*) and the defendant (*Y and Z*) appear interchangeably. Each description related to the plaintiff is followed by a contrasting description related to the defendant. Drawing on the content of this text, the first four sentences are found to supply a general description of the disputed contract, and the last two sentences establish the contrast between the parties' intentions to fulfil their respective contractual duties.

Sentence 1 is the topic sentence of the whole text because it is the place where the judges introduce the parties (*X* and *Y and Z*) and the dispute ('co-operation contract'). Sentences 2, 3 and 4 report the content of the disputed contract. Sentence 2 reports the defendants' major duties in establishing and managing the joint company, and sentence 3 reports the plaintiff's duty. Since the dispute occurred at the beginning of the parties' attempt to implement the contract, their rights in management are not reported in detail; rather, they are contracted into one concise sentence (sentence 4).

Sentences 5 and 6 go beyond simple reporting and tacitly attribute blame to the defendant. From a linguistic perspective, the theme of sentence 5 is *X*, and the theme of sentence 6 is *Y and Z*. The connection between the two themes, already built in sentence 1, indicates the judges' intention to compare them. This linguistic understanding of coherence is imprecise in the sense that it cannot explain the actual realization of responsibility attribution. To realize the plaintiff's implicit blame, one needs to consider the content of the two sentences including 'preparation work, the contract, entrusted, experienced and qualified technical-service provider, preparatory technical work, fulfil their contractual duties', and 'provide the ownership certificate (of the land)'. Further, one needs to notice the contrast between the plaintiff ('X has done a large amount of preparatory work') and the defendants ('Y and Z refused to fulfil, refused to provide, and signed a new contract with another company'). The implied conclusion is that the plaintiff expended much effort to implement the contract only to find the defendant had made this implementation impossible. The judges have carefully chosen and aranged the sentence topics (themes) to produce a coherent recontextualization of the plaintiffs' description of the facts. This coherent contextualization exactly reflects the plaintiff's private intention (Bhatia, 2004, p. 145) of blame and his public intention of describing facts according to his understanding. This provides more evidence suggesting that the highly standardized and structured genre of civil judgments still affords considerable room for specialists' manipulations and variations.

6.2.2.2 The discussion of the defendants only

Some plaintiffs discuss only the defendants in their description of facts because they believe they have sufficient evidence to prove their innocence and the defendants' faults. For example, the plaintiffs' rights may be unknowingly infringed by defendants, for example copyright being unknowingly infringed, patent rights being illegally infringed, and property being stolen. In such cases the plaintiffs are 'inactive'; their rights are passively infringed so there is nothing to state about their actions. Although it is possible that the plaintiffs may have failed to exercise reasonable attention to prevent the occurrence of the dispute, they are allowed to overlook this and focus on the discussion of the defendant only, on condition that they speak truthfully and without distorting the facts.

In the case below, the plaintiff was a famous writer in Mainland China and a number of his novels were very popular in the 1980s and 1990s. The defendants (Y and Z) published and distributed a collection of the plaintiff's novels. They did not ask for the plaintiff's authorization for this publication and did not pay the plaintiff until he filed this lawsuit. The following example text is the judges' recontextualization with regard to the plaintiff's description of facts:

> The plaintiff claimed: **Defendant Y**, in April 2004, distributed a **novel collection which was published by defendant Z. 30 novels in this collection** were authored by the plaintiff. **Defendant Z** collected and published these novels without the plaintiff's authorization and did not pay. **The titles, choices and arrangements of these novels** do not conform to the plaintiff's wish. The **defendants' actions** infringed the plaintiff's lawful copyrights (rights to use and rights to be paid) over his created works and brought material and mental suffering to the plaintiff. (Example text 31, case 14, emphasis added by the present author)

This is a typical point-driven text containing no narrative elements. The verbs in individual sentences demonstrate how judges use each sentence of this text to report different aspects of the defendants' tortious (law-breaking) actions. The judges' effort to write coherently in this text is demonstrated in the re-organization below:

(sentence1)	Defendant Y **distributed** [...]
(**sentence2**)	30 novels in this collection were **authored** by the plaintiff [...]
(sentence3)	Defendant Z **collected and published** [...]
(sentence4)	(it) **did not pay** [...]
(**sentence5**)	The titles, choices and arrangements of these novels **do not conform** [...]
(sentence6)	The defendants' actions **infringed** [...] **and brought** [...] **suffering to** the plaintiff

A careful reading reveals that four sentences (sentences 1, 3, 4, and 6) out of the six discuss the defendants' actions and the other two (sentences 2 and 5) discuss the plaintiff's actions. The consistent choices of simple and active sentences in reporting the defendants' actions are direct and unambiguous, indicating the judges' understanding of the plaintiff's intention to attribute blame. However, the discussion of the plaintiff is textualized by two passive sentences (sentences 2 and 5). The inanimate subjects of these two sentences ('30 novels in this collection', and 'the titles, choices and arrangements of these novels') keep the consistent choice of the defendants as sentence subjects; it implies that the plaintiff was thoroughly dissatisfied with the defendant's edition of his novels.

If sentences 2 and 5 are changed into active voices by positioning the plaintiff as subject, the intended rhetorical effect will be changed. This may not influence the propositional meaning of this text, but the plaintiff's intention of attributing blame, as reflected in the judges' recontextualization, will be mitigated. Each individual sentence in the text above reports a specific aspect of the defendants' tortious (law-breaking) actions. For example, sentence 1 reports that Defendant Y distributed the pirated collections to earn a profit; sentence 2 states that the novels published by Z were actually written by the plaintiff, and sentence 5 reports the disputed collection edited the plaintiff's novels without the plaintiff's authorization. The consistent choice of the defendants-related theme and the consistent choice of action verbs demonstrate the judges' legal analysis of the plaintiff's description of facts and reflect their effort to produce a readable and coherent recontextualization of this description.

It can be seen here that the judges' refusal to use the plaintiff as themes also indicates that they recognize the plaintiff's intention to show his innocence in the dispute: the cited actions of the defendant break the law and bring suffering to the plaintiffs. When the plaintiffs discuss only defendants in their description of facts, the judges' recontextualization of this description in civil judgments also concentrates on the defendants only. If it is necessary to discuss the plaintiffs in a number of places, judges will introduce the plaintiffs as the rheme of the passive sentences used. This not only keeps a consistent and coherent choice of themes (sentence topics), but also stresses the plaintiffs intention to describe themselves as victims and the defendants as wrong-doers.

6.2.3 Point-driven texts in the judges' recontextualization of the plaintiff's description of suffering

In the step *Plaintiffs' Claim*, the judges also recontextualize the plaintiff's description of suffering. In addition to giving a direct description of their suffering, plaintiffs normally report a causal relationship between their suffering and the defendants' actions. The plaintiffs' writing focuses on the causal relationship, not on their the suffering, which is reflected in the judges' recontextualization. The case below is the previously cited food safety case. The plaintiff had dinner in the defendant's restaurant and became seriously ill after eating improperly cooked food. The plaintiff's description of suffering is recontextualized by the judges as below:

Since the this incident, the plaintiff not only **suffered** great body pains and the side effects of medical treatments, but also **suffered** mental distress because of […].		*Description of suffering*
Subsequent inspection proved the defendants' improper cooking methods […] were the actual reason why this **serious public health incident** happened […].	*Sentence 1*	*Causal relationship between the suffering and the defendant's action*
The defendant **was** the **food provider** and he **should be** the **person in full charge of the food safety**; it **is** food providers' legal obligation to ensure the safety and hygiene of food served to customers.	*Sentence 2*	
In this case, the defendant's **wrong-doings caused** the plaintiff's suffering and **seriously harmed** the plaintiff's health and mental right.	*Sentence 3*	

Table 6.1. The plaintiffs' description of suffering in the step *Plaintiffs' Claim* (Example text 32, case 19, author's emphasis added).

Certain textual features make this text highly specialized and legalized. For example, there is no instance of language of doing (Halliday, 1989, p. 7) and no personal referring expressions, except 'the plaintiff' and 'the defendant'; other referring expressions are all general like 'subsequent inspection', 'improper cooking methods', and 'wrong-doings'. The heavy use of language of thinking suggests that what is discussed in the text is specialized (Bhatia, 1993, p. 161) and the result of the judges' professional thinking and analysis.

The above table suggests that judges make much rhetorical effort in their recontextualization. This text has a coherent internal structure, including a direct description of the plaintiff's suffering and a report of the causal relationship between the suffering and the defendant' action. The judges devote the majority of the textual space to the reported causal relationship. The use of referring expressions indicates that the three sentences (1, 2, and 3) are not parallel, but are structured from general to particular. Each of these sentences refers to the defendant's action with a different nominal expression, 'serious public health incident', 'the person in full charge of the food safety' and 'the defendant's wrong-doings'. The change of referring nominal expressions represents a successful completion of attributing blame to the defendant. Firstly, the judges use 'serious public health incident' to directly define the legal nature of the defendant's action, which not only infringed the plaintiff's right but also infringed the social interest. If accepted, this is a sufficient reason for the judges to award higher compensation.

Secondly, after broadly defining the defendant's action, the judges continue to discuss the defendant's responsibility ('the person in full charge of food safety'), which recontextualizes the plaintiff's argument that the defendant should be held responsible for the whole incident, regardless of excuses. The defendant is the restaurant manager and responsible for food safety in the restaurant. Even if a third party such as a food supplier may have caused this food safety incident, the defendant still bears shared responsibility to compensate the plaintiff, who may initiate another lawsuit for compensation against the supplier. Thirdly, the judges conclude this section with 'the defendant's wrong-doings [...] infringed the plaintiff's health and mental rights'. Without the proper support of the first two sentences, this conclusion cannot stand.

It can be seen that the judges' recontextualization in this text is carefully structured. Every sentence is coherently connected by logic and reasoning, rather than explicit cohesive devices like anaphoric or conjunctive expressions. The judges' writing here demonstrates their legal and rhetorical effort in analyzing and synthesizing the plaintiff's description of suffering and his report of the causal relationship between the suffering and the defendant's action. The realization of the judges' such writing effort is necessary for specialist and non-specialist readers to read the above text coherently and to become familiar with the discussed field and law.

6.3 Coherence in the step *Defendants' Defence*

No judges in the corpus use plot-driven texts to recontextualize the defendants' arguments in the step *Defendants' Defences*, whether the defendants argue against the plaintiffs' description of facts or against their claims. The judges usually concentrate on the points on which the defendants have a different understanding and explain this accordingly. As discussed in chapter 5 (section 5.3.2), the judges arrange the *Plaintiffs' Claim* and the *Defendants' Defence* steps closely. Although both the plaintiffs and defendants may supply their respective understandings of the disputed facts, the judges do not recontextualize them separately in the *Plaintiffs' Claims* and *Defendants' Defence* steps. Rather, they analyze and synthesize both parties' understandings and recontextualize them in the *Plaintiffs' Claim* step, which is the professional convention. A coherent reading of the Defendants' Defence step thus requires readers to identify the close connection between these two steps.

Since the judges report neither the facts identified by the judges nor the defendants, they seldom write plot-driven stories of the parties' dispute in this step. The judges' writing in this step only reports their analysis of the defendants' arguments, including the main points and the points where the defendants disagree with the plaintiffs' claim. The judges writing usually itemizes these points, giving considerable linguistic coherence[12]. However, specialist and non-specialist readers may not easily recognize the discursive coherency between reported points because the judges seem to assume readers can place these individual reported points coherently into a context they have presupposed in their writing. The judges' presupposition of contextual knowledge in judgments is discussed in White (1995), Zhang (1999) and Su (2001a). If specialist or non-specialist readers cannot retrieve the presupposed contextual knowledge, they have no way to understand coherently the judges' writing in this step. Judges presuppose both social knowledge and legal knowledge when they write the

12 In order to study the coherence of the move *Judges' Opinions*, the researcher draws on the discussion of coherence in Chapter 3 and proposes two levels coherence: the linguistic coherence and the discursive coherence. In this research, linguistic coherence means that a text is logically organized through cohesive devices. Discursive coherence means a linguistically coherent text appropriately fulfills the purpose required by the situation. For example, the move *Judges' Opinions* is meant to adequately disclose judges' reasoning process. When the judges' writing in this move, possibly a linguistically coherent text, is constructed in a too broad and imprecise way and cannot sufficiently disclose the judges' reasoning process, it is of low discursive coherence.

Defendants' Defence step in specific cases. The following two sections study what difficulty the presupposed social and legal knowledge can create for specialist and non-specialist readers when they try to capture the discursive coherence of this step.

6.3.1 The judges' presupposition of social knowledge

This section draws on a typical case where the parties' dispute occurs in everyday life and which can be understood by non-specialist readers if given proper explanation of the involved social knowledge. In the case quoted below, the plaintiff was scalded by boiling water when she was shopping in a supermarket managed by the defendant. After the incident, the defendant's staff sent the plaintiff to hospital. The plaintiff's injury was so serious that she had to stay in the hospital for several months, which brought physical and emotional suffering to the plaintiff. After recovering from the injury, the plaintiff filed a lawsuit requesting compensation. The defendant counter-argued as follows:

> The defendant argued: **1. our company makes a sincere apology** for the loss the plaintiff suffered [...]. The damages claimed by plaintiff are real, but the occurrence of the incident is not all in agreement with the plaintiff's arguments [...]. [T]he plaintiff should also bear some responsibility for her own suffering. **2. After the accident, we sent** the plaintiff to the chemist's and hospital, thus we have fulfilled the duty [...]. **3. We are willing to compensate the plaintiff's reasonable loss**, but she must provide evidence for any claimed compensation [...]. The claimed transportation fees should be proved by official receipts [...] we do not accept the claimed nutrition fees because there is no testimony from the medical unit [...] (Example text 33, case 22).

The judges' recontextualization in this text is concise and itemized and presupposes some social knowledge, a coherent understanding of which requires specialist and non-specialist readers to restore the presupposed social knowledge. The three topic sentences emphasized in this text argue against the plaintiff's claim not through verbal arguments but through reports of the defendant's actions ('our company makes a sincere apology – after the incident we sent – we are willing to compensate the plaintiff's reasonable loss'). These three actions are simple to understand, but capturing the coherent connection among them requires some effort.

The action 'makes a sincere apology' indicates that the defendant acknowledges some responsibility for the plaintiff's suffering. The social knowledge presupposed here is that an oral apology, although necessary, is seldom sufficient for serious mistakes; material remedies are also needed, such as the immediate cessation of the harmful action, the restoration of recoverable damages, the replacement of destroyed property, and financial compensation. The defendant's action in this case brought serious physical and mental suffering to the plaintiff, who expected the defendant to take appropriate action beyond a verbal apology. Two further remedies are reported in this text. The immediate remedial action taken by the defendant was to send the injured plaintiff to hospital for treatment. The subsequent remedy was the defendant's promise to compensate the plaintiff's reasonable loss. The two remedies, plus the apology, are sufficient to atone for the defendant's mistake. By demonstrating that all these actions were taken willingly, the judges indicate the defendant's understanding that the plaintiff should not have filed the lawsuit in the first place, since he had already been properly dealt with.

The judges' recontextualization in this text also carries the defendant's intention to avoid blame. While 'a sincere apology' shows the defendant's acknowledgement of the plaintiff's blame, 'the plaintiff should also bear some responsibility for her own suffering' shows his effort in avoiding it. The contrast and co-existence between the initial acknowledgment and the subsequent avoidance in this short text suggest that the judges are able to capture clearly the defendant's main argument and his background intention. The acknowledgement of responsibility comes first because it indicates that the defendant is a socially responsible company taking responsibility for its mistake. Of course, the defendant does not abrogate his lawful right to avoid unreasonable blame: 'are willing to compensate the plaintiff's reasonable loss' means he would not accept any claim without proper supporting evidence.

To conclude, the judges' recontextualization of the defendant's arguments in this text achieves conciseness through three clearly itemized points. While the linguistic coherence in this point-driven text is easy to capture, its discursive coherence is difficult to capture not only because specialist and non-specialist readers must refer to the step *Plaintiffs' Claim* in the same judgment for necessary background information (facts of this case) but also because the judges have presupposed some social knowledge in their point-driven writing. In order to understand the coherent connection between the three recontextualized points/arguments, readers have to retrieve the social knowledge presupposed by the judges. For example, they should know how people who make mistakes should behave and should make remedies for victims and should know a company in today' highly commercialized world can use any opportunities, even its mistakes in litigation, to construct its public image of being socially responsible. Such knowledge may not be legally specialized, but it requires a clear awareness of the areas where the parties' dispute happens, which is new for outsiders, i.e. specialist and non-specialist readers other than litigation participants, but the judges may know too well through litigation.

6.3.2 The judges' presupposition of legal knowledge

When the cases involve specialized areas like maritime, contract, patent, insurance, copyrights, and administration, the judges' recontextualization of the defendants' arguments may presuppose legal knowledge. In this situation, a coherent understanding of the step *Defendant's Defence* targets specialist readers who have a mastery of the presupposed legal knowledge. In the following case, the defendant was accused of infringing plaintiff's patent. The defendant in the example text provided two major arguments against the plaintiff's:

> The defendant argued: **First, the plaintiff's patent does not possess novelty and inventiveness** and should not be registered as patent. The defendant has applied the Patent Reexamination Board of the State Intellectual Property Office of PRC to declare the invalidity of this patent. **Second, the technology which was ac-**

cused of has material difference with the plaintiff's patent and does not infringe the plaintiff's patented technology. **So,** we require the court to dismiss the plaintiff's claim. (Example text 34, case 15, emphasis added by the present author)

This text consists of two arguments without an explicit connection. In fact, even the individual arguments are difficult to understand because of the highly specialized patent issue. Readers' social knowledge of everyday life is insufficient; specialist knowledge of patent law is presupposed in the judges' writing.

In this text, the discourse marker 'so' indicates both arguments are used by the judges to support the final conclusion ('we require the court to dismiss the plaintiff's claim'), but it is difficult to understand specific questions like why a technology 'which does not possess novelty and inventiveness' cannot 'be registered as a patent', why 'material difference' between the accused technology and the plaintiffs' patent can dismiss the present lawsuit, and why the first argument comes before the second one. Some of these questions concern content, and others rhetoric.

For example, in order to understand the first argument 'the plaintiff's patent does not possess novelty and inventiveness should not be registered as patent', it is necessary to know the related article of the Patent Law of the PRC (2000):

> Article 22: Any invention or utility model for which patent right may be granted must possess **novelty, inventiveness** and **practical applicability**. (Author's emphasis)

This article stipulates the basic properties a technology should have in order to be registered as a patent, which include 'novelty', 'inventiveness' and 'practical applicability'. The absence of any one of these invalidates the technology's patent status. The defendant argues the plaintiff's patent does not possess 'novelty' and 'inventiveness' to challenge the basic legitimacy of the plaintiff's claim.

If the plaintiff's patent does not qualify as a patent, the focus of the trial will shift from whether the court should approve the plaintiff's claim to whether it should annul his patent. This shift is legally sufficient for the court to set the defendant free from the present accusation.

Even if this effort to challenge the legitimacy of the plaintiff's patent is fruitless, the defendant's other arguments will be unharmed. The defendant prepared for this by challenging the plaintiff's specific claims in the second argument ('the technology which was accused of has material difference with the plaintiff's patent and does not infringe the plaintiff's patented technology'). Similarly, understanding of this argument requires a basic knowledge about the scope of patent protection:

> Article 17: [...] The **scope of patent protection** should be determined by **necessary technical features** prescribed [...] including technical features which are equivalent to these necessary features.
> **Equivalent features** refers to technical features which, compared with necessary technical features, use **primarily similar** methods to realize **primarily similar** functions, reaching **primarily similar** results [...]. (*Provisions of Law Application in Patent Dispute Cases, the Supreme People's Court of PRC, 2001*) (*Excerpt 11*)

This article stipulates that the patent protection is decided by the 'necessary technical features'. The 'necessary technical features' include the features registered in the official patent documents and the features ('equivalent features') which are not registered but are similar to the 'necessary technical features'. This doctrine of equivalence is crucial in deciding whether the defendant illegally used the plaintiff's patent. The text shows the defendant attempts to prove the patent was not infringed and the technology he used is not equivalent to the registered 'necessary technical features' of the plaintiff's patent: 'the technology which was accused has material difference with the plaintiff's patent'.

It can be concluded that the two arguments in this point-driven text are not arranged randomly, but coherently connected. The judges use the first argument demonstrating the defendant's attempt to end the lawsuit at an earlier stage. If this is rejected, the second argument is still sufficient to challenge the plaintiff's specific claims. A simple textual reading is not sufficient to achieve this coherent understanding because the judges presuppose some specialized legal knowledge, i.e. the knowledge about patent law. A coherent understanding of the text requires readers to retrieve the presupposed knowledge, which non-specialists may not be able to do.

6.4 Coherence in the move *Judges' Opinions*

The move *Judges' Opinions* is always written in a point-driven way, consisting of the judges' discussions of a number of distinctive yet interconnected issues. In this move, the judges are expected to do three tasks at one time:

- interpreting the law,
- applying the law in relation to the plaintiffs and defendants, and
- giving legal opinions.

These tasks are all intended to be analytical and argumentative, so it is neither desirable nor possible for the judges to tell plot-driven stories in this move. Questions to be studied in this section include how the judges textualize their completion of each of the three tasks, in what way they are coherently connected, what the typical patterns in this connection are, in what sense the patterns vary, and how one can achieve a coherent reading of the text.

The judges' writing in this move is coherent not because the judges have explicitly used cohesive devices but because they complete the three expected tasks appropriately. However, they do not always finish all these tasks in specific cases. When these tasks are completed, the judges' writing is of a higher level of discursive coherence, and when specific tasks are omitted, the judges' writing is of a lower level of discursive coherence.

In order to analyze coherence in this move, the cases in the corpus are divided into three types:

- the plaintiffs win[13] the case,
  - when the defendants break the law,
  - when the defendants breach the contract;

13 In litigation, it is rare to see one specific party, either a plaintiff or a defendant, win the case in all aspects, and it is more common for a party to win in some aspects and to lose in others. As long as the major purpose for which a party initiates or participates in the litigation is realized, one is said to win.

– the defendants win the case,
  – when the plaintiffs' claim is unreasonable,
  – when the plaintiffs' evidence is insufficient;
– neither party wins the case.

As stated earlier, the plaintiffs win the case either because the defendants break the related law or because they breach the disputed contract. The defendants win the case either because the plaintiffs' claim is unreasonable or because the plaintiffs supply insufficient evidence to support their claim. According to the case types and the above tasks to be completed by the judges in the move *Judges' Opinions*, the results of coherence research in this move are reported in the table below:

Case types		**Tasks completed by the judges**	**Tasks omitted by the judges**
The plaintiffs win the case	When the defendants break the law (the defendants' legal liability)	1. The interpretation of law 2. The application of law in relation to the defendants only 3. The judges' legal opinion	1. The application of the law in relation to the plaintiffs
	When the defendants breach the contract (the defendants' contractual liability)	1. The interpretation of law 2. The application of the law in relation to the plaintiffs' claims and the judges' legal opinion 3. The application of the law in relation to the defendants' action and the judges' legal opinion	None
The defendants win the case	When the plaintiffs' claim is unreasonable	1. The application of law in relation to the plaintiffs only (analyzing the facts in relation to the plaintiffs and giving the reason for rejecting the plaintiffs' claim) 2. The judges' legal opinion	1. The interpretation of law 2. The application of law in relation to the defendants
	When the plaintiffs' evidence is insufficient	1. The application of law in relation to the plaintiffs and the judges' legal opinion 2. The application of law in relation to the defendants and the judges' legal opinion	1. The interpretation of law
Neither party wins the case (the parties are decided to be responsible for their respective loss/suffering)		3. The application of law in relation to the party bearing more responsibility and the judges' *legal opinion* 4. The application of law in relation to the party bearing less responsibility and the judges' *legal opinion*	1. The interpretation of law

Table 6.2. Coherence of the judges' writing in the move *Judges' Opinions* in different types of cases.

It can be seen that judges include or omit tasks depending on the nature of the case. The judges do not complete all three tasks in each of the five types of cases. As a result, discursive coherence in the writing varies according to the tasks completed and omitted by the judges. The more tasks are completed in this move, the more coherent the judges' writing is; the more tasks are omitted in this move, the less coherent the judges' writing is. It is further discovered that the omission of specific tasks is usually conventional in all judges' professional practices, but not individual judges' personal preferences. These five types of cases will be studied in the following analysis to examine why judges omit particular tasks in specific cases, how such omissions influence the discursive coherence of judges' writing, and what specific measures judges take to improve the discursive coherence of their writing in this move.

6.4.1 Judges' Opinions: The plaintiffs win the case

The plaintiffs win the case when the judges support their claims and decide that the defendants have broken the related law or breached the disputed contract[14]. Accordingly, the judges need to handle the defendants' legal and contractual liability in the move *Judges' Opinions* of a civil judgment. As discovered in this research, the judges' writing in the move *Judges' Opinions* varies significantly according to the above case types when they handle the defendants' legal liability, while their writing is comparatively consistent when they handle the defendants' contractual liability. In both situations, coherence in the judges' writing is acquired through the co-existence of the conventional three tasks, which are interpreting law, applying the law

14 The involved legal knowledge is that a civil case is either about tort, i.e. law-breaking actions, or about contract. Accordingly, the defendants lose the case either because they harm the plaintiffs' rights with their tortious, i.e. law-breaking actions, or because they breach the contract of which they and the plaintiffs are both parties.

and giving legal opinions, not by the use of explicit cohesive devices. The following section studies judges' efforts to write coherently when they discuss the defendants' legal liability.

6.4.1.1 The judges' discussion of the defendants' legal liability

When judges discuss the defendants' legal liability in the move *Judges' Opinions*, they finish their conventional three tasks in two different ways, as demonstrated in the corpus. Firstly, some judges interpret the law, apply the law to evaluate and analyze the defendants' tortious (law-breaking) action, and finally give legal opinions. The variation appears when the judges give legal opinions, where their opinions may be related to the plaintiffs' claim or related to the defendants' action. Secondly, other judges seem to complete only two of the three conventional tasks: applying the law and giving legal opinions by omitting the interpretation of law. This way of writing is not discursively coherent because specialist and non-specialist readers cannot know the legal basis for the judges' opinions. The opinions thus given are not supported by sufficient explanation and argumentation.

In the following lawsuit, the plaintiff's daughter was murdered by her boyfriend in a hotel managed by the defendant. The murder was not discovered by the defendant until seven days after the plaintiff's daughter had been killed. In this civil lawsuit, the plaintiff claimed the defendant did not fulfil the duty of a hotel manager by failing to prevent the murder from happening and by failing to discover the murder at an earlier time. The following text illustrates how the judges interpret the law and use the law to analyze the defendant's duty:

<table>
<tr><td>This court holds: If **damaging results** are caused by **a third party**'s tortious (law-breaking) action, **the person who** has responsibility to protect the victim's safety should bear responsibility to the extent that **he** can prevent or stop the damaging action.</td><td colspan="2">*The interpretation of law*</td></tr>
<tr><td>**The defendant**, as the manager of hotel, should protect customers' safety **and** should follow regulations of *Methods for administering security of hotels (the Central Government of PRC)* and *Rules in applying 'Methods for administering security of hotels' (Beijing Government)*, taking measures like [...].</td><td>*The invoking of specific law*</td><td rowspan="3">*The application of law*</td></tr>
<tr><td>**The defendant** found X (the murderer), after checking out, still stayed in Y's (the plaintiff's daughter) room and did not take measures according to regulations of the above *Methods for* [...] and *Rules in Applying* [...]. On matters like X killed Y, Y alone stayed in X's room for days [...] the **defendant** bore the responsibility of negligence.</td><td>*The application of law*</td></tr>
<tr><td>In this murder incident, the **defendant** did not fulfil its obligation to protect public safety **and** should bear compensation responsibility to the extent that it can prevent or stop the damaging action.</td><td>*The conclusion*</td></tr>
<tr><td>Accordingly, the **plaintiff's** claim of requiring the defendant to compensate [...] is legitimate and lawful. But the amount claimed by the **plaintiff** is too high [...] this court will decide this according to the situation [...]. (syntax)</td><td colspan="2">*The judges' legal opinion*</td></tr>
</table>

Table 6.3. The coherence of *Judges' Opinions* in cases where the plaintiffs win (Example text 35, case 9, emphasis added by the present author).

In this text, the judges conduct the three conventional tasks: interpreting the law, applying the law to analyze the defendant's tortious (law-breaking) action, and giving a legal opinion on this action. The interpreted law includes both general legal principles ('the interpretation of law' in the above table) and specific laws ('the invoking of specific law' in the above table). In order to differentiate the interpretation of law from the discussion of case-specific issues, the judges in this text use general referring nominal expressions which are not confined to the parties of the case. For example, in other sections of this move, specific referring nominal phrases are used, such as 'the defendant', and 'the plaintiff'. Only when the judges need to discuss general legal principles or law do they shift to a general referring nominal, like 'damaging results', 'a third party', and 'the person' in the above text. The shift from specific to general enables the judges to temporarily distance themselves from the immediate situation of the litigation and create a textual space in which to express their professional understanding of a general legal issue, a specific law, or a related social norm.

The judges in this text express their understanding of the legal principle: when damage is caused by a third party, how responsibility should be divided among the victim, the infringing party (the third party) and the party responsible for the victim's safety. The interpretation of this principle is important because the defendant is a hotel manager and one of his customers was murdered in his hotel. The defendant was accused of having not properly fulfilled his duty to protect the customer's safety, although he was not involved in the murder. As shown in this text, the judges argued that the defendant should bear a certain amount of responsibility for the customer's death ('The defendant, as the manager of hotel, should protect customers' safety and should follow regulations').

Next follows the judges' analysis of the defendant's tortious (law-breaking) action ('the application of law' in the above table). The judges begin each of their sentences with the same subject, 'the defendant', which makes this section read like a list of parallel statements. However, there is an internal structure in the judges' analysis. For example, this text is consistent in the choice of sentence theme ('defendant'), as shown by the emphasized expressions. There are four explicit and two implicit (after 'and') themes: 'defendant – and (defendant) – defendant – defendant – defendant – and (defendant)'. The six sentences are sequenced from general (first two 'defendants') to specific (the middle two 'defendants') and return to general (the last two 'defendants') again. The first sentence reports the result of applying the law ('the defendant should protect customers' safety'), and the second one invokes two related government regulations. The middle two sentences supply detailed illustrations of the defendant's responsibility, which include not expelling X from the hotel after finding X had checked out but still stayed in Y's room, not taking appropriate measures to protect Y from being killed, and not discovering Y's body for several days. The detailed illustration brings significant substance to the judges' argument in the first two sentences; otherwise, the argument is general and makes little sense. After invoking the regulations and applying them to the facts, the judges give their authoritative decision in the last two sentences ('the defendant did not fulfil its obligation to protect public safety and should bear compensation responsibility').

In this text, the judges choose to give legal opinions in relation to the plaintiff's claim: 'the plaintiff's claim of requiring the defendant to compensate is legitimate and lawful', which is clear and convincing based on the foregoing arguments. However, the second part of the judges' opinion ('the amount claimed by the plaintiff is too high [...] this court will decide this according to the situation') seems to indicate the judges' analysis in the above text is not all-inclusive and that more work is not being reported here ('decide this according to the situation'). The judges refuse the plaintiff's claim for an imprecise reason ('it is too high'), and their identification of the accepted amount is even more imprecise ('according to the situation'). The two imprecise expressions indicate the judges have also done some work on determining the compensation award, which is completely omitted in this *Judges' Opinion* move.

The conclusion is that the judges in this text have completed all three conventional tasks, which are interpreting law, applying the law and giving legal opinions. The judges' writing is coherent because it follows the related professional convention in writing civil judgments and because it mostly discloses the process of the judges' analysis and reasoning. Although an understanding of such coherence requires a familiarity with the related professional convention, which is more likely for specialist readers, the judges' legal opinions are understandable for both specialist and non-specialist readers. However, minor discursive incoherence does appear in this text. Because the judges do not apply the law to discuss the plaintiff's daughter's (victim of the involved murder) misbehaviour to allow the murderer to stay in the hotel room, specialist and non-specialist readers cannot know to what extent the defendant should be held responsible for preventing the murder. Consequently, the judges' reasoning behind the compensation award is not sufficiently disclosed, which fails to meet the judicial reform aims ('litigations documents should record the process of litigation and open the judges' reasoning in judgments') required by the Supreme People's Court of the PRC.

Alternatively, some judges in the corpus complete only two of the three conventional tasks in *Judges' Opinions*: to apply the law and to give legal opinions; they do not explicitly interpret the law. The omission of the explicit interpretation of law makes the judges' legal basis for deciding the case unclear. In the case below, the defendant was a transportation company. When one of its drivers (X) transported some goods, the truck hit and badly injured a pedestrian. After recovering from his injury, the pedestrian (plaintiff) sued the defendant to get compensation for his suffering. The judges wrote their opinions in the following text:

<table>
<tr><td>This court holds: X drove a truck owned by the defendant, hit the plaintiff when he (Z) was on duty and wounded the plaintiff badly.</td><td>Legal fact in relation to the defendant</td><td rowspan="2">The application of law</td></tr>
<tr><td>The traffic Police examined and investigated this traffic accident: X was fully responsible for the accident and the plaintiff had no fault. The traffic Police's responsibility allocation is appropriate and supported by this court.</td><td>Allocation of responsibility</td></tr>
<tr><td>X should compensate for reasonable loss borne by the plaintiff. Because X is a driver employed by the defendant and X was on duty when the accident happened, the defendant should bear full joint compensation responsibility.</td><td colspan="2">The judges' legal opinion</td></tr>
</table>

Table 6.4. The lack of coherence in *Judges' Opinions* of civil judgment (Example text 36, case 23, emphasis added by the present author).

This text is linguistically coherent because most sentences are about the defendant and its employee (X), as shown by the emphasized themes above. Because the judges report the facts in relation to X and the traffic police's allocation of responsibility, the final legal opinion seems well supported. However, the judges' omission of the interpretation of law conceals the legal basis. The following analysis attempts to study why the judges do not interpret the law explicitly and how its omission influences the coherence of this text.

In this text, 'the traffic police' are introduced not as another litigation participant, but as an administrative unit with an authoritative status like the court. Traffic accidents are usually examined and investigated by the traffic police, who record the on-site investigation of the accident and officially allocate responsibility between the parties involved. It is possible for a particular party to feel dissatisfied with the police decision and file a lawsuit afterwards, but the police decision is usually final. In Mainland China, if a dispute is processed first by an administrative unit like the traffic police, the judges are theoretically empowered to examine how the administrative decision was reached, which may be accepted or denied in civil judgments. In this example text, the judges exercise their right to review the traffic police's decision ('the traffic police's responsibility allocation is appropriate and supported by this court'), but the judges do not detail the traffic police's decision nor explain its legitimacy. The judges' intention seems more to cite its authority than examine its legitimacy. Two legal opinions are made by the judges: 'X should compensate for reasonable loss borne by the plaintiff', and 'the defendant should bear full joint compensation responsibility'. The judges turn to the traffic police's decision ('X was fully responsible for the accident and the plaintiff had no fault') as the legal basis to render the first. This also explains why one cannot find the interpretation of law in this text. As for the second opinion ('the defendant should bear full joint compensation responsibility'), the only support is 'because X is a driver employed by the defendant and X was on duty when the accident happened'. The connection between this reason and the judges' second opinion needs a careful interpretation of related law, which is omitted in this text. The omitted explanation of legitimacy in the first opinion and the omitted interpretation of law in the second one demonstrate that insufficient information about the judges' reasoning has been disclosed. An intentional omission of this information prevents civil judgments from being constructed in a discursively coherent way, because specialist and non-specialist readers cannot see the litigation practices through the judges' writing in this move.

As can be seen in the foregoing analysis, the coherence of the judges' writing in the move *Judges' Opinions* is opaque because the judges do not make an explicit use of cohesive devices to achieve it.

The coherence is achieved by the judges' following of professional conventions: to finish the three conventional tasks in this move. While non-specialist readers may be able to read the legal opinions given, only specialist readers may make sense of the judges' interpretation and application of law. The omission of any of these three conventional tasks will negatively influence the coherence of the judges' writing, examples of which are found in the corpus. Judges do not explicitly interpret the law and do not disclose sufficient information relating to their reasoning in civil judgments.

6.4.1.2 The judges' discussion of the defendants' contractual liability

This section looks at the coherence of judges' writing in cases involving contractual disputes between the parties. Judges' handling of tortious (law-breaking) cases and contractual cases is significantly different in Mainland China. The defendants in tortious cases break the law, which not only harms the plaintiffs' rights but also harms the law's authority. The judges enforce the law usually by concentrating on the discussion of the defendants' law-breaking actions and giving negative analysis and evaluation. However, the defendants in contractual cases only infringe the plaintiffs' rights and negligibly harms the authority of law. Judges' writing in the move *Judges' Opinions* is therefore more balanced between the defendants and the plaintiffs. The following case illustrates this.

The plaintiff in this case opened a savings account with a fake name, which was permitted before the central bank of the PRC (*People's Bank of PRC*) implemented the real-name-system savings regulation in April 2000. The plaintiff wanted to withdraw his money after April 2000, so the bank required him to submit the ID card bearing the same name as written in the passbook. However, the plaintiff had no ID card for the fake name used for the savings account and could only supply his own ID card. The bank therefore refused the withdrawal. The judges express their opinions on this dispute as follows:

This court holds: **Contracts**, made lawfully, have **binding** force over the **parties**. When **banks** issue saving **passbooks** to **customers,** the deposit contractual relationship is established. Both **parties** should fulfil their contractual duties. When **parties** have not given clear explanations on a number of unforeseeable issues in contracts, they should implement contracts in ways that help to **realize the contractual purpose**.	*The interpretation of law*	
The plaintiff's passbook in this case was issued before People's Bank of PRC put the real-name-system into force. According to Article 2 (1) of the 126 file (2000) of People's Bank of PRC [...] when the **plaintiff** in this case wants to withdraw his money, the defendant should pay after verifying the plaintiff's ID files.	*The evaluation of the plaintiff's claim and the judges' legal opinion*	*The application of law and the judges' legal opinion*
The defendant argued the plaintiff could not provide an ID card bearing the same name with the passbook [...] because the issue of this passbook was before the People's Bank of PRC put real-name-system into force, it is not the plaintiff's fault that he used a fake name [...] the **defendant's** arguments have no legal support.	*The evaluation of the defendant's action and the judges' legal opinion*	

Table 6.5. The judges' discussion of the defendants' contractual liability in *Judge's Opinions* (Example text 37, case 24, emphasis added by the present author).

In this text, the judges interpret the law, use the law to evaluate the plaintiff and defendant respectively, and give their legal opinions at the end of each evaluation. All three conventional tasks (interpreting the law, applying the law and giving legal opinions) are completed by the judges, so this text is coherent at the discursive level. Unlike the judges' discussion of the defendants' legal liability in this move, the judges here not only apply the interpreted law to evaluate the defendant's action but also apply the interpreted law to evaluate the plaintiff's claim. By putting their evaluation of the plaintiff's claim before their evaluation of the defendant's action, the judges start with the initiating party, making their writing temporally coherent.

Moreover this text illustrates that the judges' evaluative effort is evenly distributed between the plaintiff's claim and the defendant's action. Both evaluations follow a similar textual pattern, as in demonstrated in the following table:

The plaintiff's passbook in this case was issued before People's Bank of PRC put the real-name-system into force. According to Article 2 (1) of the 126 file (2000) of People's Bank of PRC [...] when the **plaintiff** in this case wants to withdraw his money	*Supporting argument*	*The evaluation of the plaintiff's claim*
the defendant should pay after verifying the plaintiff's ID files.	*The judges' legal opinion*	
The defendant argued the plaintiff could not provide an ID card bearing the same name with the passbook [...] because the issue of this passbook was before the People's Bank of PRC put real-name-system into force, it is not the plaintiff's fault that he used a fake name [...]	*Supporting argument*	*The evaluation of the defendant's action*
the **defendant's** arguments have no legal support.	*The judges' legal opinion*	

Table 6.6. An equal discussion of the plaintiff and the defendant in the move *Judges' Opinions.*

This table shows that judges follow a widely used pattern of producing supporting argument before giving legal opinions. This pattern is repeatedly used when numerous opinions are given. The judges in this text use this pattern giving two opinions about the plaintiff and defendant respectively ('the defendant should pay after verifying the plaintiff's ID files' and 'the defendant's arguments have no legal support').

This repeatedly used pattern enables specialist and non-specialist readers to directly access the judge's opinions at the end of each issue. The judges use the two above supporting arguments to disclose their reasoning process. Firstly, they specifically invoke a law (*Article 2 (1) of the 126 file (2000) of People's Bank of PRC*). Secondly, the text reports the necessary legal facts in order to make the judges' legal opinions evidence-based, such as 'an ID card', 'the same name with the passbook', 'real-name-system', and 'a fake name'. The judges in this text demonstrate an intention to construct this move in an argumentative way, thus producing comparatively high linguistic and discursive coherence.

The corpus reveals that most judges' discussions of defendants' contractual liability are linguistically and discursively coherent, while their discussions of defendants' legal liability is sometimes more linguistically than discursively coherent. This contrast occurs for a number of reasons. When the law is broken, the judges are required to go beyond the parties' personal interests and also consider broad social and ethical interests, as discussed in previous sections (Xu, 2002, p. 39). For example, in a case where a defendant breaks the traffic law and harms pedestrians, it is actually unavoidable for the judges to interpret the traffic law and to discuss the legal and social results of breaking the law. The judges' major task in a civil trial is theoretically to rule on the parties' dispute and to award compensation, but the practice in Mainland China differs slightly because the discussion of law necessarily includes a political dimension. It is revealing that law schools in Mainland China are conventionally called 'school of political sciences and law' (政法学院, or Zhengfa Xueyuan). Nowadays, law is still a discipline closely related to politics. It is not uncommon for judges to write their argumentation in a similar way to how political discourse is constructed, i.e. imprecise, diplomatic and emotive. These values, however, decrease the discursive coherence of civil judgments as a legal genre.

When the parties' dispute concerns contractual rights and duties, judges can usually focus on the parties' personal disputes and avoid a broad discussion of law. They can confine their argumentation to the adjudication of the contractual dispute only. Because contract items are all recorded and explained in written documents, judges can carefully examine various items and supply detailed description and argumentation of them. One judge who has been practicing law for 18 years explained this contrast:

> Contract expresses the negotiation and agreement among parties. Although what is contracted may vary from the selling of a book to the leasing of an oil tank, a contract is somehow a private matter influencing contracting parties only. However, we will consider completely different things when the law is broken. We will take on board the political and socio-ethical perspectives of the law-breaking action because we should *serve the People's interests* (为人民服务). (Excerpt 12, judge E)

6.4.2 *Judges' Opinions: The defendants win the case*

When the defendants win the case, the judges in the corpus usually complete two of the three conventional tasks in the move *Judges' Opinions*: applying the law and giving legal opinions; they ignore the task of interpreting the law. The omission of the interpretation of law can negatively influence the coherence of the judges' writing, as demonstrated in the following analysis. The judges seem to believe the explicit interpretation of law is not necessary if the plaintiffs lose the case, namely, their claims are not reasonable or not supported by sufficient evidence. In the move *Judges' Opinions*, the judges usually focus their attention on the analysis and explanation of the plaintiffs' claim and evidence, paying no attention to the accessible invoking of law and the discussion of the defendants. Although the judges' sole focus on the plaintiffs' unreasonable claim or insufficient evidence is good enough for the judges to close the litigation by deciding the defendants win the case, it fails to report the judges' reasoning process, which is required by law and by the judicial reform initiated by the Supreme People's Court of the PRC. The judges' main intention in this move seems to produce linguistic coherence, not discursive coherence.

6.4.2.1 The plaintiffs' claim is unreasonable

The defendants win the case when the plaintiffs' claim is unreasonable or when the plaintiffs cannot produce sufficient evidential support. If the plaintiffs' claim is not reasonable, the judges' writing in *Judges' Opinions* will concentrate on the discussion of the illegitimacy of this claim, paying little attention to the defendant. The judges' focus on the plaintiff is supported by a principle in civil trial, i.e. the one who claims should bear the burden of proof, and the judges are entitled to dismiss the trial when the plaintiffs cannot prove the legitimacy of their claim. In the case quoted below, the plaintiff sued the defendant (a bus company in Beijing) and required the court to order the defendant to relocate one of its terminals. The plaintiff's central claim is that the particular bus terminal caused excessive noise disturbance to him. The judges ordered an organization to test the noise levels and used the results as evidence. However, the judges decided the plaintiff's claim was not reasonable, as demonstrated below:

<table>
<tr><td>This court holds: It is a person's lawful right to pursue the comfortable living surroundings and happy life. The plaintiff in this case lives in an area which belongs to Area II defined by the state. Noise in such mixed areas of business and living community, according to the testing of related organization, comes from multiple sources.</td><td>The facts in relation to the plaintiff</td><td rowspan="2">The application of law</td></tr>
<tr><td>Testing results shows noise level in the plaintiff's area is slightly above the standard level set by the state and the noise will influence the plaintiff's life to some degree. But the noise sources are multiple and it is not possible to identify the defendant's individual liability. Testing results also demonstrates that the noise level is still above the standard level even after the defendant stops running its buses during the night.</td><td>The reason for rejecting the plaintiffs' claim (results of courtroom investigation)</td></tr>
<tr><td>The plaintiffs' claims for [...] are not accepted by this court.</td><td colspan="2">The judges' legal opinion</td></tr>
</table>

Table 6.7. The move *Judges' Opinions* in cases where the defendants win (Example text 38, case 25, emphasis added by the present author).

The text shows that the judges complete two (the application of law and the giving of legal opinions) tasks instead of the conventional three. An analysis of the sentence themes identifies three sections in this text: the facts in relation to the plaintiff, the results of courtroom investigation, and the legal opinion. The judges' writing purpose in these sections suggests the plaintiff's claim against the defendant is unreasonable.

When introducing the facts in relation to the plaintiff, the judges use a general and imprecise social norm to indicate the plaintiff's motivation to claim ('it is a person's lawful right to pursue the comfortable living surroundings and happy life'), which refers rather to emotions than the law. This social norm indicates the judges' emotional support and sympathetic understanding of the plaintiff's suffering. In addition to an effort to make the facts more convincingly constructed, this imprecise social norm also demonstrates that the judges do not take the plaintiff's claim as law-based.

Unlike the social norm explaining the plaintiff's motivation, the result of courtroom investigation is law-based and used as evidence to challenge the plaintiff's claim. This section also implicitly includes the judges' sympathetic understanding of the plaintiff's suffering: 'the noise will influence the plaintiff's life to some degree'. However, the noise measurement results suggest that the plaintiff's claim is not reasonable because 'the noise sources are multiple' and because 'the noise level is still above the standard level even after the defendant stops running its buses during the night'.

Although the judges in this text have sufficient law-based reasons to reject the plaintiff's emotion-based claim, they show an intention to be considerate and sympathetic in giving their legal opinion. The judges here intend to give opinions in a more persuasive way, demonstrating that legal analysis and argumentation in civil judgments can be improved, as advocated by the Supreme People's Court of the PRC. However, the judges' omission of the interpretation of law makes this text discursively incoherent in places. Nonspecialist readers cannot capture the legal issues related to the parties' dispute. The judges use imprecise expressions to discuss the facts and courtroom investigation, like 'area II defined by the state' and 'testing results', which need further explanations; otherwise, readers not party to the case cannot get a coherent reading of the judges' writing.

Effort on the part of judges to write coherently by showing their sympathy and considerateness is new and follows the recent judicial reform initiated by the Supreme People's Court of the PRC, while their effort not to write discursively incoherent judgments has been a professional convention for some time. This convention indicates a lack of professionalism in the Chinese judicial system. One background factor that can explain this professional convention is that a number of Chinese judges do not receive academic legal education and systematic legal training. The normal practice is to acquire the PRC certificate for legal professions through the national examination (*Bar Exam of the PRC*) and then directly enter practice without any systematic legal training. It is fewer than ten years since China tried to change a tradition of recruiting demobilized soldiers as judges by requiring all judge candidates to have the PRC certificate for legal professions (HE, 1998; LIU, 2010). Some newly recruited judges are insufficiently prepared for the highly specialized litigation practices, which possibly leads to a lack of legal professionalism in the judicial system.

6.4.2.2 The plaintiffs' evidence is insufficient

If the defendants win the case because the plaintiffs have provided insufficient evidence, the judges' sole concentration on the discussion of the plaintiffs' claim and evidence is sufficient to dismiss the lawsuit, according to the above principle that the one who claims should bear the burden of proof. However, the judges cannot resolve the parties' dispute by the simple dismissal of the plaintiffs' claim. If the plaintiffs find future new evidence, they may initiate a new lawsuit. Therefore, to finalize this type of parties' dispute, judges not only discuss the plaintiffs' claim and insufficient evidence, but also discuss the defendants' action to prove the innocence of the defendants.

In the case below, the plaintiff received a heart operation in a hospital (the defendant) and recovered very well after the operation. Six months after the operation, the plaintiff learned from the media that the defendant had been using used heart tubes in heart operations. The plaintiff began to worry about his implanted heart tube and decided to sue the defendant for compensation. The judges believed that the plaintiff's claim was based solely on the media report and did not support his claim, as indicated in the following text:

<table>
<tr><td>This court holds: The plaintiff stayed in the hospital (the defendant) receiving treatment and medical contract thus came into being between these two parties […] the plaintiff paid the full medical fees when he checked out after recovery; this means both parties had their contractual rights and duties realized. Now the plaintiff learned that the defendant was reported as having used the used heart tubes in treating patients and it is understandable for him to suspect the heart tubes used in his case […].</td><td>The first discussion of the plaintiff and the judges' legal opinion</td><td rowspan="3">The application of law and the judges' legal opinion</td></tr>
<tr><td>In this dispute, the defendant has responsibility to prove that its actions in treating the plaintiff conform to the required medical regulations. In the court trial, the defendant provided evidence […] and these are sufficient to demonstrate Y's actions are proper and conform to the required medical regulations.</td><td>The discussion of the defendant and the judges' legal opinion</td></tr>
<tr><td>The plaintiff, after operation and treatments, recovered very well and suffers no after-effects. His claim that he himself had been given the used heart tubes is solely based on related news reports […] and is obviously without sufficient evidence. Because of this and the fact that Y has proved […], the plaintiff's claim is not accepted by this court.</td><td>The second discussion of the plaintiff and the judges' legal opinion</td></tr>
</table>

Table 6.8. The move *Judges' Opinions* in cases where the plaintiffs provide insufficient evidence (Example text 39, case 1, emphasis added by the present author).

In this text, the judges' discussion of the plaintiff and defendant is linguistically coherent because of the respective consistent choice of themes (sentence topics) in the three sections, which are the discussion of the plaintiff, the discussion of the defendant, and the second discussion of the defendant. The discursive coherence of the judges' writing here is somewhat problematic because the judges' omission of the interpretation of law decreases the discursive coherence, while the judges' effort to resolve the parties' dispute increases the discursive coherence.

The researcher presented this text to several specialist informants for feedback on the judges' omission of the interpretation of law. One lawyer explained the omission of the interpretation of law with the following statement:

> It is possible that the related law might be known to legal specialists, i. e. lawyers and judges, and the judges may believe it is not necessary to repeat it in judgment. This is true in practice but it does not help to improve the argumentation quality of civil judgment. It is also possible that the judges have no such consideration when writing civil judgment for interested readers other than the litiga-

tion participants, namely, the plaintiffs, the defendants and their agents. They do not pay much attention to the argumentation quality advocated by the Supreme Court's judicial reform. (Excerpt 13, lawyer F)

This omission of the interpretation of law complicates understanding of the judges' specific arguments, like 'medical contract thus came into being, both parties had their contractual rights and duties realized', and 'the defendant has responsibility to prove'. The first two arguments require an explanation of the medical contract and contract law, and the third argument requires an explanation of the allocation of the burden of proof. All required explanations are highly legalized and may make little sense for non-specialist readers, which decreases the discursive coherence of this text.

However, the discursive coherence of this text is increased by the judges' effort to discuss the defendant in this case where the plaintiff did not provide sufficient evidence. In order to close the lawsuit, it should have been sufficient for the judges to discuss only the plaintiff's insufficient evidence, but the judges seem unwilling to close the lawsuit with a simple dismissal of the plaintiff's claim. Their consideration here is to finally resolve the medical dispute, so they introduce the defendant's burden of proof fulfilment ('the defendant provided evidence and these are sufficient'). Since the defendant lawfully proved that its treatment of the plaintiff conformed to medical regulations, the plaintiff should have no reason to further challenge the legitimacy of the defendant's operation. The judges' discussion of the defendant resolves the parties' dispute, in addition to supplying a further supportive argument to dismiss the plaintiffs' claim. As discussed in the previous section, Xiao (2005) points out that the judges' omission of the interpretation of law is not be entirely new in the Chinese judicial system, but their effort to make litigation more efficient by settling down the parties' dispute forever is recent. Such effort suggests judges' intentions to enhance the legal professionalism of the Chinese judicial system, which naturally increases the discursive coherence of civil judgments.

6.4.3 Judges' Opinions: Neither party wins the case

In some cases in the corpus, the judges decide the plaintiffs and defendants should share respective suffering, or loss and blame is attributed to neither party. In this situation, neither the plaintiffs nor the defendants claims/arguments are supported by the judges, namely, neither party wins the case. If the case is about tort, i.e. law-breaking actions, it is possible that the plaintiffs are partially responsible for their own suffering. For example, a plaintiff may get hurt by a moving car if he crosses a road by climbing over the barriers in the middle of the road rather than by using the zebra crossing. Since the plaintiff contributes significantly to the occurrence of the road accident, he may get only a small proportion of the compensation claimed. If the case is about contract law, the contract may be annulled by the judges because of illegal elements such as the parties' civil conduct incompetence, malicious or fraudulent intentions, and illegal contract purposes.

In both situations, neither party can effectively exploit the opposing side, and wrongdoing can be attributed to both. This normally results in rejection of the plaintiffs' claim, with the plaintiffs and defendants bearing their respective losses. In the judges' writing in the move *Judges' Opinions*, the difference between tort and contract law does not influence the judges' writing patterns as much as rhetorical convenience does. To give opinions in these cases, the judges conventionally begin with the party who bears most responsibility and end with the party who bears the least, which makes the judges' writing highly coherent at the linguistic level. At the same time, the judges' writing is discursively coherent because they base their specific opinions on specific facts.

In the following case, the plaintiff (X) had breakfast in a restaurant managed by the defendant (Z). The second defendant (Y), the neighbour of (Z), parked his motorbike in their common exit. When X was leaving the restaurant, he tried to move the motorbike to clear the way. He started the engine with Z's key that had been left in the ignition. The motorbike became out of control and hit Y's oil pan. X was burnt by the spilt hot oil. The text below demonstrates the judges' allocation of responsibility among the three parties:

This court holds: In this traffic accident, **plaintiff X** improperly moved defendant Y's three-wheeled motorbike, hit a pot full of hot oil set in front of defendant Z' restaurant, and was burned. **Plaintiff X should bear major responsibility for this traffic accident**.	*The discussion of the plaintiff and the judges' legal opinion (bearing the most responsibility)*	*The application of law and the judges' legal opinion*
Defendant Y put his three-wheeled motorbike on the road, blocked the traffic, and carelessly forgot to take out the ignition key. These led to the fact that X improperly moved the motorbike, hit the oil pot and was burned [...]. Defendant Y's action is partially related to plaintiff X's injuries, so **defendant Y should bear a certain proportion of responsibility** [...].	*The discussion of defendant Y and the judges' legal opinion (bearing less responsibility)*	
Defendant Z, running her restaurant, set up oil pot in front of her restaurant and occupied the road to run her business. **Z** did not fulfil her obligation of securing public safety within a reasonable extension and should **bear limited responsibility as well**.	*The discussion of defendant Z and the judges' opinion (bearing the least responsibility)*	

Table 6.9. The move *Judges' Opinions* in cases where neither party wins (Example text 40, case 23, emphasis added by the present author).

The judges in this text discuss the three parties' responsibility according to their individual responsibilities. One textual pattern is repeatedly used: facts plus the judges' opinion. Facts here are particularly related to the judges' evaluation of specific party's actions. For example, in the discussion of Plaintiff X, the judges use three sentences: 'improperly moved defendant Y's three-wheeled motorbike', 'hit a pot', and 'was burned'. The use of modification ('improperly') and the choice of passive voice ('was burned') demonstrates the judges' negative attitude towards the plaintiff, namely, the plaintiff's improper behaviour led solely to his injury.

Following the facts in relation to the specific parties' actions is the judges' opinion on the amount of responsibility each should bear: 'Plaintiff X should bear major responsibility for this traffic accident, defendant Y should bear a certain proportion of responsibility' and 'Z should bear limited responsibility as well'. The division of responsibility is realized by three modifications, 'major', 'a certain proportion', and 'limited', which indicates that Plaintiff X contributed most to his own injury, Defendant Y contributed less, and Defendant Z the least. This research reveals that this way of arranging writing and opinions is preferred not only by judges writing civil judgments, but also by lawyers writing in a number of other legal genres like indictments, statements of defence, cases, and legal opinions. They conventionally handle the important problem first, with less important ones coming after.

This textual arrangement differs from the traditional Chinese way of writing, which is to lay groundwork first and then highlight important problems. This difference demonstrates that at least some Chinese judges are accommodated to professional legal argumentation. This is significant because huge differences exist between the requirements of the rule of law and traditional Chinese culture. The rule of law originates in Europe and North America and was not introduced to China until a century ago. Even today, it is not uncommon for the rule of law to be manipulated in order to serve the interests of political authorities. Mainland Chinese judges very often have to face a contradiction between their professional beliefs and Chinese culture which is dominated by political and administrative discourse. Individual judges may struggle to improve significantly the discursive coherence of civil judgments by disclosing all the necessary information related to background litigation practices, but they can make their reasoning process more accessible through argumentative writing in civil judgments, as shown in the above text. A lawyer expressed his views with the following statement:

> There is a long way to go before the Mainland Chinese context will enable the judges to enjoy judicial independence, free of any political and administrative influence. But changes are actually happening, and some legal documents in litigation practices are becoming more coherent. In some trials, there is practical difficulty in disclosing information to the public which we personally believe the public has a lawful right to know. The judges may solve this problem by supplying more elaborative reports of facts and more focused and comprehensive analyses of law and legal opinions. The judges, at least, can try to write coherently on those aspects of litigation practices which can be disclosed. (Excerpt 14, lawyer G)

The coherence of judges' writing in the move *Judges' Opinions* is complicated. They should usually finish three conventional tasks in this move: the interpretation of the law, the application of the law in relation to the plaintiffs and defendants, and the giving of legal opinions; the omission of any one of these tasks jeopardizes the coherence of judges' writing in the legal sense, because it is required by law. Judges do not always complete all three tasks in the five types of cases identified in the corpus. One or two tasks are conventionally omitted in some types of cases, which negatively influences the discursive coherence of the judge's writing, because the more tasks the judges complete, the more discursively coherent their writing is. Although such omissions are usually conventional practices for some judges who strongly intend to follow these practices in order to establish solidarity with other judges, the previous analysis has shown that some judges do break these conventions in certain cases in order to make their writing more discursively coherent.

6.5 Conclusion

Although coherence is primarily a rhetorical concept, judges' consideration in achieving it is usually legal. The judges' major intention is not to make their writing in civil judgments explicitly connected by cohesive devices, but to reach a discursive coherence between their writing and litigation practices. Judges have to consider whether their writing has followed both the law and conventional rhetorical practices accepted by other judges. These considerations strongly influence judges' writing of civil judgments so that judges will follow a convention even when they know this will harm the discursive coherence of civil judgments, as indicated by the omission of the interpretation of law in some types of cases.

The judges' choice of specific coherence strategies also depends more on the nature of cases than on their personal rhetorical preferences. In order to write a coherent recontextualization of the plaintiffs' and defendants' arguments, they may choose between using plot-driven texts and point-driven texts. Judges can choose to tell narrative stories or to list only main arguments when they recontextualize plaintiffs' arguments in the *Plaintiffs' Claim* step. In cases involving everyday issues like neighbourhood disputes, customers' rights and family disputes, judges usually arrange their writing into coherent stories, while in cases involving specialized issues like contract, copyright, patent, and insurance, judges usually arrange their writing in point form. Both stories and lists of points perform considerable effort to achieve coherence at discursive levels.

Since judges concentrate on the legal aspect of coherence in writing civil judgments, they usually pay little attention to the use of explicit cohesive devices. As a result, coherence in civil judgments is mostly implicit, rather than explicit for non-specialist readers. Judges tend to presuppose considerable legal or social background knowledge when they write to achieve coherence. They may be so familiar with some of the knowledge that they assume it needs no explanation. Some sections of civil judgments make little sense for outsiders, i.e. non-specialist readers, and sometimes also for specialist readers. One has to retrieve the knowledge presupposed by the judges in order to discover the implicit coherence, which negatively influences the coherence of this genre.

Chapter 7
Conclusion

7.1 Discussion

This research is one of the first attempts to study Mainland Chinese legal genres from an empirical perspective. Context-based studies of professional and academic discourse are not new for discourse analysts in Hong Kong, Great Britain, the U.S., and Australia, but this is a new research method for discourse researchers in Mainland China. The focus of discourse research in Mainland China is usually to introduce and explain established analytical models like Critical Discourse Analysis, Conversation Analysis, and Speech Act Theory, and then apply those models to real-world texts. The academic trend in Mainland China largely consolidates classical theories, instead of doing grounded studies and developing new adoptable, analytical models.

To explain the established models, many discourse studies in Mainland China are conducted in fields where those models were initially born, such as the media, pedagogy, business, and everyday communication, because these fields include data which can supply immediate evidential illustrations for those established models. Less, if there is any, research has been conducted in the fields like the law, the politics, and the administration, although the discourses of these three fields actually occupy high profile positions in Mainland China and deserve a lot of research effort. The present research attempts to explore aspects of both Chinese legal discourse and Chinese judges' professional practices in relation to the genre of civil judgments.

Civil judgments and most other written legal genres in Mainland China are considered unworthy of serious research because discourse researchers mostly believe these genres to be highly structured and standardized. It is believed that the conventional and standardized expressions used in civil judgments can be captured through a simple reading of judgment exemplars, which is sufficient for specialist and non-specialist readers to understand this genre. Judges' professional competence in writing civil judgments is taken for granted. However, judges' writing in civil judgments reflects aspects of the Chinese legal context and its on-going judicial reform, and thereby judges' understanding and conducting of this reform. In order to understand this legal context and judges' professional skills in conducting this judicial reform from a discursive perspective, the present researcher takes civil judgments back to the litigation practices from which they originate, hoping to describe, explain and interpret the rhetorical and legal process of judges' writing.

Civil judgments are the most important textual artefact in civil litigation, because they decide the respective rights and obligations of the parties who submit their disputes to the court for litigation (George, 2000). It is based on a civil judgment that the parties can take further remedies to protect their rights, such as the application of enforcement, appealing to a court of appeal, and claiming priority for their rights/interests. The use of civil judgments in these further remedies requires judges' writing in civil judgments to be clear, precise and unambiguous.

This research suggests that civil judgments are the one channel in Chinese civil litigation in which judges write official reports that demonstrate their understanding and analysis of and opinions on parties' litigation disputes. Consequently, judges accomplish a number of other tasks like the identification of facts, the analysis of issues, and the interpretation of law in their writing, in addition to the task of declaring judgment, i.e. court decisions. Two factors here require judges' writing in civil judgments to be sufficiently versatile and flexible. Firstly, the disputes to be litigated are not universal; judges' discussions may embrace different fields, such as finance, commerce, banking, trade, computing, entertainment, etc. Judges have to research and understand the issues in specific fields, and their writing should vary according to the type of case. Secondly, the interpretation of law requires judges to write flexibly; otherwise they cannot establish a convincing legal basis for litigation. The law in Mainland China, as in other civil law countries, is concise, 'systematized and structured and relies on declarations of broad, general principles, often ignoring the details' (Tetley, 1999, p. 596). Although Mainland China has a systematic system of laws, many specific legal stipulations and regulations are imprecise and demand interpretive effort. It is even possible that no immediately applicable law exists in cases where a newly surfaced dispute has not been handled before by judges. In both situations, judges must flexibly choose from three alternatives: to directly quote the law, to interpret the law, and to interpret related legal principles/social norms, to build an appropriate legal basis for litigation.

As can be seen in previous chapters, the above two requirements (to be clear, precise and unambiguous and to be flexible and versatile) are reflected in this genre, namely, civil judgments are often written in a formalistic style, and judges' writing varies according to specific situations. This investigation has demonstrated that all civil judgments in Mainland China include universal moves. Some of the moves are strictly standardized so that the judges' task is reduced to filling in the blanks. The formalistic and standardized writing in civil judgments is usually clear; specialist and non-specialist readers can easily access reported information like the parties' names, the dispute, and the court's decisions, as demonstrated in the moves *Heading*, *Introduction*, and *Court Decisions*. The standardization of judges' writing in civil judgments is not only a conventional litigation practice; it is also required by the Supreme People's Court of the PRC. The Supreme People's Court governs judges' writing of civil judgments and other litigation genres, and it issued *The Formality of Litigation Documents (Provisional)* (法院诉讼文书样式(试行)) in 1993, which remains in effect. The sample of civil judgments from within this law is highly standardized, and few changes are allowed in the form of this genre. Although this high standardization does make the writing of civil judgments a manageable task for most judges, it nevertheless sacrifices a fuller discloser of information about litigation practices, which underpins the Supreme People's Court's initiative to improve argumentation and legal reasoning in this genre.

Judges' analysis of facts and law cannot be regulated in a similar standardized way because the disputes to be litigated vary greatly. The writing of facts in civil judgments is based on the judges' analysis of the parties' arguments, the evidential examination, and the courtroom investigation; the discussion of law is based on the judges' choice of the related law and their interpretation of the law. Judges are required to use their legal and rhetorical competence to handle different situations, as demonstrated in the moves *Parties' Arguments, Judges' Arguments* and *Judges' Opinions*.

Legal competence means that judges are familiar with the related laws and know how to interpret and apply them. Two possible situations have been discussed in this book. The first situation is that more than one authority may have given their respective regulations on the same issue, and these different regulations are not always consistent. When inconsistency does appear, judges need to analyze and decide which regulation prevails over others. An inappropriate choice of law in civil judgments will harm the generic authority of this genre and the credibility of civil litigation. The second situation is that there is no applicable law on a certain issue. In this situation, judges' established practice in Mainland China is to invoke related social norms as authority. Since most norms are unwritten, judges are required to spend much effort explaining the chosen norm and building its legitimacy.

Rhetorical competence means that judges are familiar with most of the conventional practices in writing civil judgments and follow these conventions in their own writing. Breaking such conventions may not affect the judgment, i.e. court decision of specific civil judgments, but it does have negative implications on the judges' credibility and professional competence. This research discovered a number of rhetorical conventions in writing civil judgments. For example, in the move *Parties' Arguments*, judges usually introduce facts only in the step *Plaintiffs' Claim*, not in the step *Defendants' Defence*, even when the two parties, i.e. the plaintiffs and defendants, have a disputed understanding of the facts. The facts introduced in the step *Plaintiffs' Claim* are not always the plaintiffs' understanding of the facts; rather, they are usually brief summaries of the facts identified by the judges, which seems to contradict the title of this step – *Plaintiffs' Claim*. Only experienced judges and lawyers can identify such writing conventions because they are not explicitly stipulated by law or discussed in law schools.

This research discovered that although Chinese judges' writing of civil judgments primarily consists of standardized rules and conventions, some of these standardized rules and conventions are being breached as a result of Chinese judges' efforts to implement judicial reform. In certain situations, judges are producing more situation-specific interpretations of law and identifications of facts in their writing of civil judgments, which gives specialist and non-specialist readers a better chance to understand civil judgments and to access background litigation practices. This gradually decreasing dominance of standardization in Chinese civil judgments will create greater flexibility for judges' individual writing, although this is not possible for the moment.

7.2 Pedagogic implications

The research findings and the judges' professional competence explained in this research can be used to design pedagogic tasks for legal academic and professional training purposes. Junior law students in Mainland China spend most of their effort on memorizing specific legal regulations and on mastering practical skills which are helpful for them to pass various tests. They pay much attention to pedagogically tailored materials including textbooks, summarized judgments, and imagined cases; they usually assume real-world legal genres are highly structured and standardized, so that they can begin to understand, read and write these genres by following some easily accessible samples. However, this research demonstrates that judges' writing includes much versatility beyond the simple following of rules and conventions. The rules and conventions may be easy to understand, but the writing versatility requires judges to make use of their professional competence in specific situations, which needs much training and experience. Raising law students' and novice lawyers' awareness of both rules and conventions and judges' professional competence will provide them with a more authentic picture of the litigation in Mainland China, at the same time facilitating them to become full participants of the Chinese legal community.

On a number of occasions in this research, the specialist informants, i.e. judges and lawyers, were pleasantly surprised by the insights and observations which were presented to them for comments. It had not occurred to them that discourse analysts (in fact they referred to the researcher as *an English teacher*, *Yingyu Laoshi*, *英语老师*) can analyze civil judgments and related legal issues in such a way that judges' specialist knowledge can be enlightened and reinforced. They further pointed out that research of this kind is greatly needed for educating junior law students to raise their awareness of the connection between legal rhetoric and its situated socio-legal context.

7.3 Directions for further research

This research is essentially qualitative and does not attempt a statistical calculation of particular lexico-grammatical items. The possibility remains of compiling a larger corpus and conducting a statistic analysis of parameters like lexico-grammatical items, signposting phrases, and temporal descriptions. This further analysis will lay immediately applicable ground for the design of pedagogic or professional training materials.

This research attempts to incorporate a number of different perspectives to interpret civil judgments, i.e. textual perspective, intertextual perspective, analysts' perspectives, and specialists' perspectives. Future research may encompass more perspectives which are equally significant for a grounded study of civil judgments. For example, researchers may try to approach a number of plaintiffs and defendants because, as participants of litigation proceedings, they have a better understanding of what actually happens in court trials and what is reported in civil judgments. Their observations on the consistency or discrepancy between actual litigation practices and judges' writing in civil judgments is valuable for the analysis of readability, accessibility, and coherence in civil judgments.

The data used in this research is trial judgments, paying no attention to judgments rendered by courts of appeal. In reality, both plaintiffs and defendants can feel dissatisfied with the decisions of trial courts and appeal to courts of appeal. Future research can be done in relation to the generic features of judgments rendered by courts of appeal; effort can be made to examine how courts of appeal handle trial courts' civil judgments. This can produce more grounded explanations on how the discursive artefact that is a civil judgment is handled in different litigation practices.

References

Atkinson, J. M., & Drew, P. (1979). *Order in court: The organization of verbal behavior in judicial settings*. London: Macmilan.

Bargiela-Chiappini, F., & Nickerson, C. (1999). *Writing business: Genres, media and discourse*. London: Longman.

Bargiela-Chiappini, F., Nickerson, C., & Planken, B. (2007). *Business discourse*. New York: Palgrave.

Barnes, J. (2006). The continuing debate about 'plain language' legislation: A law reform conundrum. *Statute Law Review*, 27(2), 83–132.

Bazerman, C. (1988). *Shaping written knowledge: The genre and activity of the experimental article in science.* Madison, Wis.: University of Wisconsin Press.

Bazerman, C. (2000). Singular Utterances: Realizing Local Activities through Typified Forms in Typified Circumstances. In A. Trosborg (Ed.), *Analysing professional genres* (pp. 25–40). Amsterdam; Philadelphia: John Benjamins.

Bazerman, C. (2002). Rhetorical Research for Reflective Practice: A Multi-layered Narrative. In C. N. Candlin (Ed.), *Research and practice in professional discourse* (pp. 79–95). Hong Kong: City University of Hong Kong Press.

Bazerman, C. (2004). Intertextuality: How Texts Rely on Other Texts. In C. Bazerman, & Prior, P. (Eds.), *What writing does and how it does it: An introduction to analyzing texts and textual practices* (pp. 83–97). Mahwah, N.J.: Lawrence Erlbaum Associates.

Beaufort, A. (1999). *Writing in the real world: Making the transition from school to work.* New York: Teachers College Press.

Berkenkotter, C., & Huckin, N. (1995). *Genre knowledge in disciplinary communication: Cognition/culture/power*. Hillsdale, NJ.: Lawrence Erlbaum Associates.

Bhatia, V. K. (1983a). *An applied discourse analysis of English legislative writing.* University of Aston: Language Studies Unit.

Bhatia, V. K. (1983b). Simplification v. Easification: The case of legal texts. *Applied Linguistics,* 4(1), 44–54.

Bhatia, V. K. (1987). Language of the law. *Language Teaching*, 20 (4), 227–234.

Bhatia, V. K. (1992). Pragmatics of the use of nominals in academic and professional genres. *Pragmatics and Language Learning*, 1992 (3), 217–230.

Bhatia, V. K. (1993). *Analysing genre: Language use in professional settings*. London: Longman.

Bhatia, V. K. (1994). Cognitive structuring in legislative provisions. In J. Gibbons (Ed.), *Language and the law* (pp. 136–155). Harlow, Essex, England: Longman.

Bhatia, V.K. (1995). Genre-mixing in professional communication: The case of 'private intentions' v. 'socially recognized purposes'. In P. Bruthiaux, T. Boswood, & B. Du-Babcock (Eds.), *Explorations in English for professional communication* (pp. 1–19). Hong Kong: City University of Hong Kong.
Bhatia, V.K. (1997a). Genre-mixing in academic introductions. *English for Specific Purposes*, 16(3), 181–195.
Bhatia, V.K. (1997b). Applied genre analysis and ESP. In T. Miller (Ed.), *Functional approaches to written text: Classroom applications* (pp. 134–149). Washington D.C.: United States Information Agency, English Language Programs.
Bhatia, V.K. (2002). LSP and professional practice: Negotiating disciplinary conflicts. In M. Gotti, D. Heller, & M. Dossena (Eds.), *Conflict and negotiation in specialized texts: Selected papers of the 2nd CERLIS conference* (pp. 41–57). Bern; New York: Peter Lang.
Bhatia, V.K. (2004). *Worlds of written discourse: A genre-based view*. London: Continuum.
Bhatia, V.K. (2008). Towards critical genre analysis. In V.K. Bhatia, J. Flowerdew, & R.H. Jones (Eds.), *Advances in discourse studies* (pp. 166–177). London; New York: Routledge.
Bhatia, V.K. (2010). Interdiscursivity in professional communication. *Discourse & Communication*, 21 (1), 32–50.
Bhatia, V.K., Candlin, C.N., & Sharma, R. (2009). Confidentiality and integrity of international commercial arbitration practice. *Arbitration*, 75, 2–13.
Bhatia, V.K., Candlin, C.N., & Engberg, J. (Eds.). (2008). *Legal discourse across cultures and systems*. Hong Kong: Hong Kong University Press.
Bhatia, V.K., Candlin, C.N., Engberg, J., & Trosborg, A. (Eds.). (2003a). *Multilingual and multicultural contexts of legislation*. Berlin: Peter Lang.
Bhatia, V.K., Candlin, C.N., & Gotti, M. (Eds.). (2003b). *Legal discourse in multilingual and multicultural contexts*. Berlin: Peter Lang.
Bhatia, V.K., Engberg, J., Gotti, M., & Heller, D. (Eds.). (2005). *Vagueness in normative texts*. Berlin: Peter Lang.
Biesecker, Barbara A. (1989). Rethinking the rhetorical situation from within the thematic of difference. *Philosophy and Rhetoric* 22(2) 110–130. Rpt. in J.L. Lucaites, C.M. Condit, & S. Caudill (Eds.), (1999). *Contemporary rhetorical theory: A reader.* New York: Guilford Press.
Bitzer, L. (1968). The rhetorical situation. *Philosophy and Rhetoric*, 1968(1), 1–14.
Bloor, T. (1995). *The functional analysis of English: A Hallidayan approach*. London: Arnold.
Bremner, S. (2008). Intertextuality and business communication textbooks: Why students need more textual support. *English for Specific Purposes.* 27(3), 306–321.
Candlin, C.N. & Maley, Y. (1997). Intertextuality and interdiscursivity in the discourse of alternative dispute resolution. In B. Gunnarsson, P. Linell, & Nordberg, B.

(Eds.), *The construction of professional discourse* (pp. 201–222). London; New York: Longman.
Carroll, C. (1995). Nuremberg: judgment and challenge-The rediscovery of the law above the statutory. *USAFA Journal of Legal Studies,* 6, 205–213.
Chang, Y.-Y. & Swales, J. M. (1999). Informal elements in English academic writing: Threats or opportunities for advanced non-native speakers? In C. N. Candlin, & K. Hyland (Eds.), *Writing: Texts, processes and practices* (pp. 145–167). Harlow: Longman.
Clandinin, D. J. & Connelly, F. M. (1994). Personal experience methods. In N. Denzin, & Y. Lincoln (Eds.), *Handbook of qualitative research* (pp. 413–427). Thousand Oaks: Sage Publishing.
Cohen, J.A. (1997). Reforming China's civil procedure: Judging the courts. *The American Journal of Comparative Law*, 45(4), 793–804.
Connelly, F. M. & Clandinin, D. J. (1990). Stories of experience and narrative inquiry. *Educational Researcher*, 19(5), 2–14.
Connor, U., & Johns, A. M. (Eds.). (1990). *Coherence in writing: Research and pedagogical perspectives*. Virginia: TESOL, Inc.
Crismore, A., Markkanen, R., & Steffensen, M. (1993). Metadiscourse in persuasive writing: A study of texts written by American and Finnish university students. *Written Communication*, 10(1), 39–71.
Devitt, A. J. (1991). Intertextuality in Tax Accounting: Generic, referential, and functional. In C. Bazerman, & J. Paradis (Eds.), *Textual dynamics of the professions: Historical and contemporary studies of writing in professional communities* (pp. 336–357). Madison, Wis.: University of Wisconsin Press.
Devitt, A. J. (2004). *Writing Genres.* Carbondale: Southern Illinois University Press.
van Dunne, J. M. (1996). Narrative coherence and its function in judicial decision making and legislation. *The American Journal of Comparative Law*, 44, 463–487.
Enkvist, N. E. (1990). Seven problems in the study of coherence and interpretability. In U. Connor, & A. M. Johns (Eds.), *Coherence in writing: Research and pedagogical perspectives* (pp. 11–28). Virginia: TESOL, Inc.
Fairclough, N. (1992). *Discourse and social change.* Cambridge: Polity Press.
Fairclough, N. (1993). Critical discourse analysis and the marketization of public discourse: The universities. *Discourse & Society*, 4(2), 133–168.
Fairclough, N. (1995). *Critical discourse analysis: The critical study of language.* London; New York: Longman.
Fairclough, N. (2003). *Analysing discourse: Textual analysis for social research.* London; New York: Routledge.
Flowerdew, J. (2002). *Academic discourse*. London: Person Education.
Freedman, A. and Medway, P. (Eds.). (1994a). *Genre and the New Rhetoric.* London: Taylor and Francis.
Freedman, A. and Medway, P. (Eds.). (1994b). *Learning and teaching genre*. Portsmouth, NH: Heinemann/Boynton-Cook.

Fu Yulin. (2000). The functions and style of civil judicial decisions (民事裁判文书的功能和风格). *Social Sciences in China* (中国社会科学), 4, 123–133.
Gao, Yun. (2009). *Thinking Lines* (思维的笔迹). Beijing: Law Press.
Gechilk, M.Y. (2005). Judicial reform in China: Lessons from Shanghai. *Columbia Journal of Asian Law*, 19 (1), 97–137.
Geertz, C. (1973). *The interpretation of culture*. New York: Basic Books.
George, J. J. (2000). *Judicial Opinion Writing Handbook*. New York: William S. Hein & Co., Inc.
Gibbons, J. (Ed.) (1994). *Language and the law*. Harlow, Essex, England: Longman.
Gu, Peidong. (2000). Macro aspects of Chinese judicial reform (中国司法改革的宏观思考). *CASS Journal of Law* (法学研究), 22(2), 3–16.
Goffman, E. (1959). *The presentation of self in everyday life*. New York: Doubleday.
Hafner, C. (2006). Understanding barristers' opinions: a discourse analytical perspective. *Clarity*, 56, 37–39.
Halliday, M.A.K. (1978). *Language as social semiotic: The social interpretation of language and meaning*. London: Edward Arnold.
Halliday, M.A.K. (1989). *Spoken and written language*. Oxford: Oxford University Press.
Halliday, M.A.K., & Hasan, R. (1976). *Cohesion in English*. London: Longman.
Halliday, M.A.K., & Matthiessen, C. (2004). *An introduction to functional grammar*. London: Arnold.
HE, Weifang. (1998). The court recruits demobilized soldiers (复转军人进法院). *Nangfang Weekend* (南方周末), January 2, 1998.
Hu, Jingtao. (2007). *Speech by Hu Jintao to the 17th National Congress, October 15, 2007*. Beijing.
Hyland, K. (1996). Talking to the academy: Forms of hedging in science research article. *Written Communication,* 13(2), 251–281.
Hyland, K. (2000). *Disciplinary discourse: Social interactions in academic writing.* Harlow: Longman.
Hyland, K. (2004). *Genre and second language writing.* Ann Arbor: University of Michigan Press.
Hyland, K. (2005). *Metadiscourse: Exploring interaction in writing*. London: Continuum.
Hyon, S. (1996). Genres in three traditions: Implications for second language teaching. *TESOL Quarterly,* 30, 693–722.
Ji, Zongru. (2005). The limitations of apology as a civil remedy (论赔礼道歉作为民事就记得局限性). *The Journal of People's Adjudication* (人民司法), 2005(9), 60–62.
Jiang, Zemin. (1997). *Report Delivered at the 15th National Congress of the Communist Party of China on September 12, 1997*. Beijing.
Johns, A.M. (1997). *Text, role, and context: Developing academic literacies.* New York: Cambridge University Press.

Jolliffe, D. A. (Ed.) (1988). *Writing in academic disciplines*. Norwood, N.J.: Ablex Pub. Corp.
Kimble, J. (1994). Answering the critics of plain language, *The Scribes Journal of Legal Writing*, 5, 51–85.
Kurzon, D. (1997). 'Legal language': Varieties, genres, registers, discourses. *International Journal of Applied Linguistics*, 7, 119–139.
Levi, J. N., & Walker, A. G. (Eds.). (1990). *Language in the judicial process*. New York: Plenum Press.
Lin, C. X. (2003). A quiet revolution: An overview of China's judicial reform. *Asian-Pacific Law & Policy Journal*, 4(2), 255–319.
LIU, Yousheng. (2010). Facilitate the professionalism of the judges (推进法官职业化建设). *People's Daily* (人民日报), January 7, 2010.
Little, L. E. (1998). Hiding with words: Obfuscation, avoidance, and federal jurisdiction opinions. *UCLA Law Review*, 46, 75–160.
Maley, Y. (1994). The language of the law. In J. Gibbons (Ed.), *Language and the law* (pp. 3–50). Harlow, Essex, England: Longman.
Martin, J. R. (1992). *English text: System and structure*. Philadelphia: John Benjamins Pub. Co.
Martin, J. R. (1997). Analysing genre: Functional parameters. In F. Christie, & J. R. Martin (Eds.), *Genre and institutions: Social processes in the workplace and school* (pp. 3–39). London: Cassell.
Martin, J. R., Christie, F. & Rothery, J. (1987). Social processed in education: A reply to Sawyer and Watson (and others). In I. Reid (Ed.), *The place of genre in learning: Current debates*. Greelong: Australia Deakin University Press.
Martin, J. R. & White, P. R. R. (2005). *The language of evaluation: Appraisal in English*. Basingstoke; New York: Palgrave Macmillan.
Mauranen, A. (1993). Contrastive ESP rhetoric: Metatext in Finnish-English economics texts. *English for Specific Purposes*, 12(1), 3–22.
Miller, C. (1984). Genre as social action. *Quarterly Journal of Speech,* 70, 151–167.
Miller, C. (1994). Rhetorical community: The cultural basis of genre. In P. Medway, & A. Freedman (Eds.), *Genre and the New Rhetoric* (pp. 67–78). London: Taylor & Francis.
Orbuch, T. L. (1997). PEOPLE'S ACCOUNTS COUNT: The Sociology of Accounts. *Annual Review of Sociology*, 23, 455–478.
Pan, W. (2003). Toward a consultative rule of law regime in China, *Journal of Contemporary China*, 12(34), 3–43.
Peerenboom, R. (2010). A government of laws: Democracy, rule of law and administrative law reform in the PRC. *Journal of Contemporary China* 12(34), 45–67.
Posner, R. A. (1995). Judges' writing styles (And do they matter?). *The University of Chicago Law Review*, 62, 1421–1451.
Rowe, S. E. (1999). Legal research, legal writing and legal analysis: Putting law school into practice. *Stetson Law Review*, 1–23.

Sanders, T. J. M., & Noordman, L. G. M. (2000). The role of coherence relations and their linguistic markers in text processing. *Discourse Processes*, 29(1), 37–60.
Sanders, T. J. M., Spooren, W. P. M., & Noordman, L. G. M. (1992). Toward a taxonomy of coherence relations. *Discourse Processes*. 15, 1–35.
Seidman, I. (1998). *Interviewing as qualitative research: A guide for researchers in education and the social sciences (2nd ed.)*. New York: Teachers College Press.
Smart, G. (2006). *Writing the economy: Activity, genre, and technology in the world of banking*. London: Equinox.
Smart, G. (2008). Ethnographic-based discourse analysis. In V. K. Bhatia, J. Flowerdew, & R. H. Jones (Eds.), *Advances in discourse studies* (pp. 56–67). London: Routledge.
Solan, L. M. (2004). Pernicious ambiguity in contracts and statutes. *Chicago-Kent Law Review*, 79, 859–888.
Sloan, L. M. (2005). Private language, public laws: The central role of legislative intent in statutory interpretation. *The Georgetown Law Journal*, 93, 426–486.
Stevenson, D. (2003). To whom is the law addressed. *Yale Law & Policy Review*, 21, 105–167.
Su Li. (2000). *Send law to the countryside* (送法下乡). Beijing: China University of Political Science and Law Press.
Su Li. (2001a). The context of judgment (判决书的背后). *CASS Journal of Law* (法学研究), 23(3), 3–18.
Su Li. (2001b). Legal professionals in countryside communities (乡土社会中的法律人). *Legal and Social Development* (法律和社会发展), 38(2), 1–11.
Sun, Yu. (2009). *Thinking as a barrister* (找回大律师). Beijing: Law Press.
Sun, Hailong, & Gao, Wei. (2007). An investigation of reliability of adjudicating documents and the study of related reforms (裁判文书及其公信力现状调查和改革路径研究). *The Journal of Law Application* (法律适用), 2007(5), 35–40.
Swales, J. M. (1981). *Aspects of article introductions*. Birmingham, UK: University of Aston Language Studies Unit.
Swales, J. M. (1986a). Citation analysis and discourse analysis. *Applied Linguistics*, 7(1), 39–56.
Swales, J. M. (1986b). A genre-based approach to language across the curriculum. In M. L. Tickoo (Ed.), *Language across the curriculum: Selected papers from the RELC deminar on "Language across the curriculum", Singapore, 22–26 April, 1985* (pp. 10–22). Singapore: SEAMEO Regional Language Centre.
Swales, J. M. (1990a). *Genre analysis: English in academic and research Settings*. Cambridge: Cambridge University Press.
Swales, J. M. (1990b). Nonnative speaker graduate engineering students and their introductions: Global coherence and local management. In U. Connor, & A. M. Johns (Eds.), *Coherence in writing: Research and pedagogical perspectives* (pp. 187–207). Virginia: TESOL, Inc.

Swales, J. M. (1998). *Other floors, other voices: A textography of a small university building*. Mahway, N.J.: Lawrence Erlbaum Associates.
Swales, J. M. (2004). *Research genres: Explorations and applications*. Cambridge, UK; New York: Cambridge University Press.
Tetley, W. (1999). Mixed jurisdictions: Common law vs civil law (codified and uncodified) (Part I). *Uniform Law Review*, 1999 (3), 591–619.
Thompson, G. (1996). *Introducing functional grammar*. London; New York: Arnold.
Tiersma, P. (2001). A message in a bottle: Text, autonomy, and statutory interpretation. *Tulane Law Review*, 76, 431–482.
Turnbull, I. (1997). Legislative drafting in plain language and statements of general principles. *Statute Law Review*, 18(1), 21–31.
Vande Kopple, W. J. (1985). Some exploratory discourse on metadiscourse. *College Composition and Communication*, 36, 82–93.
Wagner, A. (2010). Mapping legal semiotics. *International Journal of Semiotics of Law*, 2010 (23), 77–82.
Wald, P. M. (1995). The rhetoric of results and the results of rhetoric: judicial writings. *The University of Chicago Law Review*, 62, 1371–1419.
Wang, Ganlin. (2009). 66 errors in one judgment. *Democracy and Legal System*, 2009(22), 71
Wengraf, T. (2001). *Qualitative research interviewing: Biographical narrative and semi-structured methods*. London: SAGE.
White, H. D. (2004). Citation analysis and discourse analysis revisited. *Applied Linguistics*. 25(1), 89–116.
White, J. B. (1995). What's an opinion for? *The University of Chicago Law Review*, 62(4), 1363–1369.
Williams, C. (2004). Legal English and plain language: An introduction. *ESP Across Cultures*, 2004(1), 111–124.
Xiao, Hui. (2005). The tradition and modern development of Chinese judicial opinions – the case of civil adjudication (unpublished PhD thesis) (中国判决理由的传统与现代转型-以民事判决为中心). Southwest University of Political Science & Law (西南政法大学).
Xiong, Jiankui. (2003). A preliminary study of Chinese law on compensation for mental distress (浅析我国精神损害赔偿的特点). *Contemporary Law Review* (当代法学), 2003(9), 156–158.
Xu, Chuanxi. (2002). The present situation of Chinese tort law: perspectives and discussions (中国侵权法现状：考察与评论). *Tribune of Political Science and Law* (政法论坛), 20(1), 34–49.
Xu, Ruibai. (2003). Aspects of reforms of civil and commercial judgments (民商事判决书改革中的几个问题). *The Journal of Law Application* (法律适用), 2003(Z1), 30–33.
Young, L., & Harrison, C. (2004). *Systemic functional linguistics and critical discourse analysis: Studies in social change*. London; New York: Continuum.

Zhao, Y., & Sharma, R. (2003). Introduction to the legal system of the People's Republic of China. In V.K. Bhatia, C.N. Candlin, J. Engberg, & A. Trosborg (Eds.), *Multilingual and multicultural contexts of legislation* (pp. 25–57). Berlin: Peter Lang.
Zhang, Qi. (1999). *Realizing justice through legal reasoning: A perspective of Chinese judicial reform* (通过法律推理实现司法公正). CASS Journal of Law (法学研究), 1999 (5), 21–27.
Zhang, Qianfan. (2003). The people's court in transition: The prospects of the Chinese judicial reform. *Journal of Contemporary China*, 12(34), 69–101.

Appendices

Appendix I. Example texts

The following texts are quoted from civil judgments in the compiled corpus. Since the Chinese case title, as shown in the end of each text, is considerably long and not manageable in the body text of this book, the researcher, alternatively, appoint Arabic numbers to each of the quoted case.

Example text 1 (case 1)

北京市朝阳区人民法院
民事判决书
2003）朝民初字第 9980 号

原告王荣福，男，1935 年 10 月 12 日出生，汉族，北京兆维电子集团退休职工，住北京市朝阳区高家园 201 楼 2 层 5 号
委托代理人王强（原告王荣福之子），男，1964 年 3 月 10 日出生，汉族，北京大学医学部教师，住北京市海淀区北京大学医学部 25 号楼 5 单元 1 层 14 号
委托代理人刘瑞爽，男， 1968 年 9 月 25 日出生，汉族，北京大学医学部教师，住北京市海淀区花园北路 49 号。

被告北京酒仙桥医院，住所：北京市 朝阳区酒仙桥一街坊六号。
法定代表人陈明哲，任该医院院长。
委托代理人邓利强，北京市华卫律师事务所律师。
委托代理人高奇英，女，1953 年 9 月 14 日出生，汉族，该医院医务处干事，住该医院宿舍

原告王荣福与被告北京酒仙桥医院（以下简称酒仙桥医院）医疗服务合同纠纷一案，本院受理后，依法组成合议庭，公开开庭进行了审理。原告王荣福的委托代理人王强、刘瑞爽、被告酒仙桥医院的委托代理人邓利强、高奇英到庭参加了诉讼。本案现已审理终结。（*北京市朝阳区人民法院审理王荣福诉北京酒仙桥医院医疗服务合同纠纷民事判决书（2003）朝民初字第 9980 号*）

Example text 2 (case 2)

原告张铁林，男，大不列颠及北爱尔兰联合王国国籍，1957 年 6 月 15 日出生，北京月亮影视艺术有限公司导演，现住北京市朝阳区慧忠北里 412 号楼 3－4 单元 1201 号。
委托代理人谢刚，北京市国方律师事务所律师。
委托代理人张智霞，北京市国方律师事务所律师。(*张铁林诉周美凝(周璇)及成都商报社名誉权纠纷案 北京市第二中级人民法院民事判决书 (2003)二中民初字第 7230 号*)

Example text 3 (case 3)

原告：李恩起，男，1936 年 3 月 12 日生，汉族，热电公司设计站职工，住天津市河东区 中山门南里*号高层*号。
委托代理人：李丹（原告之女），1961 年 5 月 24 日生，汉族，…
委托代理人：罗鹏（原告亲属），男，…

被告：乔静娟，女，1934 年 8 月 10 日生，…
委托代理人：钟声（被告之子），…（*天津市河东区人民法院审理李恩起诉乔静娟、钟声相邻关系纠纷一案民事判决书（2007）东民初字第 139 号*）

Example text 4 (case 4)

原告秦涛诉称， 2006 年搜狐公司未经许可转载了我在个人博客上写的文章，我诉至法院要求搜狐公司承担侵犯著作权的责任。诉讼中，搜狐公司和我于 2006 年 5 月 12 日签订《和解协议》，约定搜狐公司赔偿我经济损失 5 万元。至今搜狐公司尚未履行《和解协议》约定的付款义务，故我诉请法院判令搜狐公司按照《和解协议》的约定向我支付 5 万元。(*秦涛诉北京搜狐互联网信息服务有限公司其他合同纠纷案 北京市海淀区人民法院 民事判决书（2007）海民初字第 6419 号*)

Example text 5 (case 5)

…
诉讼请求：
1、请求法院判令被告立即停止侵权行为…
2、请求法院判令被告赔偿原告经济损失 100，000 元；

3、请求法院判令被告赔偿原告为本案支出的合理费用 2000 元；

4、请求法院判令被告承担本案的全部诉讼费用

事实和理由：

… 原告也已有明确声明："如有任何转载引用请预先协商并获取授权。" 2005 年 8 月 9 日，原告在博客网发表的《百度疯了，麦莎来了，阿里巴巴卖了的六种感觉》一文，由被告在未与原告协商获得授权，未注明出处，也未向原告支付任何报酬的情况下，于 2005 年 8 月 9 日在其网站刊登… 原告认为，原告作为上述博客文章的作者，其著作权受法律保护。被告… 应尊重作者的合法著作权益，却未与原告协商获得授权多次非法刊登原告文章，非法获利巨大，依法应承担著作权侵权的法律责任。故原告特诉至人民法院，请求人民法院依法判允所请… (*秦涛诉搜狐公司侵犯博客著作权起诉书*)

Example text 6 (case 6)

本院经对当事人提交的证据进行质证、认证，认定为有效证据并予以采纳的证据及理由为：①原告提供的在债务人位置签有"李玉璞"名字的 5 份债务逾期催收通知书。因为该 5 份通知书均有"李玉璞"的名字，被告否认签名行为，辩称系原告伪造，但在举证期限内未申请本院对签名字迹进行鉴定，即没有提供不是李玉璞亲笔签名的任何证据，故应视为 5 份催收通知书上的"李玉璞"名字均系李玉璞亲笔签名。②…
认定为无效证据，不予采纳的证据及理由为：①原告提供的赵太宽的证明一份，因为…证人赵太宽没有出庭，并未经人民法院许可，且被告对该证言的真实性提出质疑，故该证据的客观真实性不能认定。②原告提供的李玉璞贷款的 13 笔清单… ③…
根据以上采纳的证据，本院查明的事实为… (*河南省泌阳县人民法院审理中国农业银行河南省泌阳县支行诉李玉璞借款合同纠纷 民事判决书（2003）泌民二初字第 994 号*)

Example text 7 (case 7)

… 2001 年，新力公司制作发行了《LEON "MUSIC MOVIES" COLLECTION DIRECTED BY :L.L》VCD 光盘，其中包括…该光盘封套背页标注有"（C）2001 Sony Music Entertainment (Hong Kong)Ltd."即新力公司版权标记。2004 年5月24日，国际唱片业协会亚洲区办事处出具证明文件，证明《LEON "MUSIC MOVIES" COLLECTION DIRECTED BY :L.L》音乐录影作品（MTV）是由新力公司向其提供，并作版权登记之用。
2003 年 12 月 12 日，国际唱片业协会北京代表处委托代理人刘莹来到西部娱乐公司经营的西部飚歌城 410 号房间，对黎明演唱的八首歌曲进行点播，并

对歌曲的播放过程进行了摄像，并刻录光盘两份。…苏州市公证处对上述取证过程进行了公证…（*江苏省苏州市中级人民法院审理新力公司与被告西部娱乐公司著作权侵权纠纷案民事判决书（2004)苏中民三初字第 062 号*）

Example text 8 (case 8)

1998 年 10 月 13 日，姚中坚与科学出版社签订图书出版合同一份，合同的主要内容是：姚中坚授予科学出版社在合同有效期内，在全国地区以图书形式出版《手册》中文版的专有使用权…上述事实有姚中坚提交的证据 1 和科学出版社提交的证据 1 在案佐证。（*北京市海淀区人民法院审理姚中坚诉科学出版社出版合同纠纷一案民事判决书（2004）海民初字第 19386 号*）

Example text 9 (case 2)

本院认为：根据民法通则的规定，公民享有的名誉权受法律保护，禁止用侮辱、诽谤等方式损害公民的名誉；涉外民事关系中侵权行为的损害赔偿，适用侵权行为地法律，故本案外国人张铁林名誉侵权诉讼，适用《中华人民共和国民法通则》。

张铁林指认周美凝在 2003 年 6 月 29 日、7 月 4 日《成都商报》涉案文章中的说法侵害其名誉权，周美凝辨称其从未说过“以性作交易”、“‘皇上’提出怪要求”的话。根据当日及事后其他新闻媒体的相关报道，周美凝在举行其小说《绝爱》的签售活动时所谈到的她去北京邀请一个影视大腕来蓉担当签售的嘉宾一事与涉案文章所用的标题、行文的词语意思相当，内容相近。现周美凝并无证据证明其在涉案文章中的说法是真实的，而此说法直接影响到张铁林的社会评价，在此情形下，周美凝的行为构成对张铁林名誉权的侵害，理应承担侵权的民事责任，其辩解本院不予采信。成都商报社对周美凝举行小说《绝爱》签售活动时“性交易事件”的报道，来源于周美凝的叙述，反映的内容基本真实，在没有对方姓名的情况下也无核实的义务；对周美凝主动约见记者，公开当众明确指出其邀请来蓉担当签售嘉宾的影视大腕----“皇阿玛”就是张铁林的报道，反映的内容亦基本真实，没有夸张、歪曲事实，故均不构成对张铁林名誉权的侵害。（*张铁林诉周美凝(周璇)及成都商报社名誉权纠纷案 北京市第二中级人民法院民事判决书（2003)二中民初字第 7230 号*）

Example text 10 (case 7)

本案争议焦点是：一、涉案的 MTV 作品的性质及著作权归属问题；二、关于西部娱乐公司是否有权使用涉案 MTV 作品的问题；三、西部娱乐公司是否侵权及承担责任的问题。
根据已查明的事实和证据，本院认为：

一、关于涉案的 MTV 作品的性质及著作权归属问题。

本院认为，…涉案的 MTV 是以确定的声乐、器乐作品作为承载主体，依据音乐体裁不同的特性和情境氛围进行视觉创意设计，形成音、画合一的视听结构，…属著作权法规定的以类似摄制电影的方法创作的作品，依法应受我国著作权法保护。…故对新力公司享有涉案三首 MTV 作品的著作权应依法予以认定。

二、关于西部娱乐公司是否有权使用涉案 MTV 作品的问题。

本院认为，…西部娱乐公司认为其已自音著协获得合法使用权的抗辩理由不能成立。

三、关于西部娱乐公司是否侵权及承担责任的问题。

本院认为，…西部娱乐公司…侵犯了新力公司对其作品享有的放映权及获得报酬权的财产权利，西部娱乐公司依法应承担停止侵害、赔偿损失的民事责任…(*江苏省苏州市中级人民法院审理新力公司与被告西部娱乐公司著作权侵权纠纷案民事判决书（2004）苏中民三初字第 062 号*)

Example text 11 (case 9)

据此，依照《中华人民共和国民法通则》第一百三十四条第七项、《最高人民法院关于审理人身损害赔偿案件适用法律若干问题的解释》第六条第二款的规定，判决如下：
自本判决生效之日起七日内，北京万程世都宾馆有限责任公司赔偿魏秀贵、刘玉杰六万元（含已付五千元）。
案件受理费六千八百七十元由魏秀贵、刘玉杰负担四千五百六十元（已交纳）；由北京万程世都宾馆有限责任公司负担二千三百一十元，自本判决生效后七日内交纳。
如不服本判决，可在判决书送达之日起十五日内，向本院递交上诉状，并按对方当事人的人数提出副本，上诉于北京市第一中级人民法院。(*北京市宣武区人民法院审理魏秀贵、刘玉杰与北京万程世都宾馆有限责任公司人身损害赔偿纠纷一案民事判决书（2005）宣民初字第 3925 号*)

Example text 12 (case 10)

原告…诉称，…该瓶的保额为人民币 120 万元。出险后，我们经现场勘验，认定符合理赔条件。我们与北京翰海拍卖有限公司签订了结案协议书，确认保险理赔金额为人民币 120 万元。…由于被告的严重过错，导致保险标的物破碎，致使我们赔付 120 万元…因此诉讼请求被告赔偿 120 万元。（*北京市宣武区人民法院审理中国人民财产保险股份有限公司北京市宣武支公司与被告房言山财产损害赔偿纠纷案 民事判决书（2005）宣民初字第 2414 号*）

Example text 13 (case 11)

原告李晓军诉称，被告因拍摄二十集电视连续剧《我和我的父亲》，聘请我担任该剧的导演，并于 2002 年 8 月 1 日与其签订了协议书。根据协议约定，被告应于该剧完成全部制作之日一次性支付原告人民币 30 万元（每集 15 000 元）。因该剧在创作上采用了我的剧本，依据剧本补充合同，被告应在该剧开机后七日内一次性支付我编剧稿酬 164 000 元。现该剧早已在全国发行公映，但被告迟迟未付原告报酬。经多次催要，被告总以资金紧张为由推拖。故诉至法院，请求判令被告支付我酬金人民币 464 000 元（其中导演酬金 300 000 元，编剧酬金 164 000 元）。（*北京市海淀区人民法院审理李晓军诉中联铭世嘉人公司劳务合同纠纷案民事判决书（2004）海民初字第 3386 号*）

Example text 14 (case 6)

原告泌阳农行诉称，被告李玉璞自 1994 年 6 月至 1999 年 10 月先后在我行贷款 9 笔，金额为 270260 元，以他人冒名贷款 4 笔金额为 42000 元，合计 13 笔，共计 312260 元，经我行多次催要，仅付了部分利息后以无钱为由拖欠至今…

…

根据以上采纳的证据，本院查明的事实为：1989 年 9 月 10 日，李玉璞以泌阳粉丝加工厂的名义在原告处贷款 63000 元，到期日为 1992 年 9 月 10 日…1994 年 6 月 26 日，李玉璞以王兴民的名义在原告处贷款 5000 元，到期日为 1995 年 6 月 26 日..1999 年 11 月 16 日李玉璞封息，尚欠本金 5000 元，1995 年 4 月 28 日，李玉璞以黄牛繁殖厂的名义在原告处贷款 10 万元，到期日为 1998 年 4 月 28 日…1995 年 12 月 11 日，李玉璞在原告处贷款 2 万元，到期日为 1996 年 12 月 11 日…（*河南省泌阳县人民法院审理中国农业银行河南省泌阳县支行诉李玉璞借款合同纠纷民事判决书（2003）泌民二初字第 994 号*）

Example text 15 (case 12)

…被告的所作所为严重侵犯了原告的合法利益，经多次找被告协商解决无果，故原告请求人民法院判令，1、被告立即将李立新的死亡证明交给原告二人。2、判令被告公开向原告二人赔礼道歉。3、判令被告给付原告二人精神抚慰金 5 万元。4、判令被告承担本案的全部诉讼费用。(*北京市宣武区人民法院审理李佳婧、张道明与李淑兰、章哲其他人身权纠纷案民事判决书（2006）宣民初字第 4827 号*)

Example text 16 (case 13)

原告诉称：2006 年 7 月 6 日，原告前往被告经营的酒楼就餐… 2006 年 7 月 19 日始，原告出现半身发麻无力症状… 7 月 24 日，原告前往北京大学第三医院就诊，医院初步诊断为疱疹，开了一些治疗药物… 7 月 28 日，北医三院请中国人民解放军总医院 309 医院医生会诊。经会诊被诊断为结核性脑膜炎… 7 月 29 日转到 309 医院结核科… 2006 年 8 月 17 日，原告前往首都医科大学附属北京友谊医院，被确诊为“广州管圆线虫病”，并于 2006 年 8 月 17 日至 2006 年 8 月 30 日住院治疗。…（*北京市朝阳区人民法院审理张征征与北京蜀国演义餐饮文化发展有限公司人身损害赔偿纠纷案民事判决书（2007）朝民初字第 07348 号*)

Example text 17 (case 13)

被告辩称：对于原告的就餐及遭受损害的事实无异议，我公司表示真诚的歉意。在事件发生后，我公司已在媒体上进行了道歉，因此不同意原告要求我公司在北京地区具有影响力的报纸或刊物上公开赔礼道歉的诉讼请求。对于原告要求的后续治疗费、误工费、住院伙食补助费，我公司同意在合理的范围内赔偿。对于原告要求的精神损害抚慰金，数额过高，希望法院酌情判决。(*北京市朝阳区人民法院审理张征征与北京蜀国演义餐饮文化发展有限公司人身损害赔偿纠纷案民事判决书（2007）朝民初字第 07348 号*)

Example text 18 (case 12)

被告剥夺了原告对李立新尸体的所有权和对李立新的哀思权，造成原告终身的痛苦。当原告二人得知李立新病故的噩耗后悲痛欲绝，之后长期的彻夜不眠，精神恍惚，不能坚持工作和学习。被告的所作所为严重侵犯了原告的合法利益，经多次找被告协商解决无果，…（*北京市宣武区人民法院审理李佳婧、张道明与李淑兰、章哲其他人身权纠纷案民事判决书（2006）宣民初字第 4827 号*)

Example text 19 (case 14)

…我们对由于工作失误，在未得到授权就出版了原告作品表示深深的歉意…我社协同执行主编查找原作者联系途径，寄送稿酬。同时已将全部应付原作者的报酬一并支付给了执行主编，4 并在该书“编辑说明”中特别注明付酬联系方法。我社实际已履行了支付报酬的义务…（*巴金(李尧堂的笔名)诉吉林摄影出版社、北京新华图书有限责任公司侵犯使用权和获得报酬权纠纷案 北京市第一中级人民法院民事判决书（２０００）一中知初字第 １１７号*）

Example text 20 (case 16)

本院认为，土地管理属国家强制管理，土地所有权、使用权的转让必须经国家土地管理部门批准。中滩第二农场、中滩村经济合作社…其在未获得国家土地管理部门批准的情况下，无权擅自将该土地所有权、使用权、经营权、收益权作为投入与他人约定合作项目…（*北京市第一中级人民法院审理夏都公司诉中滩第二农场合作合同纠纷案判决书*）*(case 16)*

Example text 21 (case 17)

本院认为，苏伯进、屈家军… 描述得清清楚楚，真实可信；…被告的证人张丁莲、黄捍美、黄德源出庭作证的证词反映了事发前张涛醉酒等情况，客观真实，本院予以采信。分析造成本案发生的原因，…在张涛不醉酒的情况下，意外翻出白云旅社内天井栏杆并摔到一楼天井地板的可能性极小…（*广西壮族自治区横县人民法院审理张继高等与白云旅社、邓金芳人身损害赔偿纠纷案 民事判决书（2004）横民一初字第 666 号*）

Example text 22 (case 17)

原告张继高在公安机关对张涛死亡而制作的《尸体勘验笔录》中明确不同意解剖检验并签名，原告林秀清同意法医尸检结论，不要求进一步解剖检验并签名，造成对张涛是否醉酒没有法医学或医学上的鉴定结论，四原告对此也应承担举证不能的责任，所以，四原告称事发当晚张涛没有醉酒，证据不足，本院不予采信。（*广西壮族自治区横县人民法院审理张继高等与白云旅社、邓金芳人身损害赔偿纠纷案 民事判决书（2004）横民一初字第 666 号*）

Example text 23 (case 18)

本院认为，…本案原告…并未特别告知纸箱内装的是什么…旅客对自己物品的注意保管程度，明显大于承运人对旅客物品的注意保管程度…原告明知自己随身携带的是具有人格象征意义的特定纪念物…而草率地交给司乘人员，并且对应该由自己控制的物品疏于注意保管，致使随身携带的物品丢失，其责任应由自己承担…被告出于道义上的原因，积极配合、协助原告多方寻找…（*甘州区法院审理原告高嘉阳与被告张掖市昌运汽车运输有限责任公司、田吉生赔偿纠纷一案 民事判决书（2007）甘民初字第 97 号*）

Example text 24 (case 19)

本院认为：…被告作为酒楼经营者，对其出售的食品的安全及卫生应负高度的注意义务。…被告…主观上具有明显过错，故其对原告所遭受的人身损害及相应的财产损害负有完全赔偿责任。（*北京市朝阳区人民法院审理黄志勇与北京蜀国演义餐饮文化发展有限公司人身损害赔偿纠纷案 民事判决书（2007）朝民初字第 07667 号*）

Example text 25 (case 2)

本院认为：…成都商报社对周美凝举行小说《绝爱》签售活动时“性交易事件”的报道，来源于周美凝的叙述，反映的内容基本真实，在没有对方姓名的情况下也无核实的义务；对周美凝主动约见记者，公开当众明确指出其邀请来蓉担当签售嘉宾的影视大腕----“皇阿玛”就是张铁林的报道，反映的内容亦基本真实…（*北京市第二中级人民法院民事判决书（2003）二中民初字第 7230 号*）

Example text 26 (case 20)

…本院认为宜富思特公司已经初步证明了华通嘉业公司在陕西国华锦界电厂工程中使用被许可专利的事实。华通嘉业公司有义务且更容易举证…其应就其举证不能承担不利后果… （*北京市高级人民法院审理北京市华通嘉业空调设备有限责任公司诉北京宜富思特科技发展有限责任公司专利使用合同纠纷案民事判决书（2007）一中民初字第 5075 号*）

Example text 27 (case 21)

…对尸体的处分一般情况下应按照死者生前的意愿依遗嘱内容进行…符合一般的社会伦理道德标准…一般情况下会得到法律的支持…在死者生前未立有遗嘱的情况下…其尸体应由死者近亲属共同处分…一般情况下亦会得到法律的认可... 另一种情况，夫妻一方死亡后另一方再婚，先夫妻的合葬习俗受到法律保护还是后夫妻的合葬习俗受到法律保护？情况比较复杂… 因法律没有明确规定…一般应根据案件的具体情况按照社会的一般认识标准区别对待… *（江苏省徐州市贾汪区人民法院审理黄呈远诉张孝清其它特殊侵权纠纷案 民事判决书（2006）贾民一初字第 604 号）*

Example text 28 (case 8)

对格式合同的解释，应考虑到多数订约者而不是个别订约者的意志和利益，以订约者可能平均、合理的理解进行解释… 格式合同是由一方制定而非双方商定的，因此各项条款可能是制作人基于自己的意志所作的有利于自己的条款，尤其是条款制作人可能会故意使用或插入意义不明确的文字以损害相对方的利益，或者*(可能)*从维持其经济上的优势地位出发，将不合理的解释强加于相对方，因此，为维护相对方的利益，在条款不清楚或存在不同理解时，对条款制作人应做不利的解释…*（北京市海淀区人民法院审理姚中坚诉科学出版社出版合同纠纷一案 民事判决书（2004）海民初字第 19386 号）*

Example text 29 (case 18)

原告高嘉阳诉称： 2006 年 8 月 29 日，原告携带父亲骨灰盒，乘坐第二被告以第一被告名义经营的甘 G07788 号由兰州开往张掖的长途汽车，按照被告票员的要求将骨灰盒放在车底货仓，8 月 30 日早晨，被告的车到张掖后，原告下车取骨灰盒时却发现不见了. 原告按照被告的意思，发广告并多次花去交通费、住宿费，往返于兰州至张掖及张掖各县寻找骨灰盒，但没有结果。原告丢失了寄托父亲哀思的骨灰盒后，精神恍惚抑郁，受到严重伤害。故起诉要求被告赔偿…*（甘州区法院审理原告高嘉阳与被告张掖市昌运汽车运输有限责任公司、田吉生赔偿纠纷一案 民事判决书（2007）甘民初字第 97 号）*

Example text 30 (case 16)

原告夏都公司诉称：2001 年 9 月 25 日，夏都公司与中滩第二农场和中滩村经济合作社签订了合作合同，中滩第二农场和中滩村经济合作社以土地投资，夏都公司负责其他全部投资，合作经营天通苑西区 32.4 亩土地。夏都公司投资做了大量前期准备工作，并委托有丰富经验、资质的技术服务企业做了大量前期技术服务工作，中滩第二农场、中滩村经济合作社拒不履行合同义务，不出具土地方应出具的规划、转制等手续，并于 2002 年 4 月 12 日，以低于与夏都公司的合同很多的价格，与其他公司另行签订了合作合同，给夏都公司造成损失。(*北京市第一中级人民法院审理夏都公司诉中滩第二农场合作合同纠纷案判决书*)

Example text 31 (case 14)

原告李尧堂诉称：２０００年４月，被告新华图书公司发行被告吉林摄影出版社出版的《二十世纪中国著名作家散文经典》系列丛书。该丛书之《寻梦》单行本，署名巴金，共收入原告创作的作品３０篇。被告吉林摄影出版社未经原告同意，擅自将原告创作的散文作品汇编成集并出版发行，未向原告支付报酬。该书的书名、选目和编排都不符合原告的意愿。被告吉林摄影出版社的行为侵犯了原告依法对其创作作品享有的著作权中的使用权和获得报酬权，给原告造成了物质上和精神上的损失。(*巴金(李尧堂的笔名)诉吉林摄影出版社、北京新华图书有限责任公司侵犯使用权和获得报酬权纠纷案 北京市第一中级人民法院民事判决书（２０００）一中知初字第 １１７号*)

Example text 32 (case 19)

…事发至今，原告不仅承受着身体上的剧烈疼痛及药物治疗带来的副作用，更是由于该病初期的无法确诊及潜在的后遗症等问题给原告精神上造成无法弥补的伤害… 后经查，被告…加工工艺不当…是导致原告无辜染病以及引发本次“重大突发公共卫生事件”的原因所在。…被告作为食品生产经营者，是食品安全的第一责任人，保护消费者的食品卫生及安全是生产经营者的法定责任。在本案中，被告的过错行为导致原告损害事实及结果的发生，严重侵害了原告的人身权利。(*北京市朝阳区人民法院审理黄志勇与北京蜀国演义餐饮文化发展有限公司人身损害赔偿纠纷案 民事判决书（2007）朝民初字第 07667 号*)

Example text 33 (case 22)

被告毛毛食品公司辩称：1、我公司对给赵明造成的损失表示道歉… 赵明所述的损害事实虽然存在，但损害的过程有出入… 赵明的法定代理人也应承担一部分责任。2、损害发生后我公司员工积极陪着赵明买药、看病，尽到了相应的责任。3、我公司同意赔偿赵明的合理损失，但赵明需要提交证据证明相应的损失，…赵明要求的交通费应有正式票据。原告赵明没有误工，因此其要求的误工费实际应是护理费，又因营养费需有医疗机构出具的证明，故我公司对于赵明要求的误工费及营养费不予认可…（*北京市通州区人民法院审理原告赵明与被告北京华普联合商业投资有限公司、哈尔滨毛毛食品有限公司一般人身损害赔偿纠纷案 民事判决书（2007）通民初字第 9225 号*）

Example text 34 (case 15)

被告矿迪公司答辩称：首先，涉案专利不具备新颖性和创造性，不应获得专利权。被告已就此向国家知识产权局专利复审委员会提出了宣告该专利权无效的申请。其次，本案被控侵权物与原告的专利有实质区别，不构成对原告专利权的侵犯。因此，请求驳回原告的诉讼请求。（*北京市第二中级人民法院审理北京恩菲通用设备科技有限公司等诉北京矿迪科技有限公司侵犯专利权纠纷案 一审民事判决书 (2007)二中民初字第 6753 号*）

Example text 35 (case 9)

本院认为，因第三人侵权导致损害结果发生，安全保障义务人有过错的，应当在其能够防止或者制止损害的范围内承担相应的补充赔偿责任。被告作为宾馆经营者，对旅客负有安全保障义务，并应该遵守《旅馆业治安管理办法》及《北京市实施〈旅馆业治安管理办法〉细则》的规定，如…

本案被告在发现陈瑜退房后留宿其女友魏巍的客房，未按照《旅馆业治安管理办法》及《北京市实施〈旅馆业治安管理办法〉细则》规定采取管理措施，违反了该规定，在防范问题上存在过错。… 被告存在疏忽大意的过失。在陈瑜杀害魏巍的事件中，被告没有尽到安全保障义务，应当在其能够防止或者制止损害的范围内承担相应的补充赔偿责任。

现原告以被告没有尽到合理限度范围内的安全保障义务、陈瑜无财产可供执行为由，要求被告承担补充赔偿责任，理由正当，本院予以支持。但原告要求被告赔偿应由陈瑜赔偿的全部损失，要求过高… 具体赔偿数额，本院酌定。（*北京市宣武区人民法院审理魏秀贵、刘玉杰与北京万程世都宾馆有限责任公司人身损害赔偿纠纷一案 民事判决书（2005）宣民初字第 3925 号*）

Example text 36 (case 23)

本院认为：林德飞驾驶被告被告宁波中外运久凌储运有限公司所有的货车，在履行职务过程中与原告发生碰撞，造成原告受伤的交通事故，经交警部门勘查认定，林德飞负事故的全部责任，原告不负事故责任，交警部门的责任认定准确，本院予以支持。原告合理部分的损失应由林德飞赔偿，由于林德飞系被告被告宁波中外运久凌储运有限公司的雇佣驾驶员，发生事故时林德飞在履行职务行为，故被告宁波中外运久凌储运有限公司应承担赔偿责任。（*浙江省丽水市莲都区人民法院审理原告张鲁兴与被告宁波中外运久凌储运有限公司道路交通事故人身损害赔偿纠纷一案 民事判决书（2006）莲民初字第 1027 号*）

Example text 37 (case 24)

本院认为：依法成立的合同，对当事人具有法律约束力。银行与储户建立储蓄存折，双方的存储合同关系即告成立。双方均应履行合同内容。当事人就有关合同履行方式约定不明确的，按照有利于实现合同目的的方式履行。该存折系在中国人民银行规定实名制之前开户，根据中国人民银行 2000 年 126 号文件中第 2 条第 1 项规定…原告取款时，被告应审核其有效身份证件后予以支付。被告辩称审核发现原告不能提供与存折姓名一致的身份证，该存折的户名也无相应有效证件印证… 因该存折开户是在中国人民银行规定实名制之前，原告与存折户名不一致及无相应有效证件印证并非原告之过错… 被告要求原告书面承诺保留对所支取款项的追索权，这种做法并无法律依据…（*北京市宣武区人民法院审理杨琳诉中国银行北京市宣武区支行储蓄存款合同纠纷案 民事判决书（2004）宣民初字第 1703 号*）

Example text 38 (case 25)

本院认为：对美好环境和幸福生活的向往是大家的共同追求。本案原告的居所区域属国家 2 类标准区域，在这种混合区域出现的噪声问题，根据有关部门的监测，噪声的来源并非是唯一的；虽然根据监测结果显示，噪声较比国家规定的标准略有超出，对原告的居住生活会造成一定的影响，但由于噪声来源的多样性，难以确认被告的单方责任；且根据监测数据反映，在被告车辆夜间停运后区域噪声亦存在超标情形。故现原告要求被告排除危害、赔偿损失，本院不予支持。（*北京市朝阳区人民法院审理王大丰诉北京市公共交通总公司第七客运分公司环境噪声污染赔偿纠纷案民事判决书（2004）朝民初字第 06781 号*）

Example text 39 (case 1)

本院认为：王荣福因病入住酒仙桥医院接受治疗，双方形成了医疗服务的合同关系，…王荣福病愈出院时，足额交纳了住院医疗费用，双方实现了医疗服务合同法律关系中各自的权利、义务内容。现王荣福因得知酒仙桥医院曾对患者进行心脏介入治疗时复用过心导管，而对自己在接受心脏介入治疗时所使用的心导管是否是一次性合格产品产生怀疑，是可以理解的。… 对此，作为提供医疗服务一方的酒仙桥医院，有责任举证证明其对王荣福的治疗过程符合医疗规范。在本案的审理过程中，酒仙桥医院提供了… 由此可以认定，酒仙桥医院在对王荣福进行心脏介入手术及治疗的过程符合医疗规范，并无不当。且王荣福术后痊愈良好，没有损害结果的发生。现王荣福仅以有关媒体报导了酒仙桥医院存在对患者进行心脏介入治疗时，有复用心导管的情况，而认定酒仙桥医院对其本人治疗时，亦复用了心导管，显属证据不足。又鉴于酒仙桥医院举证证明了其对王荣福的治疗过程符合医疗规范，故对王荣福要求酒仙桥医院返还医疗费之请求，本院不予支持。（*北京市朝阳区人民法院审理王荣福诉北京酒仙桥医院医疗服务合同纠纷民事判决书（2003）朝民初字第 9980 号*）

Example text 40 (case 23)

本院认为：…在本起交通事故中，…原告…在推行电动三轮车过程中因操作不当，导致电动三轮车失控，撞翻被告谭亚萍摆放早餐店门口油锅，造成原告…烫伤，…应负本起交通事故主要责任。…被告李春峰将电动三轮车停放店门口道路上，致使道路受阻，且疏忽大意未将车钥匙拔下，致使周翠凤在推行三轮车过程中失控，撞翻油窝，造成原告烫伤，被告的行为与原告受伤有一定因果关系，故被告李春峰应承担一定的赔偿责任。…被告谭亚萍从事餐饮经营活动，将油锅置放于店门口道路上，占道经营，被告未尽合理限度范围内的安全保障义务致使原告受伤，故被告谭亚萍也应承担一定的赔偿责任。（*浙江丽水市莲都区人民法院审理原告徐上根与被告李春峰、赵荣平、谭亚萍道路交通事故人身损害赔偿纠纷一案民事判决书（2007）莲民初字第 458 号*）

Appendix II. Excerpts

Excerpt 1

在国外打官司不请律师这是不可想象的，在国内这种情况却比较普遍。这八成多没请律师代理的案件包括不请律师和公民以个人身份代理两种情况。虽然近几年律师行业发展较快，但对普通百姓来说，仍然比较神秘。对于收费标准、服务质量等问题，老百姓仍然存在着不少疑虑。因此在打官司时，不少人认为请律师作用不大，或者不知道怎么请到最合适的律师。（“八成民事案件不请律师”，*北京青年报*，2004 年 2 月 12 日）

Excerpt 2

法官总是想把概括地把所有的信息都讲出来 … 诉讼的过程太复杂，用一两段话根本讲不透彻. 法官所做的也只是粗略的提一下这些信息. 如果有需要，他们可以汇报庭审中关键的事情，但不需要用以这么粗略的方式汇报所有的事情. （*律师 A 采访录音*）

Excerpt 3

加快裁判文书的改革步伐，提高裁判文书的质量。改革的重点是加强对质证中有争议证据的分析、认证，增强判决的说理性；通过裁判文书，不仅记录裁判过程，而且公开裁判理由，使裁判文书成为向社会公众展示司法公正形象的载体，进行法制教育的生动教材. （*《人民法院一五改革纲要》中华人民共和国最高人民法院*）

Excerpt 4

中共中央政治局委员、书记处书记、中央政法委书记罗干…对海淀区人民法院荣获“全国优秀法院”称号并荣立集体一等功表示祝贺。他说，海淀法院是一个好典型，…海淀法院在提高政治素质的同时，很注意提高自己的业务素质，法官们把法律知识和科技知识结合起来，很好地审结了一大批案件，得到了人民群众的赞赏。（*罗干接见海淀区法院代表时强调公正执法是政法工作的永恒主题海淀法院先进事迹报告会在京举行《人民日报 》1998-12-05*）

Excerpt 5

作为全国 3000 多个基层法院的优秀代表，海淀法院以司法公正为根本目标，建立了一流队伍，创造了一流业绩，赢得了…人民的信任，在人民群众中树立了人民法院和人民法官的良好形象。（*"科技高地"上的公正天平，《人民法院报》，2008-1-31*）

Excerpt 6

十、…公民、法人因名誉权受到侵害要求赔偿的，侵权人应赔偿侵权行为造成的经济损失；公民并提出精神损害赔偿要求的，人民法院可根据侵权人的过错程度、侵权行为的具体情节、给受害人造成精神损害的后果等情况酌定。（*最高人民法院关于审理名誉权案件若干问题的解答*）

Excerpt 7

…目前在大部分民事案件中，原告要求赔偿精神损害的现象越来越普遍。这一方面反映了公众权利意识的觉醒，同时也透露出公众在行使权利时存在很多模糊空间。因此法官提醒公众，在提起诉讼请求时应慎而又慎，不可一味地为了满足自己的心理需求而漫无目的地要求对方赔偿精神损害。这样的话，不但需要支付更高的诉讼费和律师费，而且还不一定能获得法院的支持。目前上海市规定，精神损害赔偿的最高额为 5 万元人民币。如果"狮子大开口"，就很有可能"赢了官司，输了钱"。（*上海规定最高 5 万元精神损害赔偿，上海商报，2004-10-15*）

Excerpt 8

法官在'原告诉称'和'被告辩称'两个部分不会原封不动的汇报当事人的观点。在原被告之间可能有多个争议和问题，他们只考虑那些和案件有法律相关性的问题。法律确实规定法官有权分析当事人的观点，以确认法律事实。可法律没有规定要在判决书的'原告诉称'和'被告辩称'两个部分汇报所认定的法律事实，这样做只是一种惯例。（*律师 B 采访录音*）

Excerpt 9

大部分民事诉讼案件的被告的确是或多或少侵犯了原告的权益. 我觉得被告作为过错方是不会像原告那样咄咄逼人的. 如果显现出太强的逃避责任的意图, 反而对被告的答辩不利. 因为我们希望被告能表现出对原告所遭遇的不幸的理解, 尽管他的主要目的是减轻自己的责任. (*律师C采访录音*)

Excerpt 10

民事诉讼中我和我的同事都会遇到许多关于日常生活的一些纠纷, 比如邻里之间的争吵, 轻微的交通事故, 轻微的人身伤害等等. 我们谈论或讲述这些纠纷的时候, 写作的目的并不仅是报告一下纠纷的发生过程. 我们写作的每句话都表述了我们对具体的法律或事实问题的专业理解和分析. 遣词造句上也许我们会有些差别, 但大家都认为不管是专业还是日常的纠纷, 律师的写作都应该讲究策略, 都应该有一定的目的. (*律师D采访录音*)

Excerpt 11

第十七条 …专利权的保护范围应当以权利要求书中明确记载的必要技术特征所确定的范围为准，也包括与该必要技术特征相等同的特征所确定的范围。等同特征是指与所记载的技术特征以基本相同的手段，实现基本相同的功能，达到基本相同的效果… (*最高人民法院关于审理专利纠纷案件适用法律问题的若干规定（２００１年6月１９日最高人民法院审判委员会第１１８０ 次会议通过）法释（２００１）２１号*)

Excerpt 12

合同是当时人之间的磋商和协议. 合同涉及的问题可以小到买一本书, 也可以大到买一个油轮, 可这些都是当事人之间的私人事务, 只影响当事人的权利和义务. 可我们诉讼中面对的是违法事件的时候, 考虑的问题就不一样了. 除了法律问题, 我们还要考虑政治和社会伦理问题… 为人民服务是我们重要的工作. (*法官E采访录音*)

Excerpt 13

可能因为所涉及的法律是律师和法官熟知的，所以法官觉得没有写的必要。司法实践有时是这样的，但对提高判决书的说理没有什么好处。也有可能法官觉得原告、被告、以及他们的律师经过庭审都知道了该用的法律，而且法官又意识不到他们的判决其他的人也会读，所以他们对高人民法院司法改革对改善判决书写作的要求不太在意。(*律师 F 采访录音*)

Excerpt 14

法官能够做到司法独立…还有很长的路要走，但这些还是在逐渐改变。 有些诉讼文书写的很流畅，能反映诉讼实践过程。有些案件视乎有必要公开信息，但也有实际的困难。 法官在这些案件里也试图解决这个矛盾，他们在撰写判决书时会把能公开的事实问题汇报清楚，把能公开的法律问题分析的深入和透彻一些。这样判决书就能比较好的反映诉讼的实践过程。(*律师 G 访谈录音*)

Appendix III. Interview questions

Move-based questions

1. How often do you read civil judgments? In what situations, you will use a civil judgment?
2. Would you please share you viewpoints on the purposes of civil judgments?
3. Can you talk in a broad sense about your professional observations on the characteristics and quality of civil judgments?
4. Why are so many details about litigation participants introduced in the beginning of civil judgment? Is it necessary?
5. Are there any differences in how individual participants are introduced and how corporate participants are introduced?
6. Why are lawyers, as counsels, absent in a number of civil trials?
7. Why is the beginning of civil judgments written in a vague and simplified way?
8. The explicit discussion and illustration of issues rarely occur in civil judgment, why so? Is this legitimate?
9. There are a few judgments where judges supply elaborative reports of evidential examination and explicit lists of disputable issues. Compared to other judgments, in what sense are these judgments special?
10. Why is there a close correspondence between the information disclosed in 'plaintiffs' claim' and 'defendants' defense' and the information in 'facts found by the court'? Anyway, the former is meant to represent parties' understanding and arguments and the latter is facts identified by the judges?
11. In 'plaintiffs' claim' and 'defendants' defense', those information in the original indictments and statement of defenses are reformulated and simplified by the judges, why?
12. Evidence is conventionally not integrated with litigation participants' arguments; rather, they are listed as isolated paragraphs. Is this way of using evidence convincing? Why?

13. The majority of civil judgments rendered by Beijing *Haidian People's Court* supply comparatively more detailed report of parties' arguments and more elaborative discussions of legal issues. Why can this court do so?
14. Why do judges write 'judges' opinions' as single paragraph essays which are difficult to read? Readers, specialist or non-specialist, may not even know how many issues are being handled? What do you comment on this phenomenon?
15. Why is the information about appealing not sufficiently told to parties? Is it necessary to telling more about it? What is judges' practical consideration to decide what information to tell in 'courts' decisions'?

Lexico-grammar based questions

1. 'Plaintiffs' claim' uses a lot of numerical expressions to report the economic loss suffered by plaintiffs. It is true that the total number is always reported, but not all specific numbers? Why? Is this missing of specific numbers created by plaintiffs or by judges?
2. When specific numbers and total number are both listed, is it possible the total number is calculated wrongly? Do you ever experience this?
3. The numerical expressions in 'plaintiffs' claim' are frequently repeated in 'facts found by the court', but in a more precise way, why so? This information correspondence is popular. Do judges have any intention to purposefully simplify expressions in 'plaintiffs' claims' when they could have been more precise?
4. In cases where plaintiffs claim the compensation of mental distress, there are big difference between the claimed amount which is normally very high and the finally awarded one which is quite small. Can you explain this difference?
5. Most plaintiffs seem to know their claimed compensation of mental distress will end up with a small sum, but they still claim

high, why? Are they aware they will be charged a high court fee because of this?

6. Defendants' original arguments use temporal numerical expressions as a useful tool to improve precision in their discussion of evidence and description of fact. Why are these expressions completely missing in 'defendants' defense' of civil judgment? Why do judges reformulate defendants' arguments in this way?
7. If plaintiffs have discussed fact and evidence in their indictments, will defendants repeat them in statements of defense, why? For what purposes?
8. Do Mainland Chinese judges explain the law only to adjudicate the dispute at hand? Do they have the intention to give examples for other judges to follow? To what extent? Who do they expect will read or refer to their civil judgments?
9. It is not uncommon that judges use a variety of rhetorical devices like emphatics and hedging to demonstrate their personal or professional attitudes towards parties. In what situations do they use more of these devices and in what situations do they restrain the use? Will they consider the difference between tort and contract?
10. Is it a coincidence that judges show a strong negative attitude towards illegal land dealers? In what way, this way of writing is (not) legally professional?
11. Parties, either plaintiffs or defendants, seldom use hedging in civil judgment. Do they not have a chance to use or do they resist to use it, why? When will they use it? For what purposes?
12. A big bus company in Beijing is sued because the noise it makes has influenced somebody's life. However, important decisions like locating terminals are made or should be approved by the government. In the final judgment, the judges do not mention the real decision-maker (government) at all in factual and legal discussions. Why can judges not introduce the government in civil judgment?
13. In some occasions, judges seem to take hedging as required not optional, why? Is it to claim their personal existence and identity? Or to avoid too strong commitment? Or simply because expressions with hedging are sufficient, no stronger expressions needed?

14. How do you comment judges' interpretation of law? Are they formulaic? To what extent do judges express their professional expertise?
15. Are judges proud of their own interpretation of law, of social norms, of newly and never-occurred issues? Why do they use hedges, usually quite a lot, then?
16. Present Example text 45 and 46 of Appendix I to specialist informants and ask for their comments and observations on the rhetorical characteristics of texts?

Coherence-based questions

1. Is it difficult to read civil judgments? Which sections are comparatively easy, and which are difficult?
2. Comment on this example text:

   > The plaintiff X claimed: August 29, 2006, the plaintiff, carrying his father's cinerary casket, got on the bus (G07788) run by the second defendant in the name of the first defendant from Lanzhou to Zhangye. Upon the request of the defendants' steward, the plaintiff put the casket into the bus' bottom luggage hold. On the morning of August 30, after the defendants' bus arrived in Zhangye, the plaintiff got off the bus only to find the casket was lost. With the defendants' advices, the plaintiff circulated advertisements and went back and forth from Lanzhou to Zhangye to find the casket. His efforts turned out fruitless and he had to pay the transportation and boarding fees many times.

   All sentences of this text begin with the word 'plaintiff'. Are these simply coincident or arranged with a purpose? When 'defendant' can have been chosen to start a sentence, the sentence will be changed into subordinate ones, why so?
3. Comment on this example text:

   > Afterwards inspection shows the defendants' improper cooking methods [...] are the actual reason why this 'serious public health accidence' has happened [...].

> The defendant is the provider of food and he should be the first person in charge of the food safety; it is food providers' legal obligation to ensure the safety and hygiene of food provided to customers.
> In this case, the defendant's wrong-doings results in the plaintiff's damages and has seriously infringed the plaintiff's personal rights.

The plaintiff of this text talks not much about his own suffering, however, he chooses to talk more about the defendant's action. What is the consideration to make this choice? Is this choice made by the plaintiff or by his lawyer? What is the connection among these three paragraphs?

4. Have you ever read civil judgments whose structure is poorly organized? What are the possible reasons for the poor organization? Comment on the example text:

> The plaintiff claimed: I, accompanied by two friends on July 26, 2003, went to see the defendant and had an operation by Y to erase under-eye bags. Before the operation, the defendant told me there would be no wrinkles and no hollow eyes. But after operation, I got two hollows under my eyes, bulges on my lower eyelids, and quite a lot wrinkles around my eyes. Through investigation, I knew defendant's business scope does not cover medical beautifying and Y does not have doctor qualification. But defendant used deceitful methods, did operation on me without official authorization, hurt my eyes and brought my severe spiritual damages.

5. In the following case, there are two defendants and only one of them is accused in civil judgment, as shown in the following text, why? Do you have any legal or social explanations?

> The plaintiff X claimed: Defendant Y, April 2004, distributes serious books – ABC published by defendant Z. *Search of Dreams* in this serious is authored by X, which collected 30 works written by X. Defendant Z, as they wish, collected and published plaintiff's works without plaintiff's authorization and it did not pay. The titles, choices and arrangements of the book does not conform the author's wish. Defendant Z's actions violated plaintiff's lawful copyrights (rights to use and rights to be paid) over his created works and brought material and spiritual damages to plaintiff.
> This defendant, as one official publishing unit of the state, publicly offended the law and randomly infringed the author's rights; its infringing actions are

serious and the nature of its actions is malicious and severe. Defendant Y's action also consists of infringement over plaintiff's copyrights.
To protect the plaintiff's lawful rights, the plaintiff, according to the related regulations of PRC Copyright Law, requested the court to order defendants: 1, to stop distributing the pirated book *Search of Dreams*; 2, to compensate the plaintiff RMB 99,000; 3 [...].

6. Comment on the following defense. Is it sufficient to defy the plaintiff's accusation related to the defendant's illegal use of patent? Can the order of two arguments be reversed?

    Defendant Y defended: First, the paten in dispute is not of novelty and inventiveness and should not be registered as patent. Defendant has applied The Patent Reexamination Board of the State Intellectual Property Office of PRC to declare the invalidity of this patent. Second, the accused technology has material difference with plaintiff's patent and does not infringe plaintiff's patented rights. So, we require the court to deny plaintiff's claims.

7. When defendants actually have done the accused action, judges normally use much effort to discuss defendants' wrong actions and little effort is spent on plaintiffs' claim. Why so? Is the somehow neglect of plaintiffs legitimate?
8. When judges have to refer to the decisions made by administrative units, how will they handle them? What is the normal practice?
9. Judges often literarily mirror the occurring of facts. What is the role of this chronological writing?
10. When plaintiffs' claims are unreasonable or without legitimate support, judges will devote most of their effort to the discussion of plaintiffs' claim, in order to defy them. Why do they not support defendants directly or just declare defendants have done nothing wrong? Is there any significant difference between these two ways of writing?
11. Why do judges seem to support the party who will lose the trial by showing their personal understanding to the party's motivation and emotion in starting the lawsuit?

12. In cases where both parties will lose, why do judges handle the party with most liability first? How about the party with less liability first?
13. What is the difference between fact in ‘facts found by the court’ and fact in ‘judges’ opinions’? Why do judges discuss facts twice in two places? Is this required or optional? Why?

Appendix IV. Interview questions in Chinese

关于民事判决书内容和总体结构的访谈问题

1. 你经常阅读民事判决书吗? 什么情况下你会使用民事判决书?
2. 关于民事判决书的作用, 你有什么看法?
3. 能不能大致谈一下你对内地民事判决书的写作质量和特点的一些看法和思考?
4. 民事判决书在开头介绍诉讼参加人的时候, 会提供很详细的信息, 为什么? 有这个必要吗?
5. 在介绍个体参加人和公司参加人的时候有什么样的区别?
6. 为什么很多的民事诉讼没有律师作为代理人出现?
7. 为什么民事判决书的"开场白"总是很模糊, 过于简单化? 有必要写这个开场白吗?
8. 很少有民事判决书清楚的列出并讨论审判的主要问题, 这样合适吗? 为什么?
9. 在所选的判决书里, 有一小部分判决书很详细的汇报了证据的质证过程, 还清楚地列出了审判的主要问题. 比起其他判决书, 这一小部分判决书有什么特殊的意义吗, 尤其考虑到中国的司法改革?
10. 为什么"原告诉称"部分披露的信息和法院认定"事实"部分汇报的信息有很多的一致性? 毕竟, 前者应再现原告的理解(诉求), 后者是法官认定为有司法效力的法定事实?
11. 在写作"原告诉称"和"被告辩称"的过程中, 原告起诉书和被告答辩书中的很多信息被从新表述, 简化, 为什么? 法官写作判决书的理论目的和实际目的是什么?
12. 民事判决书提到的证据通常单独汇报, 而不是和要支持的论述融合在一起。这样的写作方式有说服力吗? 为什么?
13. 北京市海淀区人民法院发布的大部分判决书对当事人的主张都有比较详细的汇报，而且会详细探讨审判涉及的法律问题? 为什么这个法院可以做到这样?
14. 法官阐述法庭意见的时候，论述很长也不分段，也没有讲述要讨论的问题。专业还是非专业读者，都不容易判断法官要分析的问题。能不能评价一下这个现象?
15. 民事判决书最后要告知当事人上述的权利，为什么这种告知披露的信息非常不具体? 有没有必要说的详细一点? 决定应该告知什么信息的时候法官又什么现实的考虑吗?

关于民事判决书遣词造句和语法使用的访谈问题

1. 为了报告自己的损失和所要求的赔偿，原告在“原告诉称”这个部分用了大量关于数字的表述. 所有的判决书都会把损失和赔偿的总的数额写明，可这个总的数额有什么具体项目和要求构成并不是都写清楚，相当一部分都被省略了.为什么？这种之列明部分损失项目和赔偿要求的写法是谁写的，出于怎样的考虑？
2. 有的判决书列明了全部的具体损失项目和赔偿要求，可这些所列数目之和和判决书写明的总的损失和赔偿数目之间有时候并部吻合？这是写作错误，还是其他原因造成的，你见过这样的判决书吗？
3. “原告诉称”部分涉及的数字表述很多都会又出现在“事实”部分，而且表述也都变得更为精确，这种写作现象又什么意义吗，为什么？这种信息的前后呼应不仅仅局限于数字表述，在事实讨论中也经常会有. 什么原因造成了这种信息呼应？这和写作判决书有关联吗？
4. 有些原告要求了精神赔偿，面对很高的要求数额，法官通常只判定极低的实际赔偿. 为什么会这样，法官的做法有什么依据和考虑？在可以预见的未来，这种现象会发生改变吗？
5. 大部分提出精神赔偿的原告似乎知道内地法官只会判定数额极低的赔偿，他们为什么还要提出很高的数额？他们不担心诉讼费会变的很高吗？
6. 被告在答辩书里会使用不少关于时间的表述，用来提高他们讨论证据和描述事实的准确性. 可这些用法在判决书的“被告辩称”部分都被省略了，被告原来的写作目的也没有得到体现. 为什么法官要这样表现被告的论述？
7. 如果原告在起诉书中已经描述过事实和证据问题，被告会以什么方式表述自己对相同问题的理解？有什么写作目的？
8. 法官在判决书中的法律解释仅仅是为了裁决手头的争议吗？他们有没有其他目的，会不会考虑其他法官的看法？多大程度上，他们会期望起他的法官和律师会使用自己写的判决书？
9. 法官经常会使用强调或模糊等修辞方式来表达他们对诉讼参加人的态度. 什么情况下他们对修辞手法的使用比较随意，什么情况下他们会克制这种使用？他们会不会考虑侵权案件和合同案件的不同？
10. 法官对土地的非法交易所持的强烈否定态度是偶然的吗？为什么？什么因素决定了他们的这种态度？
11. 不管原告还是被告，在写作中都较少的使用模糊语，是因为他们拒绝使用还是没有机会使用？他们会出于什么目的使用模糊语？
12. 有人起诉北京的一家大的公交公司，理由是公交公司制造的噪音严重干扰了他的生活. 但对于公交公司，像选择公交站场之类的重大决定都是由政府做出或批准的. 在最后的判决中，法官对政府作为决策者的事实只字不提，为什么？法官可不可以在民事诉讼中探讨政府的责任？

13. 一些民事诉讼中，为什么法官似乎必须使用模糊语来表明他们对法律和事实的看法和理解？是为了表示法官作为个体的存在？为了避免太过肯定的语气？还是因为模糊的表达已经很充分了，不需要语气强烈的表达？
14. 你对法官在判决书中的法律解释有什么看法？是格式化的写作？还是自己专业的论述？
15. 法官会不会对自己对法律，社会规则，以及新生社会问题的解释感到自豪？如果自豪，他们为什么还要用模糊语来和这些解释保持一定的距离？
16. 请看附录 A 中的 32 和 33，能不能就这两个文本的修辞特点给与评价和分析？

关于判决书文本连贯性的访谈问题

1. 你觉得阅读民事判决书困难吗？对非法律认识呢？那部分相对容易理解，那部分困难一些，为什么？
2. 请阅读并评价下面一段话：
   原告高嘉阳诉称： 2006 年 8 月 29 日，原告携带父亲骨灰盒，乘坐第二被告以第一被告名义经营的甘 G07788 号由兰州开往张掖的长途汽车，按照被告票员的要求将骨灰盒放在车底货仓，8 月 30 日早晨，被告的车到张掖后，原告下车取骨灰盒时却发现不见了. 原告按照被告的意思，发广告并多次花去交通费、住宿费，往返于兰州至张掖及张掖各县寻找骨灰盒，但没有结果。原告丢失了寄托父亲哀思的骨灰盒后，精神恍惚抑郁，受到严重伤害。故起诉要求被告赔偿…（*甘州区法院审理原告高嘉阳与被告张掖市昌运汽车运输有限责任公司、田吉生赔偿纠纷一案民事判决书（2007）甘民初字第 97 号*）
   这段话中的句子都已“原告”开始，这是一种巧合还是有意的写作安排？即使本来应该以“被告”开头的句子，也通过句子时态的变化让“原告”位于句首，为什么这样安排，有什么目的？
3. 阅读并评价下面一段话：
   …事发至今，原告不仅承受着身体上的剧烈疼痛及药物治疗带来的副作用，更是由于该病初期的无法确诊及潜在的后遗症等问题给原告精神上造成无法弥补的伤害… 后经查，被告…加工工艺不当…是导致原告无辜染病以及引发本次“重大突发公共卫生事件”的原因所在。
   …被告作为食品生产经营者，是食品安全的第一责任人，保护消费者的食品卫生及安全是生产经营者的法定责任。
   在本案中，被告的过错行为导致原告损害事实及结果的发生，严重侵害了原告的人身权利。（*北京市朝阳区人民法院审理黄志勇与北京蜀国演义餐饮文化发展有限公司人身损害赔偿纠纷案 民事判决书（2007）朝民初字第 07667 号*）

原告的写作并没有集中在自己所受的“痛苦”上面，他反而更多的是讨论被告行为的法律性质。在这两种写作方式之间做出选择的时候，原告有什考虑？这种写作方式是原告的选择还是代理律师的选择？这三段话之间的逻辑关系是什么？

4. 你有没有遇到过“原告诉称”这个部分组织的不好的判决书？什么原因会造成这个部分写的不好？请评价下面这段话：
   原告诉称：2003 年 7 月 26 日，我由两个朋友陪同到被告处由任学会主刀做了祛除眼袋手术。术前，被告承诺我不会出现皱纹，不会眼窝凹陷。但术后，我眼睛下面出现了两个坑，形成了凹陷，下眼脸边缘突起，眼周围出现多处皱纹。经我调查，得知被告没有医疗美容的经营范围，任学会也无医师资格。但被告却对我采用欺骗的手段，擅自开刀做手术，伤害了我的眼睛，致使我精神上受到极大打击。（*北京市朝阳区人民法院审理李桂凤诉北京任伊美美容中心医疗美容损害赔偿纠纷案民事判决书（2004）朝民初字第 04683 号*）

5. 下面这个案件有两个被告，为什么只有一个被强烈的控诉？原告的选择有没有法律或社会层面的解释？
   原告李尧堂诉称：２０００年４月，被告新华图书公司发行被告吉林摄影出版社出版的《二十世纪中国著名作家散文经典》系列丛书。该丛书之《寻梦》单行本，署名巴金，共收入原告创作的作品３０篇。被告吉林摄影出版社未经原告同意，擅自将原告创作的散文作品汇编成集并出版发行，未向原告支付报酬。该书的书名、选目和编排都不符合原告的意愿。被告吉林摄影出版社的行为侵犯了原告依法对其创作作品享有的著作权中的使用权和获得报酬权，给原告造成了物质上和精神上的损失。该被告作为国家的正式出版单位，公然无视法律规定，肆意侵犯作者权益，侵权情节十分严重，侵权性质十分恶劣。被告新华图书公司的行为也构成对原告的侵权。（*巴金（李尧堂的笔名）诉吉林摄影出版社、北京新华图书有限责任公司侵犯使用权和获得报酬权纠纷案 北京市第一中级人民法院民事判决书（２０００）一中知初字第 １１７号*）

6. 请评价下面一个被告的答辩。原告起诉被告非法使用了他的专利，被告的答辩够不够充分，能不能驳斥原告的诉求？这里的两个论述能颠倒顺序吗？
   被告矿迪公司答辩称：首先，涉案专利不具备新颖性和创造性，不应获得专利权。被告已就此向国家知识产权局专利复审委员会提出了宣告该专利权无效的申请。其次，本案被控侵权物与原告的专利有实质区别，不构成对原告专利权的侵犯。因此，请求驳回原告的诉讼请求。（*北京市第二中级人民法院审理北京恩菲通用设备科技有限公司等诉北京矿迪科技有限公司侵犯专利权纠纷案 一审民事判决书（2007）二中民初字第 6753 号*）

7. 当原告的诉求不合理或者没有合法依据时，法官会把写作精力集中在探讨这样的诉求如何不合理和为什么法庭不能接受上面．法官为什么不直接分析或宣称被告的行为没有过错？这两种写作侧重点有什么不同？
8. 如果被告被起诉的行为的确存在，法官通常将主要精力放在讨论被告的违法行为上，而极少谈到原告的权利和诉求本身，为什么？这种情况下的对原告的忽视和不合理？
9. 主持民事诉讼的法官如果不得不使用行政机构做出的决定，他们会怎么处理？有没有惯常的做法？
10. 法官讲述事实问题的时候，都是直白的叙述．这样顺序的写作方式有什么作用？
11. 在一些判决书里，法官写清楚他们对原告的起诉目的和情绪的理解和分析，即使这些目的和情绪可能没有法律支持，法官这样做的目的是什么？
12. 为什么在原被告都有过错的案件中，法官通常先处理有较多过错一方的责任，然后是过错较少的一方？ 能不能顺序反一下？
13. "事实"部分和"法庭意见"部分，法官都会讲到法庭对事实问题的认定．为什么要在不同的地方重复探讨事实问题，二者之间有差别吗？这样写是因为有要求还是法官自己的选择？

Appendix V. The move analysis of a full judgment

This judgment is taken verbatim from the official website of a court and the underlined part is added by the present researcher for the purpose of analysis.

It should be further pointed out that some linguistic and discursive features of the original Chinese texts are unavoidably lost in the process of translation. So research findings which are all based on the analysis of the original texts might not be evidenced in this appendix.

Civil Judgment

- Move 1: Heading
  - Step 1: Case Number
  - Step 2: List of Litigation Participants
- Move 2: Introduction
- Move 3: Parties' Arguments
  - Step 1: Plaintiffs' Claim
  - Step 2: Defendants' Defense
  - Step 3: Evidence (*optional*)
- Move 4: Judges' Arguments
  - Step 1: Facts
  - Step 2: Issues (*optional*)
  - Step 3: Evidence (*optional*)
- Move: 5 Judges' Opinions
  - Step 1: Interpretation of Law
  - Step 2: Application of Law
  - Step 4: Opinions
  - Step 5: Opposite Opinions (*rarely available*)
- Move 6: Court Decisions
  - Step 1: Decisions
  - Step 2: Notification of the Right to Appeal
  - Step 3: Signature Line

MOVE 1: HEADING

STEP 1 OF MOVE1: CASE NUMBER

XYZ Court of the PRC
Civil Judgment
(2001) GHFCZ No. ABC

STEP 2 OF MOVE 1: LIST OF LITIGATION PARTICIPANTS

Plaintiff: Shenzhen Bao An Gaoke Electronic Co., Ltd.
Address: High-tech Industrial Park, No. 8 Tang Hang Rd.,
Shiyan County, Shenzhen
Legal Representative: Zhao Jinhai, General Manager
Agent ad litem: Yan Tieying, lawyer of Guangdong Wanshang Law Firm

Defendant: Beijing Hui Hang International Forwarding Ltd.
Shenzhen Branch
Address: Room AB, 26/F, Shenzhen Development Bank Tower,
No.5047, Shen Nan Dong Rd., Luo Hu District, Shenzhen
Representative: Li Ming, Manager
Agents ad litem: Zhao Shuzhou, Sun Jingliang,
lawyers of Wang Jing & Co. Law Firm

Defendant: Wan Hai Lines Ltd.
Address: 10/F, No. 136, Song Jiang Rd., Taipei, Taiwan, China
Legal Representative: Chen Chaoheng, Chairman of the Board of Directors
Agents ad litem: Zhao Shuzhou, Sun Jingliang,
lawyers of Wang Jing & Co. Law Firm

MOVE 2: INTRODUCTION

As filed by the Plaintiff, Shenzhen Bao An Gaoke Electronics Co., Ltd. (hereinafter referred to as "Bao An Gaoke Co.") against the Defendants, Beijing Hui Hang International Forwarding Ltd. Shenzhen Branch (hereinafter referred to as "Hui Hang Shenzhen") and Wan Hai Lines Ltd. (hereinafter referred to as "Wan Hai Lines") with respect to the dispute over the release of goods without collecting the original bill of lading this court accepted the case on September 26th, 2001. On November 30th, the judge, Huang Qingnan, heard the case by public hearing according to law. Yan Tieying, the agent ad litem of Bao An Gaoke Co., and Zhao Shuzhou and Sun Jingliang, the agents ad litem of Hui Hang Shenzhen and Wan Hai Lines, participated in the proceedings. This case has now been concluded.

MOVE 3: PARTIES' ARGUMENTS

STEP 1 OF MOVE 3: PLAINTIFFS' CLAIM

The Plaintiff, Bao An Gaoke Co. claimed that: on March 24th, 2001, the Plaintiff, Bao An Gaoke Co., through its agent, Shenzhen Construction Equipment and Materials Import & Export Head Company (hereinafter referred to as "Shenzhen Construction Co."), entrusted Hui Hang Shenzhen to transport 1,736 cartons of telephone sets valued at USD250,250 from Shenzhen, China to Semarang, Indonesia. Having received the goods consigned by the Plaintiff Bao An Gaoke Co., the Defendant Hui Hang Shenzhen issued on April 2nd the shipped on board clean bill of lading No. SKSM00222 in triplicate. As the actual shipper, the Plaintiff, Bao An Gaoke Co. obtained the bills of lading and held them till now. After the goods arrived at the destination port, the Defendant, Wan Hai Lines, as the actual carrier of the goods in this case, delivered the goods to a third party, in consequence of which the Plaintiff, Bao An Gaoke Co., could not collect the payment for the goods. The court is applied to adjudge that both Defendants shall jointly and severally compensate the losses of the Plaintiff, Bao An Gaoke Co., i.e. the losses of goods in the sum of USD250,250 and the interests accrued thereon pursuant to the loan interest rate stipulated by People's Bank of China in the corresponding period (from April 24th to the day when both Defendants actually compensate the Plaintiff), plus lawyer's fees in the amount of RMB80,000, the translation fee at RMB6,488 as well as the inquiry fee of Administration for Industry and Commerce at RMB58, which were all paid by the Plaintiff, Bao An Gaoke Co.; and to order the two defendants to bear the court fees.

STEP 3 OF MOVE 3: EVIDENCE

The plaintiff Bao An Gaoke Co. provided this court with 28 pieces of evidence.

STEP 2 OF MOVE 3: DEFENDANTS' DEFENSE

The Defendant Hui Hang Shenzhen defended that: 1. The Defendant, Hui Hang Shenzhen issued the said B/L as the agent of Wan Hai Lines, and it was not the carrier of the goods in this case; hence, it was not a qualified defendant. In addition, Hui Hang Shenzhen is not an independent legal person of enterprise, but is affiliated to Beijing Hui Hang International Forwarding Ltd., thus it is not qualified to take on the civil responsibility. 2. The said B/L is a straight bill of lading in which the Plaintiff, Bao An Gaoke Co. is not stated as the shipper nor the consignee. Hence, the Plaintiff is not a party to the contract of carriage of goods by sea as evidenced by the said B/L, nor is it entitled to lodge the complaint based on the bills of lading and without the capacity as the plaintiff.

STEP 3 OF MOVE 3: EVIDENCE

The Defendant, Hui Hang Shenzhen provided this court with 3 groups of evidences.

STEP 2 OF MOVE 3: DEFENDANTS' DEFENSE

The Defendant, Wan Hai Lines defended that: 1. The Plaintiff, Bao An Gaoke Co. is not the shipper or the consignee stated in the said B/L, thus is not entitled to file an action based on the B/L. 2. The party who signed the shipping order with the Defendant, Hui Hang Shenzhen, is Shenzhen Foreign Trade Import & Export Combined Transport Co., rather than the Plaintiff, Bao An Gaoke Co.; besides, the Plaintiff cannot be verified to be the actual shipper, for if the party who handed over the goods for shipment is to become the actual shipper, it needs to certify not only that it has handed over the goods to the carrier, but also that the goods are handed over in its own interests. However, the Plaintiff, Bao An Gaoke Co. has not completed their burden of proofs in these two regards. Furthermore, even if the Plaintiff, Bao An Gaoke Co. was the actual shipper, the relationship between the Plaintiff and the Defendant, Wan Hai Lines., was merely the legal relationship as provided in the Maritime Code of the PRC, rather than the legal relationship of contract of carriage of goods by sea evidenced by or contained in the bills of lading. Maritime Code of the PRC does not entitle the actual shipper to ask the carrier to deliver the goods to him, nor does it regulate that the carrier has the obligation to deliver the goods to the actual shipper. Therefore, the Plaintiff, Bao An Gaoke Co. cannot excise the rights of requesting delivery of goods under contract of carriage of goods by sea as contained in or evidenced by the bills of lading. 3. The straight Bs/L, as in this case does not have the function as document of title. The party to whom the goods should be delivered can only be the consignee stated in bill of lading, while any third party beyond the bill of lading relation is not entitled to enjoy the rights connecting to goods. Therefore, even if the Plaintiff, Bao An Gaoke Co. held the B/L, it could not claim its rights in respect of the goods. In summary, it is applied to the court to reject the litigation requests of the Plaintiff, Bao An Gaoke Co..

STEP 3 OF MOVE 3: EVIDENCE

The Defendant, Wan Hai Lines provided this court with 3 groups of evidences.

MOVE 4: JUDGES' ARGUMENTS

STEP 1 OF MOVE 4: FACTS

It is found out through court trials:

I. Facts relating to transaction of the goods

The Plaintiff, Bao An Gaoke Co. submitted to this court the following evidences: 1. The original Sales Contract No. GK2001-001 signed by the Plaintiff and P. T. KARYA MAKMUR SEJATI (hereinafter referred to as KARYA Co.); 2. The faxes that KARYA Co. sent to the Plaintiff, Bao An Gaoke Co.; 3. The original Agreement concluded between the Plaintiff and PRIMA BRIGHT LIMITED (hereinafter BRIGHT Co.); 4. The original Packing List issued by the Plaintiff, certifying facts of the sales of the goods in this case. The Defendants, Hui Hang Shenzhen and Wan Hai Lines did not accept the authenticity of the four groups of evidences mentioned above, but no contrary evidence was submitted. This judge holds the opinions that: Sales Contract, Agreement and Packing List are all originals; furthermore, the faxes sent by KARYA Co. to the Plaintiff, Bao An Gaoke Co. conform to the three groups of evidences mentioned above. Therefore, the four groups of evidences above can be admitted as grounds to ascertain the facts of this case, and the following facts certified by them shall be confirmed.

On February 15th, 2001, the Plaintiff, Bao An Gaoke Co., and KARYA Co. concluded Sales Contract No. GK2001-001. It is agreed that: the Plaintiff sells to KARYA Co. 28,000 telephone sets worthy of USD250,250 (CNF Semarang, Indonesia); KARYA Co. should pay USD 60,000 as the deposit and the balance should be paid when it received the facsimile copy of the original B/L provided by the Plaintiff; the time of delivery by the Plaintiff is within 30 days upon the receipt of the deposit.

On March 20th, after putting the telephone sets purchased by KARYA Co. into cartons, the Plaintiff issued the Packing list. It records that: there are altogether 1,736 cartons with 28,085 telephone sets, of which 85 sets are spare ones.

On March 21st, KARYA Co. faxed to the Plaintiff, Bao An Gaoke Co., requesting that the "shipper" on the B/L should not be in the authentic name, nor should the name of company in Mainland China appear hereon; and the B/L shall state the "consignee" as PT TRIDHARMA DJAYA SELARAS (hereinafter referred to as DJAYA Co.).

On the same day, the plaintiff, Bao An Gaoke Co. and BRIGHT Co. concluded an Agreement. It is agreed that: because clients of the Plaintiff requested that the shipper stated in the B/L should not be in the name of a company in Mainland, BRIGHT Co. agreed that: the Plaintiff could name BRIGHT Co. as shipper in the box of shipper in the B/L when the Plaintiff handled the shipping procedures for the 1,736 cartons of telephone sets whose consignee is DJAYA Co.; the Plaintiff handles by itself other issues relating to the shipment of the goods, and BRIGHT Co. is not responsible for the same; the Plaintiff obtains the B/L by itself and enjoys the property rights under the B/L.

The Defendants, Hui Hang Shenzhen and Wan Hai Lines claim that the Plaintiff, Bao An Gaoke Co. has received USD60,000 as deposit paid by KARYA Co. However, no corresponding evidence is submitted. Hence, this judge does not accept such claim.

II. Facts relating to the consignment of the goods

The Plaintiff, Bao An Gaoke Co. submitted to this court the following evidences: 1. The original Agreement on Agency for Export signed by the Plaintiff, Bao An Gaoke Co. and Shenzhen Construction Co.; 2. The original Letter of Entrustment for Custom Declaration issued by Shenzhen Construction Co. to Donglian Customs Declaration

Co. Ltd. (hereinafter referred to as Donglian Co.); 3. Original Declaration Form of Exported Cargo by which Donglian Co. declared to Shenzhen Custom for exportation; 4. The original Agreement entered into by Shenzhen Construction Co. and Connect Channel International Transportation Co., Ltd. (hereinafter referred to as Connect Channel Co.); 5. The original Shipping Order issued by Shenzhen Construction Co. to Connect Channel Co.; 6. Copies of Shipping Order issued by Connect Channel Co. to Shenzhen Foreign Trade Import and Export Combined Transport Co. (hereinafter referred to as Shenzhen Combined Transport Co.); 7. The original Statement with respect to Shipment of the Goods under B/L No. SKSMC00222 issued by Shenzhen Combined Transport Co. to the Defendant, Hui Hang Shenzhen; 8. the original shipping confirmation issued by Shenzhen Combimed Transport Co. to the Defendant Beijing Huihang; 9. The original Certificate for Carriage of Container issued by Shenzhen Xihu Huayu Trailer Transport Co. Ltd. (hereinafter referred to as Shenzhen Xihu Trailer Co.); 10. Copies of Export FCL Collection Order issued by the agent of Wan Hai Lines Ltd.–Wan Hai Lines (HK) Ltd. (hereinafter referred to as Wan Hai HK); 11. The original of Container In/Out Order issued by Shekou Container Terminals Ltd. (hereinafter referred to as Shekou Container Terminal.), certifying that the Plaintiff, Bao An Gaoke Co., through the agent, Shenzhen Construction Co., entrusted the Defendant, Hui Hang Shenzhen to carry 1,736 cartons of telephone sets; Shenzhen Xihu Trailer Co. transported the telephone sets consigned by the Plaintiff to Shekou Container Terminal, and finally the telephone sets were carried by the Defendant, Wan Hai Lines.

With regard to the foregoing 11 groups of evidences, the Defendants, Hui Hang Shenzhen and Wan Hai Lines only agreed with the Shipping Order issued by Shenzhen Combined Transport Co. and submitted to Hui Hang Shenzhen; as for the other evidences, the Defendants did not admit their authenticity, but no contrary evidence was submitted.

This judge holds that: among the 11 groups of evidences provided by the Plaintiff, Bao An Gaoke Co., except for the Shipping Order issued by Connect Channel Co. to Shenzhen Combined Transport Co. and Export FCL Collection Order issued by WH, HK being in photo copies, all other evidences are all original ones, thus they can be admitted as grounds to ascertain the facts of this case;0in addition, the Shipping Order issued by Connect Channel Co. to Shenzhen Combined Transport Co. and Statement with regard to Shipment of Goods under B/L No. SKSMC00222 issued by Shenzhen Combined Transport Co. can certify each other; Export FCL Collection Order issued by Wan Hai HK and the Certificate for Carriage of Container issued by Shenzhen Xihu Trailer Co. and Container In/Out Order issued by Shekou Container Co. can verify each other, therefore, the Shipping Order issued by Connect Channel Co. to Shenzhen Combined Transport Co. and Export FCL Collection Order issued by Wan Hai HK can also be taken as the grounds for ascertainment of the facts in this case. In summary, the following facts certified by the foregoing 11 groups of evidences shall be confirmed.

On March 18th, 2001, the Plaintiff, Bao An Gaoke Co. signed the Agreement on Agency for Export with Shenzhen Construction Co. It was agreed that: Shenzhen Construction Co. acts as the agent of the plaintiff to handle the procedures for exporting telecommunication products such as telephone sets; after Shenzhen Construction Co. received confirmation of the agency for export by the Plaintiff, it is responsible for arranging the procedures in respect of inspection, transportation, custom declaration and so on; 0the Plaintiff is responsible by itself for stipulations under the contracts it signed with buyer abroad, such as the time of delivery, quality of the goods and so on.

On March 20th, Shenzhen Construction Co. and Connect Channel Co. entered into an Agreement. It agrees that: Connect Channel Co. accepts the entrustment of Shenzhen Construction Co. and is responsible for going through all related procedures for shipment of 1,736 cartons with 28,000 sets of telephone sets (85 sets for spare) therein from Shekou, Shenzhen to Semarang. Indonesia; The actual expenses incurred during the procedures shall be settled by Connect Channel Co. with the carrier, and Shenzhen Construction Co. shall correspondingly make the payment to Connect Channel Co.; Shenzhen Construction Co. shall pay Connect Channel Co. the agency fees within 3 days when getting bill of lading. On the next day, Shenzhen Construction Co. issued a Consignment Bill to Connect Channel Co.

After accepting the entrustment, Connect Channel Co. issued Shipping Order to Shenzhen Combined Transport Co., sub-contracting Shenzhen Combined Transport Co. to handle the procedures for shipment of goods which Shenzhen Construction Co. was authorized to handle as the agent of the Plaintiff, Bao An Gaoke Co.

On March 23rd, having accepted the entrustment, Shenzhen Combined Transport Co. issued Shipping Order to Hui Hang Shenzhen, entrusting M/V "Wan Hai 202" to carry the goods of this case from Shekou, Shenzhen to Semarang, Indonesia. The Shipping Order records: the Defendant, Hui Hang Shenzhen is the agent appointed by the Defendant, Wan Hai Lines.

On March 24th, in accordance with the Export FCL Collection Order issued by the agent of Wan Hai Lines–Wan Hai HK, the Plaintiff, Bao An Gaoke Co., entrusted Shenzhen Xihu Trailer Co. to send container trucks, Yue B-31707 and Yue B-31708 to pick up two empty 40' containers, numbering CLHU8304038 and CAXU9708118 respectively from the bonded area of Yantian, Shenzhen. After the two container trucks took delivery of the empty containers, the trucks went to the Plaintiff, Bao An Gaoke Co. for loading the subject goods. There were 953 cartons of telephone sets loaded into container CLHU8304038, and 783 cartons into container CAXU9708118, totaling 1,736 cartons. Later, the container truck Yue B-31707 and Yue B-31708 carried the said goods to Shekou Container Terminal. Shekou Container Terminal issued the Container Collection/Acceptance Order.

On March 26th, with the approval of the Plaintiff Bao An Gaoke Co., Shenzhen Construction Co. entrusted Donglian Co. to handle the customs declaration procedures for export. On the next day, Donglian declared the exported goods to Shenzhen Shekou Custom. After examining the goods, the Custom affixed the Cargo Release Chop on the Declaration Form For Exported Goods. The Form records that: Export Agent is Shenzhen Construction Co., Manufacturer is the Plaintiff, Bao An Gaoke Co., the Sales Contract Number is GK2001-001, Container Numbers are CLHU8304038, CAXU9708118, the goods are 28,085 telephone sets, the value of the goods is USD 250,250, CNF Indonesia.

III. Facts relating to the issuance and receipt of the B/L

The Plaintiff submitted to this court the following evidences: 1. The original B/L No. SKSMC00222 in triplicate issued by Defendant, Hui Hang Shenzhen; 2. The original Receipt for B/L issued by Shenzhen Combined Transport Co.; 3. The original Certificate of Connect Channel Co. for getting the B/L, to evidence that after receiving the goods consigned by the Plaintiff Bao An Gaoke Co., the Defendant Hui Hang Shenzhen issued the ocean B/L No. SKSMC00222; having obtained the B/L from the Defendant Hui Hang Shenzhen, Shenzhen Combined Transport Co. handed the B/L to Connect Channel Co., and Connect Channel Co. to Shenzhen Construction Co., then Shenzhen Construction Co. to the Plaintiff, Bao An Gaoke Co.. The Defendants Hui Hang Shenzhen and Wan Hai Lines had no objection to the authenticity of the B/L No. SKSMC00222, but they did not recognize the authenticity of the other 2 groups of evidences. Neither Defendants submitted evidences to the contrary. This judge holds that: all parties concerned agreed with the authenticity of B/L No. SKSMC00222, thus the B/L may serve as the grounds to ascertain the facts of this case. In addition, other 2 groups of evidences submitted by the Plaintiff Bao An Gaoke Co. are originals, although the Defendants Hui Hang Shenzhen and Wan Hai Lines dissented from them, but no contrary evidence was submitted. Furthermore, the foregoing 2 groups of evidences and other evidences submitted by the Plaintiff can cross-verify each other. Therefore, the two groups of evidences can be adopted as grounds to ascertain the facts of this case. The following facts certified by the foregoing evidences should be confirmed.

After receiving the said goods in Shekou, Shenzhen, the Defendant Hui Hang Shenzhen issued the ocean straight clean bill of lading No.SKSMC00222 in triplicates on behalf of the Defendant Wan Hai Lines on April 2nd, 2001. It was recorded on the bill of lading that: Consigner, BRIGHT Co.; Consignee, DJAYA Co.; Carrier, the Defendant Wan Hai Lines; Carrying Vessel, M/V "Wan Hai 202"; Port of Loading, Hong Kong; Port of Discharge, Semarang, Indonesia; Containers No., CLHU8304038 & CAXU9708118; Quantity of Goods, 1,736 cartons. Afterwards, the Defendant Hui Hang Shenzhen handed the whole set of bills of lading to Shenzhen Combined Transport Co. On April 6th, Shenzhen Combined Transport Co. handed over the same bills of lading to Lai Fulong, an employee of Connect Channel Co.. On receipt of the above bills of lading, Lai

Fulong handed them over to Shenzhen Construction Co. The Plaintiff Bao An Gaoke Co. obtained the bills of lading from Shenzhen Construction Co. and has kept them till now.

IV. Facts Concerning the Release of the Goods

The Plaintiff Bao An Gaoke Co. submitted to this Court the forged bill of lading against presentation of which a third party took delivery of the goods at the port of destination. The said fake bill of lading was shown to the Plaintiff Bao An Gaoke Co. by the Defendant Hui Hang Shenzhen when the former inquired about the whereabouts of the goods. The Defendant Hui Hang Shenzhen affixed a company seal on the fake bill of lading. From the above, the Plaintiff Bao An Gaoke Co. claimed that the cargo had been taken away by the third party on the strength of the fake bill of lading. The Defendants Hui Hang Shenzhen and Wan Hai Lines did not confirm the authenticity of the mentioned evidence. This Judge holds that since Hui Hang Shenzhen had affixed an official chop on the fake bill of lading, this fake bill of lading should be taken as the same one that the Defendant Hui Hang Shenzhen showed to the Plaintiff Bao An Gaoke Co. when the latter inquired the whereabouts of the cargo of the former; and that the cargo in question had been taken away by the third party on the strength of the fake bill of lading.

The Defendants Hui Hang Shenzhen and Wan Hai Lines contended that the party that actually took away the said goods was the consignee DJAYA Co. under the straight bill of lading No.SKSMC00222. To prove that, the Defendants Hui Hang Shenzhen and Wan Hai Lines submitted to this Court a copy of the bill of lading shown to them by DJAYA Co. when it went to take delivery of the goods; a copy of the Commercial Invoice issued by BRIGHT Co., the consigner under the bill of lading, and a copy of the Packing List. The Plaintiff Bao An Gaoke Co. did not confirm the authenticity of the said evidences. This Judge holds that all the above documents were copies only, and they could not be taken as the effective evidence for determining the facts of this case in the absence of other proofs. Therefore, it could not be inferred from the said available evidences that the party that actually took delivery of the goods was DJAYA Co.

The Defendant Wan Hai Lines argued that it released the cargo at the request of BRIGHT Co., the consigner under the bill of lading. However, the Defendant failed to provide the corresponding evidences for its argument, and the Plaintiff Bao An Gaoke Co. raised a dissention from it. So this Judge would not accept the Defendant's claim.

It was confirmed by the Defendants Hui Hang Shenzhen and Wan Hai Lines during the court hearing that they did not contact Shenzhen Combined Transport Co. when the cargo in question was released. The Plaintiff did not have dissention from this. So this Judge accepts this point.

V. Other Facts

The Plaintiff Bao An Gaoke Co. claimed that it had paid the attorney fee for this case in amount of RMB80,000, the translation fee in amount of RMB6,488 and the inquiry fee to the industrial and commercial bureau in amount of RMB58, and, to prove the above claims, submitted to this Court the original Invoice of Attorney Fee issued by Guangdong Wanshang Law Firm, the original Invoice of Translation Fee issued by Shenzhen Shanghua Translation & Consultant Co. Ltd., and the original Invoice of Industrial and Commercial Inquiry Fee issued by Shenzhen Industrial and Commercial Commodity Price Information Center. The Defendants Hui Hang Shenzhen and Wan Hai Lines held that the above evidences had nothing to do with the dispute in this case, and could not be adopted as the evidences for determining the facts of this case. However, the Defendants Hui Hang Shenzhen and Wan Hai Lines did not provide any contrary evidence in this respect. This Judge believes that, in the absence of contrary evidence from the Defendants Hui Hang Shenzhen and Wan Hai Lines, the original documents provided by the Plaintiff Bao An Gaoke Co. could be used as evidences for determining the facts of this case. So it was ascertained that the Plaintiff Bao An Gaoke Co. paid attorney fees in amounts of RMB48,000 and RMB32,000 to Guangdong Wanshang Law Firm on July 20 and September 5, 2001 respectively; paid translation fees in amounts of RMB5,538 and RMB950 to Shenzhen Shanghua Translation & Consultant Co. on September 6 and September 26 respectively; and paid inquiry fee in amount of RMB58 to Shenzhen Industrial and Commercial Commodity Price Information Center on August 20.

The Defendant Hui Hang Shenzhen does not enjoy the capacity of a legal person of an enterprises as it is affiliated to Beijing Hui Hang International Forwarding Ltd.

The Plaintiff Bao An Gaoke Co. chose breach of contract as cause of action to file a lawsuit against the Defendants Hui Hang Shenzhen and Wan Hai Lines. All parties concerned agreed to apply Chinese law to govern settlement of the substantive dispute of the subject case.

MOVE 5: JUDGES' OPINIONS

STEP 1 OF MOVE 5: INTERPRETATION OF LAW

This Judge holds that this case is about a dispute over the release of goods without original bill of lading with respect to carriage of goods by sea, and that the law of the People's Republic of China shall be applied to govern the settlement of substantive dispute of the subject case.

According to the Maritime Code of the People's Republic of China, "shipper" means a) The person by whom or in whose name or on whose behalf a contract of carriage of goods by sea has been concluded with a carrier; b) The person by whom or in whose name or on whose behalf the goods have been delivered to the carrier. "On whose behalf a contract of carriage of goods by sea has been concluded with a carrier" means that the trustee, in accordance with the entrustment of the principal and in order to realize the principal's interests, is entitled to conclude a contract of carriage of goods by sea with a carrier in its own name. Therefore, when judging a shipper, one should have a comprehensive analysis, taking into consideration not only the party stated in the contract of carriage of goods by sea, but also the relative entrustment relationship.

STEP 2 AND 3 OF MOVE 5: APPLICATION OF LAW AND OPINIONS

In this case, the Plaintiff Bao An Gaoke Co. entrusted Shenzhen Construction Co. to go through the export formalities for the said cargo on its behalf, with a view to fulfilling its obligation under the Purchase and Sales Contract it entered into with KARYA Co. As the agent of Bao An Gaoke Co., Shenzhen Construction Co. re-entrusted DL to apply to the Customs, and Connect Channel Co. to go through the shipping formalities, both with the consent of the Plaintiff Bao An Gaoke Co.. So it can be seen that the Plaintiff Bao An Gaoke Co. was the principal, while Shenzhen Construction Co., Donglian Co., Connect Channel Co. and Shenzhen Combined Transport Co. were all agents of the Plaintiff Bao An Gaoke Co. in this case. For the interest of the Plaintiff Bao An Gaoke Co., Shenzhen Combined Transport Co. concluded a contract of carriage of goods by sea with a foreign party, and handed over the bill of lading it obtained to the Plaintiff Bao An Gaoke Co. via Connect Channel Co. and Shenzhen Construction Co.. The above-mentioned facts were enough to prove that the shipper of the cargo in the subject case was the Plaintiff Bao An Gaoke Co., while Shenzhen Combined Transport Co., who issued a shipping order to the Defendant Hui Hang Shenzhen, was only the agent of the shipper.

The Defendants Hui Hang Shenzhen and Wan Hai Lines defended that the Plaintiff Bao An Gaoke Co. failed to prove that it had actually delivered the goods to the carrier, nor could it prove that the delivery of goods was done in its own interest, so the Plaintiff Bao An Gaoke Co. was not the shipper of the said goods in the subject case. In view of the facts that the Purchase and Sales Contract with KARYA Co., the Certificate for Taking Delivery of the Container issued by Shenzhen Xihu Trailer Transport Co. Ltd., and the Collection/Acceptance Order issued by Shekou Containers Terminal all submitted by the Plaintiff Bao An Gaoke Co. were sufficient to prove that the Plaintiff entrusted the cargo in question for carriage by sea to the carrier for its own interest. Therefore, the defence of the Defendants Hui Hang Shenzhen and Wan Hai Lines should be rejected.

According to the records on the shipping order and the bill of lading No.SKSMC00222 of the subject case, the Defendant Hui Hang Shenzhen was the agent of the Defendant Wan Hai Lines, and Hui Hang Shenzhen issued the ocean bill of lading on behalf of Wan Hai Lines. Therefore, Wan Hai Lines should be ascertained as the actual carrier of the cargo in question; a contractual relationship of carriage of goods by sea did exist between the carrier and the Plaintiff. As such contractual relationship was not in violation of law and lawful and effective, and should be protected. As to the Defendant Hui Hang Shenzhen, it was only the agent of the carrier. It was not a party in the contractual relationship of carriage of goods by sea, and was free from the obligation of delivering the goods against the original bill of lading. Therefore, the request of the Plaintiff that the Defendant Hui Hang Shenzhen should be liable for the release of the goods without the original bill of lading lacked legal grounds and should be turned down.

As the carrier of said cargo in the subject case, the Defendant Wan Hai Lines failed to deliver the goods consigned by the Plaintiff to a third party against production of the original bill of lading, as a result, the Plaintiff, though still holding the original bill of lading, lost control over the cargo under the said bill of lading, and finally had no way to collect the cargo value. The Defendant Wan Hai Lines' act of releasing the goods without collecting the original bill of lading breached the contract. The Plaintiff Bao An Gaoke Co., as the shipper and the holder of the original bill of lading, was entitled to claim against Wan Hai Lines for its loss thereof. According to relative regulations of the Maritime Code of PRC, the scope of loss of the goods in question should be calculated in accordance with the actual value of the goods. In accordance with the stipulation of the mentioned Purchase and Sales Contract and the record of the Declaration Form of Goods for Export, the actual value of the goods in question was USD250,250. The Plaintiff Bao An Gaoke Co.'s request that Wan Hai Lines should compensate to it the loss of cargo price in amount of USD250,250 and the loss of interest thereof (calculating from April 24, 2001 at the loan interest of the People's Bank of China at that time) was in conformity with the provision of law and therefore should be supported. The other request of the Plaintiff that Wan Hai Lines should indemnify it for the attorney fee, translation fee and industrial and commercial inquiry fee related to the litigation was legally groundless and should be dismissed.

The Defendant Wan Hai Lines' defence that the Plaintiff was not the shipper or the consignee as stated on the bill of lading, therefore it was not a party related to the bill of lading, and it was not entitled to initiate a lawsuit in reliance on the bill of lading was not tenable, the reasons for which were as follows: according to the regulations of the Maritime Code of the PRC, a bill of lading was only evidence of a contract of carriage, but it was not the contract of carriage itself. After receiving the goods, the carrier shall issue a bill of lading to the shipper at the shipper's request. The bill of lading in this case stated as requested by the buyer KARYA Co. that the shipper was "BRIGHT Co.", and the consignee was "DJAYA Co.", and the Defendant Hui Hang Shenzhen then issued the said bill of lading at the request of the Plaintiff's agent Shenzhen Combined Transport Co.. As long as the Plaintiff Bao An Gaoke Co. did not transfer the bill of lading to a third party, it was at the same time the shipper and the holder of the said bill of lading, and was entitled to initiate a lawsuit against the carrier on basis of the contract of carriage and the original bill of lading to claim its right in the cargo.

The Defendant Wan Hai Lines also defended that since the bill of lading in question was a straight bill of lading, it was justified to let the consignee DJAYA Co. named under the bill of lading take delivery of the goods, and should not be liable for releasing the goods without the original bill of lading. As the Defendant Wan Hai Lines failed to prove that DJAYA Co. was the party that had actually taken delivery of the goods, its above argument shall not be supported. Besides, even if DJAYA Co. was the party that had actually taken delivery of the goods, it was not right for Wan Hai Lines to have the goods taken delivery of, the reasons for which are as below: according to the stipulations of the Maritime Code of the PRC, a bill of lading is a document which serves as an evidence of the contract of carriage of goods by sea, and based on which the carrier undertakes to deliver the goods against surrendering the same. Although the bill of lading in question issued by the carrier was a straight bill of lading, the carrier, when delivering the goods, should verify both the identity of the consignee and whether it holds the original bill of lading. The purpose of such stipulation is to make sure that if the named consignee refuses to make payment for the goods, the shipper may choose not to transfer the bill of lading to prevent the named consignee from taking delivery of the goods and to keep control over the goods under this bill of lading. If there was no need for the named consignee to show the original bill of lading to the carrier when taking delivery of the goods, then the party that had actually taken delivery of the goods in this case should have had no need to make a fake bill of lading in order to take delivery of the cargo from the carrier. He might just have to prove his identity as the consignee and taken away the goods. However, the fact was that the party that had actually taken delivery of the goods showed a fake bill of lading to the carrier, who failed to discern the forgery during the examination and wrongfully released the goods.

The Defendant Wan Hai Lines further argued that Shenzhen Combined Transport Co. entered into the shipping order with the carrier in its own name, so the Plaintiff was not the shipper. Even if this argument of Wan Hai Lines was tenable, the Plaintiff was still entitled to a request for compensation against the Defendant Wan Hai Lines for the latter's releasing the cargo without the original bill of lading. The reasons are: according to Article 403 of the Contract Law of the PRC, under a contract concluded by the agent in the agent's name with a third party who is not aware of the proxy relationship between the agent and its principal, when the agent fails to perform obligations toward its principal because of the third party, the agent shall disclose the third party to the principal, and the principal may then exercise the rights of the agent against the third party. In this case, Shenzhen Combined Transport Co. was the agent of the Plaintiff. So under the circumstance that the Defendant Wan Hai Lines committed mistakes when delivering the goods, the Plaintiff Bao An Gaoke Co. may directly ask Wan Hai Lines to indemnify it for losses incurred thereof.

MOVE 6: COURT DECISIONS

STEP 1 OF MOVE 6: DECISIONS

To sum up the above, and in accordance with the stipulations of Article 42 (1) 1–3, Article 55, Article 71 and Article 72 of the Maritime Code of the PRC, the Judgment is hereby given as follows:

- The Defendant Wan Hai Lines shall compensate to the Plaintiff Bao An Gaoke Co. the loss of cargo in amount of USD250,250 and the loss of interest thereof based on the loan interest of the People's Bank of China applied in the corresponding period (calculating from April 24, 2001 to the date of payment as specified by this Judgment);
- Other litigation requests of the Plaintiff Bao An Gaoke Co. shall be dismissed.

Of the acceptance fee of this case in amount of RMB55,514, the Plaintiff Bao An Gaoke Co. shall pay RMB2,220, and the remaining RMB53,294 shall be borne by the Defendant Wan Hai Lines. This Court shall not refund to the Plaintiff the acceptance fee paid in advance by the Plaintiff. The Defendant Wan Hai Lines shall pay its apportionment to the Plaintiff directly.

The payment of the above sums shall be completed within 10 days upon coming into effect of this Judgment.

STEP 2 OF MOVE 6: NOTIFICATION OF THE RIGHT TO APPEAL

Should there be any objection to this Judgment, a statement of appeal with copy/copies in the number of the opponent party/parties may be submitted to this Court within 15 days upon the service of this Judgment, for appealing before the appeal court Guangdong Higher People's Court.

STEP 3 OF MOVE 6: SIGNATURE LINE

Judge: H Q

Secretary: L Y

(XYZ Court)

December 26, 2001

This copy is verified as true to the original.